Danny Dorling has been a Professor of Human Geography at the University of Sheffield since 2003. He is also Adjunct Professor in the Department of Geography, University of Canterbury, New Zealand, and Visiting Professor in the Department of Social Medicine, University of Bristol, UK. He is an Academician of the Academy of the Learned Societies in the Social Sciences, and Honorary President of the Society of Cartographers. In 2009 he was awarded the Gold Award of the Geographical Association and the Back Award of the Royal Geographical Society for his work on national and international public policy. He has worked both with the British government and the World Health Organization and is frequently asked to comment on current issues on TV and the radio. He has published more than twenty-five books, most recently *Injustice: Why Social Inequality Exists*, which was described by Richard Wilkinson, author of *The Spirit Level*, as 'provid[ing] the brain-cleaning software we need to begin creating a happier society.' He lives in Sheffield with his family.

So You Think You Know About Britain?

Danny Dorling

Constable • London

Constable & Robinson Ltd
3 The Lanchesters
162 Fulham Palace Road
London W6 9ER
www.constablerobinson.com

First published in the UK by Constable,
an imprint of Constable & Robinson Ltd, 2011

A copy of the British Library Cataloguing in
Publication Data is available from the British Library

ISBN: 978-1-84901-391-8

Printed and bound in the UK

1 3 5 7 9 10 8 6 4 2

For Eric Charlesworth

CONTENTS

ACKNOWLEDGEMENTS

I am extremely grateful to Leo Hollis of Constable & Robinson for editing far beyond the call of duty. He turned this book from an idea into an argument, and with his merciless red pen, saved you a great deal of grief. Carl Lee read through the whole manuscript and was not backward in coming forward to let me know where he thought I was going wrong. I'm in debt. My colleagues at the University of Sheffield, especially Dan Vickers, Bethan Thomas, Ben Hennig, Anna Barford and Dimitris Ballas, have had to put up with me being more than usually preoccupied, and I am very grateful for their patience and their advice. Paul Coles, also of the University of Sheffield, very carefully redrew all the figures, maps and graphs contained here, and I am very grateful to him for this huge help. Ideas from parts of this book were tested on different audiences who attended about fifty public lectures held during 2010. I am grateful to everyone who put up with me during those lectures, especially those who asked questions and offered criticism. Bronwen and Alison Dorling corrected numerous drafts of my writing yet again, initially getting it into a form good enough for Leo to cross out, and then helping to make my corrections literate: I've always preferred numbers to words, but numbers do not make an argument. Lastly I should thank my grandfather, Eric Charlesworth, to whom this book is dedicated, and who taught me many years ago that geography matters, and who also corrected a part of a draft of Chapter 1 when I got muddled up about mills, water, steam, iron, coal, North and South. Eric taught geography from 1939 to 1978, bar six years in the Second World War. He was the first to show me how to read a map. Over the years, there have been many people who've helped to put me in my place. Thank you.

INTRODUCTION – GEOGRAPHY MATTERS

This book concerns eight big questions about Britain. In trying to answer them we often find that the bigger picture, the macro scale, reveals a very different story to the one that perhaps we tend to assume at ground level, the one often reported in newspaper headlines. For instance, at ground level it sometimes looks as if there might be too many people to fit on this island; but at macro level we discover that it is the areas with declining population that are finding it hardest to cope, economically and socially. Our country is in need of more young people, and compared to the world level we find that our share of global population is about to halve, and that other parts of the globe are more densely populated.[1]

How can it feel so crowded in Britain when there is, in fact, so much empty land on this island? This is one of the eight big questions about life in Britain today. The other seven concern whether Britain is irreconcilably divided between North and South; how the balance of the sexes is altering and whether the shortage of young men is increasing; just how many immigrants there are, and their effect, or lack thereof; whether we are becoming more ethnically segregated; why town and country are separating even further; how the aging population might tax our resources, and, finally, what hope is there for the future?

The geography you may have been taught late on a Thursday afternoon at school is not the geography that is taught in universities today. When I was at school I was told that an Ice Age was coming. I was taught things I might need to know if I were to rule West Africa: what crops grew there; what languages the people spoke; and how to dress to survive life in a desert (do not wear nylon in the Sahara, else the fabric will melt and stick to you). My teachers were enthusiastic and friendly but I cannot remember much more than that. Geography then was about tea from Ceylon and rubber-tapping in the Amazon, about who *we*, the British, could exploit, about what *they* had, where *they* were, and how to rule *them*. The younger teachers told us that the textbooks were wrong but that we had to repeat such things to get good marks at A level.

Geography today is taught differently; for example, the main concerns are how human life might be ending with climate catastrophe and the impact of the extinction of so many plant and animal species, and of how growing worldwide inequalities of resources unfairly shape all human life across the planet. We now know, and teach routinely, that no one starves due to bad harvests in the world but because of the greed, poor organisation and a lack of understanding by those in power. Today there are always warehouses full of grain located very near to people who are hungry.

What is being taught about Britain in schools and universities is changing too; however, some teachers may well be getting it wrong, as a few of my teachers did, even if they were right about no longer referring to the rest of the world as some kind of resource that we British could exploit. Maybe climate change won't be as abrupt as we think; maybe those in power are getting better at getting the grain out of those warehouses. Yet maybe there is still too much rhetoric about 'us' having to 'fight' our way in the world in order to 'compete' ever more fiercely with our economic rivals.

Nevertheless, when it comes to Britain, those who teach and study and profess to try to understand the human geography of this island now think we are living somewhere very different to where we were before. The human geography of Britain has changed in terms of people's lives being less strictly ordered, but even more in terms of how we understand our population to be spaced geographically – as compared to when I was (and *probably* when you were) at school.

You may know some of your neighbours, but access to new kinds of data means we can get to know far more about people online than we find out by living next door to them![2] You may watch television or read the papers but, remember, many of the people who make television programmes or edit the papers were taught in a pre-Internet age. Our media is also incredibly focused in and around southern England. The BBC has a 'North of England' correspondent, but no 'South of England' one, because for the BBC to report from the Home Counties is to report from home, from where the elite sleep at night before driving in along the M40. Likewise for those reporting on behalf of Sky, who often seem to think that Britain is in some ways just the London office of an American corporation.

Our national newspapers are little better: all are based in the capital. This, and the often select education of those who tell much of Britain's news stories, means that an unrepresentative account is often told to the rest of us. It is not the fault of the elite: if you were at school in the 1970s, were lucky enough to attend university in the 1980s, made your career in London in the 1990s, and settled in or near Surrey within the last ten years then you also would need a 'North of England' correspondent to explain to you what happens in the provinces and the other 'nations and regions'.

This book uses contemporary news stories as launching points to talk about Britain; however, it is not a book about the news. It is a book about where we really live, who is really around us, how things are actually changing, what you find when you count and survey and ask people – and what you see when you do this across the whole country and consider all walks of life. It is a book about a place that roughly sixty-one million people call home,[3] not including the other millions who live abroad but who also call this country 'home'. It is a book not only for the British but also for ex-pats, for tourists, for students, and for anyone who wants a different guide to some of the key issues affecting the human geography of this island today.

Britain is not an easy island to understand and we are living in the curse – and possibly the promise – of especially interesting times; however, it is at just such a time that we most need to question the assumptions often held about Britain and the British. These are the commonly accepted assumptions held by policymakers whose decisions form the bedrock of much of our everyday news. But how much of what we think we know about Britain is true?

The credit crisis shook our faith in banks. We now know that one day the cashpoint machines could dry up. This might be a revelation that changes our thinking as much as when many began to doubt the omnipotence of God. Our Prime Minister told us that Britain was broken and said that (with our help) he will fix it. But is it so shattered? And if so do we have the will and the tools to mend it? How do we know that apparent certainties are certainties? Who should we believe? I think we need to get back to some basic facts and work from there . . .

CHAPTER 1

DIRTY OLD TOWN – NORTH AND SOUTH

'North-south divide wider than ever'

Guardian, 19 June 2007[1]

All was not well at the height of the longest ever economic boom. In June 2007, three months before police had to ask groups of middle-aged and retired savers to disperse from branches of Northern Rock,[2] it was reported that a two-tier economy had re-emerged in Britain, with the North trailing behind: 'Only a handful of cities outside the south-east such as Cardiff, Edinburgh, Leeds and Nottingham are delivering robust growth, Experian says.' Experian, the credit-reference agency, had written the report that this *Guardian* story was based on. But, as it turned out, Edinburgh and Leeds, who relied so much on banking and finance, had been enjoying growth that was far from robust. Nottingham, home to Experian's operational headquarters, did well when more people were taking out credit and so suffered as a result of the credit crisis; and Cardiff relied on high levels of public-sector jobs, which were also particularly affected by the crisis, making Cardiff no longer so 'robust'.

We were told it was to be a southern England and middle-class recession, and that the divide that was growing wider at the height of the boom would narrow when the economic crash came and the credit crunch followed. Bankers would suffer, though maybe not so much the rest of us. But it didn't work out that way. By 2010 it was revealed that it had been the North that had been hardest hit and that the divide might be both deepening and shifting further south as towns and cities just within the North-South border appeared most vulnerable, with some showing signs of being economically discarded.[3] To be discarded was to be grouped with the North.

As companies retrenched their expenditure, it became clear that it was best to be as near to the capital as you could be. And that was before the £81 billion of government spending cuts and the half-million public-sector job losses announced by George Osborne on 20 October 2010.[4] Rising unemployment in the North was being contrasted, yet again, with rising employment in the South. In the year to March 2010 an extra thirty-five jobs were recorded as having been created in London for every new position opening up in Yorkshire and the Humber.[5] Huge increases in unemployment in northern, Scottish and Welsh cities were being predicted for 2011–12, simply reflecting the geography of the cuts to come.

The phrase 'unemployment' was first used in Britain around 1888. Men had been losing paid work with increasing frequency since the economic slump that had started slowly in the 1870s. This greatly dampened the celebrations of 1887, the jubilee year of Queen Victoria's reign, which ended in a harsh winter when many people froze to death, especially those who were poor – among them the families of the men who were newly 'unemployed'. During the 1880s the lowest life expectancy recorded in Britain was in Liverpool – at thirty-six years; in Bristol it was ten years higher.[6]

Many would agree that good health is what matters most to people; however, inequalities in health and longevity, in connection with the North-South divide, have been recognized for years. If we use this as a gauge to judge the divide it quickly becomes apparent that something far more important than wages, or house prices, or even experience of unemployment, fundamentally separates people living in different parts of the country.

Today life expectancy at birth in Liverpool is only between two and three years lower than that in contemporary Bristol, a much smaller gap than that which existed in the 1880s. So has the North-South divide diminished? Perhaps we should look elsewhere for a comparison: the boroughs of Glasgow City and Kensington & Chelsea, for example, indicate that there is still a great divide. When life expectancy is measured from birth in Kensington & Chelsea, women now live eleven years longer, and men thirteen years longer, than the women and men of Glasgow City.[7]

The combined average life expectancy for men and women today is 74.3 in Glasgow City and 86.7 in Kensington & Chelsea; therefore, the gap between an affluent enclave of London and one of the most run-down enclaves of Glasgow is now twelve years, or an additional 17 per cent for those in Kensington & Chelsea. In the 1880s an extra ten years on top of an expectancy of thirty-six was an additional 28 per cent.

As a result, we see that the divide today is undoubtedly narrower than it was between different parts of Britain in the 1880s; however, it is wider than at any time since at least the early 1920s. (I know this because when I was in my first job as a university lecturer, I spent hundreds of hours typing in columns of figures from dusty old decennial reports concerning how many people had died in remote parts of the country in the 1950s and 1960s.

Also, in the 1990s I had spent far too long in the library squinting at faint numbers that recorded deaths in the 1970s and which survive only as a record in aggregate on microfiche transparencies. The cuts to official statistical reports made by the incoming 1979 government, which did not think we needed so many official statisticians, had made reconstructing the record a time-consuming process. For deaths occurring from the 1980s onwards, digital records were available, and I was given access to these, courtesy of a civil servant concerned by my increasing squint.)

When I put together all this data in 2010, along with the most recent statistics, as well as data some of my colleagues have collected from even earlier, I found that inequalities in mortality between areas in Britain were at their peak since any time after at least 1921. Premature death was the great measurer of the North-South divide, which in 2010 was at its widest for at least ninety years.[8]

While the divide has grown, it has also moved. Over the years, in collaboration with researchers from various disciplines, I compared a whole set of statistics either side of the line, not just mortality rates but also house prices, joblessness and voting patterns. I have even studied statistics on how the size of the head on beer varies across the country (this also has a North-South divide, with the head higher in the North).[9] In 2007 I was looking at a map of health inequalities when I received a phone call from an art gallery asking me if I could draw the line of the divide on a map. The gallery was called the Lowry; the line I drew for them was ridiculously detailed. Here's the whole route and a section of it:

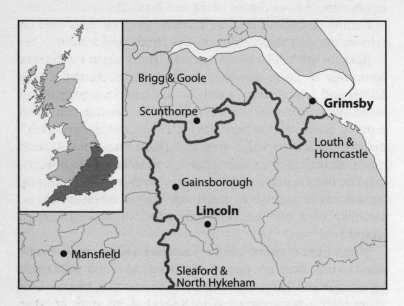

FIGURE 1: Detail of the North-South Divide:
from Newark to Louth

Source: Work with the SASI group, University of Sheffield[10]

This line tells where life-chances divide. Near where I live that line is somewhere just south of the Humber and lying along much of the Trent ('wrong side of t'river' you might say – depending on which side of the river you are from). Elsewhere along its length, the new line can be argued to be part of the furthest outer boundary of London; thus, claims can be made that something has changed distinctly from the past – when this outer boundary really was the divide between highland and lowland Britain. The line now divides on the one hand the outermost commuting suburbs and exclaves of a metropolis, and on the other hand the runt of the country that is left over and beyond – the North, the bit that is being left behind.[11]

I came to believe in the divide when I tried to explain why some people in some places died earlier than other people in other places in Britain. Many things influence how soon or late a group of people might die, but having accounted for as many of those as I can in my results, I have always been left with this divide on the map, this pattern to which statisticians refer to as the 'residuals'. To understand how I got to this point and what I think explains the divide – what the usual suspects of poverty, behaviour and history cannot alone account for – let's step back a little. All the way back to 1877, when it was so cold in the winter that the British Medical Journal warned against the use of perambulators.[12]

Towards the end of Queen Victoria's jubilee year a baby was born in Barrett Street in Stretford, Lancashire, a town just a mile or so south of what was to become, twenty-two years later, Manchester United's football ground; another mile north was Salford, the smoke-stack punctuated exemplification of an emerging industrialized nation. The baby was named Laurence Stephen Lowry. He died eighty-eight years later at the beginning of 1976, the year in which (as measurements confirm) the people of Britain had 'never had it so good'.[13] Lowry missed out on that long hot summer of 1976, which seems a little unfair given how cold his first winter had been.

Today when people think of the North-South divide in Britain they often recollect Lowry's paintings of the North, complete with images of grey matchstick figures who appear to trudge through flat industrial urban landscapes. In contrast to these rather bleak Northern scenes

11

you might imagine men wearing white against a lush green backdrop – playing cricket in the south of England, even though cricket was far more popular in the North in the 1880s than it was in the South. Notably, all sports were more popular in that bit of the North, east of the Pennines, where self-employed weavers and other such people who worked from home could choose their own hours and play when they liked, unlike the cotton weavers in towns such as Salford, where they would have been tied to factory hours.

Despite these great differences within the north of England, and between places such as Lancashire and Yorkshire, and Wales and Scotland, the divide that has almost always mattered most has been between the south-east of England and the rest of Britain. Why? And why has it existed for such a long time? Today it is bolstered by the country's reliance on financial industries and the concentration of these industries in London but, in addition to this, geology, topography and even chemistry have all had their parts to play.

Records of the North-South divide can be found as far back as 1086 when the Doomsday book was collated and documented the outcome of the Norman harrowing of northern England. Evidence has emerged recently that before 1066 the population of England had been far higher than it was shortly after 1066, and that people had lived far more sustainably than was ever understood by the Victorian historians and scholars whose studies still influence our current view, which has been tempered by the fact that we now understand that, even though flatter, more fertile land towards the south-east of England made for more prosperous farming; many more people lived in the North before the Normans razed so many of their villages.[14]

Seven hundred years later it was the water of the North (with its particular chemical properties) – and the power of the stream to turn wheels – that led to industrialization beginning in narrow Derbyshire valleys, spreading to wide Yorkshire valleys, and then (with the coal of the North producing steam) across the great flat expanse of south Lancashire, where the softer water was more suited to cleaning cotton than wool. Industrialization created, at its best, economic power and wealth and, at its worst, the depravity of conditions in its 'dark, satanic' mills and factories.

Superficially, the geology of Britain can appear to underlie the great geographical social divide. For example, apart from in significant regions of Yorkshire, water north of the dividing line is soft, as the (hard) rock it passes through filters away some of the waters' calcium carbonate and so makes it more efficient at dissolving soap. But soon the divide became much more than a matter of where the water runs fast and/or soft, and more a matter of where coal and iron were deposited. The steam age required coal more than fast-running water and partly enabled the mechanization of cloth production, which then required a labour force to become nomadic in order to survive and so move away from their villages to factory towns and cities.

Friedrich Engels lived in Manchester in the 1840s and in 1844 published *The Condition of the Working Class in England*,[15] which he wrote in reaction to his first-hand experience of life in the 'Capital of the North'. He writes, for example, of when he vomited from the stench of the open sewers in little Ireland, one of Manchester's most notorious slums. In turn, these various experiences led to his collaboration with Karl Marx and their joint publication of *The Communist Manifesto* in 1848.

A few years later, in 1855, Elizabeth Gaskell's novel *North and South* was published.[16] It was in reaction to

13

what she also saw first-hand in Manchester. From different political perspectives these books told similar stories of the poverty peculiarly intensive in the North. Gaskell also entitled a chapter of her earlier book, *Mary Barton* (1848) 'Poverty and Death' and described the consequences of lay-offs at the mills: 'when week after week passed by, and there was no work to be had, and consequently no wages to pay for the bread [which] the children cried aloud for in their young impatience of suffering.'[17]

We know from reconstructed life tables that what both Engels and Gaskell witnessed in the north-west of England were some of the worst ever living conditions and highest ever death rates recorded during peacetime and outside of a pandemic anywhere in the world.[18] For the first fifty years of the nineteenth century, staggering levels of infant and childhood mortality meant that life expectancy in Manchester rarely exceeded an average of twenty-five years.[19]

It was just as much international geography as topography that mattered in determining where the industrial revolution took place, hence where people, especially children, would first be treated as disposable parts in the world's first giant machine – the mill, the production and raison d'être of which depended on resources from abroad and on the control and coercion of great markets such as those in India, where vast quantities of 'Manchester' cotton were sold.[20]

Manchester's reliance on the rest of the world became starkly obvious when, during the American Civil War of 1861–5, the ships of the north of that country blockaded the ports of the south, thus preventing the shipment of one of the South's main exports: cotton. As a result, Manchester experienced a 'cotton famine', which duly affected the newly created working classes, who, like the factory owners, depended on the labour of slaves who picked the cotton, and the impoverishment of India, which imported the cloth. (Such was the global dominance of Manchester cotton that the word 'Manchester' is still used as a moniker for cotton goods in New Zealand.)

Although the cotton famine of the 1860s led to thousands being laid off in Manchester, by the 1880s it was within London that some of the most acute unemployment was experienced. One of the earliest uses of the word 'unemployment' was to describe the state of some 500 men subsequently re-employed as an act of charity to, among many other tasks, turf a cricket field within London's Paddington recreation grounds in 1888. The men were employed both to relieve a little of their poverty and to create a field for nearby gentry who wished to play the game. (Among those members of the gentry was Lord Randolph Churchill, father to Winston. Notably, one of the gates to the Paddington cricket ground is named after Churchill senior).[21]

There is no clear indication of where the word 'unemployment' was first used, but we know it was around the time when economic depression swept from North to South and ushered in an era when a Manchester-born Welshman, David Lloyd George would be appointed Chancellor of the Exchequer and as such introduce pensions, reduce poverty and later become Prime Minister, during the First World War. Lloyd George's policies did, at least, go some way to change how we thought of people, of how disposable they should be, or not.

It was in the years directly after the First World War that the image of the North-South divide we have today was cast – by the artist Lowry. Later, this image was reinforced by novelists such as Walter Greenwood, whose *Love on the Dole*, set in Salford in 1931 and published in 1933, left an enduring impression on the middle classes. It was adapted for the stage in 1934 and a million people had seen this stage version by 1935. The play 'moved the mostly middle-class audiences without blaming them'; the playwright succeeded when he 'aimed to touch the heart'.[22]

Seventy-five years later *Love on the Dole* formed the basis for a full-page retrospective in what had been the Manchester *Guardian*[23] and which mentioned George Orwell's 1937 *Road to Wigan Pier*. But it was Lowry who impressed us first.

Lowry's best known images are of life in Salford and Manchester during, between and just after the First and Second World Wars. His depictions have become iconic, if not stereotypical: the traipsing mill workers in their thousands dragging their feet on the way to and from work; the crowds heading for football matches; the factories, mills and chimneys; the flat-capped men bent slightly forward – stereotypes of 'Northern toil'. His depictions entered the mainstream during his lifetime and one of his paintings, *The Pond* (1950), was printed on the then Prime Minister Harold Wilson's Christmas card in 1964, not just because it highlighted Wilson's northern origins but also because it was an image of a time and place where much was beginning to improve.

The North-South divide narrowed in the 1950s, 1960s and 1970s and this is highlighted by mortality records, along with a decline in the production of popular images from the northern part of the divide. I was born towards the end of this period, in the South in 1968; later, I emigrated to the North by travelling as far as I could from Oxford while remaining in England: to university in Newcastle upon Tyne in 1986, coming 'up' from Oxford.

In the snobbish world of academic convention everywhere

is located geographically 'down' from Oxford. Trying to explain conventions such as this to people from other countries is very difficult, not least because most people even in Britain have no need to know of such snobbishness, even though academia remains rife with it. Most academics have a university homepage on the Internet and many start this page with a short description of where they are from. Mine begins: 'Danny Dorling was educated at The University of Newcastle upon Tyne', which is true, even though I did not learn as much in lectures and from the library as I did from being in a city different to the one I grew up in, and where I was conventionally educated – at school.[24]

When I was school-age, I learnt that it matters where you grow up within a city, from which quarter you come from. At university I learnt that the fate of large cities, in Britain, depended on their geographical location in the North or South. When I turned up in Newcastle in 1986 it soon became obvious to me that if I had been born and brought up there, my prospects would have been different to those I had benefitted from when growing up in Oxford, even if everything else about my life – my social class, my nutrition and whatever else – had been identical.[25]

It seemed to me that the young men of my age hanging around the streets in Newcastle upon Tyne in the late 1980s had a look in their eyes that was often a little more haunted than was usual in Oxford. In Newcastle the neighbourhoods I lived in were different to those I'd known as a child growing up in the South. In Oxford, I learned to dislike tourists and affluent students alike, but to Newcastle's young men, many of whom were without work since leaving school, students like me looked as ridiculously privileged and as much tourists in their town, as did the *Brideshead Revisited* lookalikes of Oxford that formed part of the background to my childhood.[26]

I lived in Newcastle for ten years and by 1991, at age twenty-three, I was awarded a PhD and had started writing academic papers and then a book.[27] I worked with a lot of people, mostly in the University's Centre for Urban and Regional Development Studies and for what was then called the Regional Research Laboratory for the North East of England. With one colleague, David Atkins, I wrote a report on population change in Britain. Among much else within that report we charted the movements of Britain's shifting population centre.[28] (The centre is the point under which you would have to place your finger to lift the island up and for it to balance perfectly, if human beings were the only objects to have any weight and if all people weighed the same.)

It is not hard to calculate the location of the centre, and not that surprising where you find it, but what shocked me was to learn just how relentlessly it had moved south over the course of almost every year of the last century, apart from a few of those very best years of the 1970s when it did stagger north for a month or twelve. It moved most quickly southwards in the 1930s and in the 1980s. Thus, I was unsurprised to find that while the population in the South was growing, the North was becoming less attractive to the young.

I added to the Northern exodus when I moved back to the South in 1996 to take up a job in Bristol. On arrival I was so shocked by the house prices that I didn't try to buy even a studio flat, despite the fact that I'd had a joint mortgage on a three-bedroom house in Newcastle, where 'decent' property cost much less than a one-bed flat did in Bristol. But I met new people, lived rent-free for a time, and within a couple of years was doing things such as helping to make TV programmes, one of which was called *The Drop-Dead Show*.[29]

The show consisted of a series of questions asked of members of the audience (at home and in the studio), to help determine when they were most likely to 'drop dead'. The answers revealed some unexpected truths about the North-South divide and unearthed previously hidden geographical bias within what appeared to be simply a social or biological division. The show illustrated what some academics like to call the 'problem of context and composition': how much of what happens to people depends on them, or on the place where the action happens.

What *The Drop Dead Show* promised to do was to give everyone an approximate date of death, with a wide margin of error – about twenty years. 'Please don't be tempted to take the following statistics too seriously! For averages of groups of people with the same characteristics, the statistics which follow are pretty accurate; for an individual the final number will almost always not be your exact age at death.'

Davina McCall, the show's presenter, began by explaining that everyone needed a starting point, that with all else being equal the nationally quoted life-expectancy figures didn't apply. Why? Because there were no babies in the audience. Had there been any babies, she said, then at the time the show was broadcast the baby boys should start with a life expectancy of 74, the baby girls with one of 79. So, after discussing how the group's life-chances didn't equate to individual certainty, and how everyone has a different life expectancy depending on the age they are, she next had to try to explain the five-year gap between men's and women's life expectancy.

Even this, of course, has geographical implications. London's increasingly female population makes the capital healthier because women generally live longer and are more careful; the same is true of parts of the coast where

19

older (more often female) people tend to settle in retirement. So, even if the only differences between people's life chances were whether they were male or female, there would still be geographical differences in life expectancy; but not necessarily based upon a great North-South divide.

So the question remained – what was the starting point for members of the audience, none of whom were babies? Well, the men in the audience were told that if they were under 36 they gained an extra year of life than those babies ('start with 75' ordered Davina), yet another year if they had made it over 35 and up to age 49 ('start with 76), yet another year between that and 59 ('start on 77'), another if they were 60 or 61 ('start at 78'), another from age 62 or 63 ('start at 79') and at 64 and 65 ('start at 80'). The numbers continue to rise after that but then begin to get a bit more depressing if you are of great old age. However, even in your later nineties you can expect each year (on average) to make it to another year, if not another two.

What about the women? Well, the benefits for women tend to come a little later. For men, growing up is great, as they are more immature in young adulthood, which is why the improvement shown in the table on page 23 begins earlier at 36. If you have a young male friend or relative who is behaving badly, try to bear in mind that if he makes it to age 36 he is much more likely from then on to be fine, not to have so many fights and use so many substances that might harm him.

Women, in contrast, are at all points from age 1 up to age 40 likely to live until age 80. Women mature earlier, which helps them score better than men on GCSE coursework. Women are still at (a small) risk from childbirth but then again women over 40 tend to have far fewer babies and from 41 women then begin to gain an extra year ('start with 81'), from 55 one more ('start on 82'), at 65

20

one more ('start on 83'), then quickly at 66 another ('start at 84'), at 70 another ('start at 85) and, again, on it rises.

The kink in the curve just described at age 66 is interesting. Why should a woman who has made it to age 66 be likely to live at least 2 years longer than one who has reached the age of 64? The retirement age for almost all women at this time was 60 (at the latest), the menopause around a decade earlier. Female babies very likely fared even better from good rations during the war than did male babies. Boys might already have been a little more favoured when there wasn't enough to go round in the 1930s. The war was good for the overall health of infants, so maybe we should not be surprised to see the echoes of the good effects of rationing on poorer infants, especially baby girls, still being played out, even sixty-five years later.[30]

You may wonder why old people have a longer life expectancy and you may kick yourself when you find out the answer, which is that they have already survived beyond the years in which, in all probability, they would most likely have died. Put simply, an 80-year-old cannot be given a life expectancy of 74 or 79. But, you might argue, surely life expectancies have been improving all the time and so these are all underestimates, especially for younger folk? You are probably right. I say 'probably' because right now in Britain things are not looking so good in some areas. In Glasgow, life expectancy stopped rising altogether from about 2008; it inched up again, given figures reported for 2009, although then came the economic cuts, which add a level of uncertainty to this topsy-turvy trend.

All the social and biological differences found among us have geographical implications and often reveal underlying social and economic influences. As already noted, the population tends to move – steadily and in aggregate as they age – southwards towards the coast. Proportionately more end up in the south-west of England than in any other spot and it has become a place where, in general, improvements in life expectancy have been greatest in the recent past.

So, if you want to play 'Drop Dead' as you read on, you should by now have a starting age. The table overleaf shows what that should be (it has been extended downwards for older readers) and, as these numbers are a decade out of date, you should add three years to account for the effects of social progress. But don't be fooled into thinking that this lengthening is a result of recent progress. Not so. It is all about after-effects – because the population were better fed in the 1960s as compared to the 1950s, and because so many people stopped smoking in the 1970s, they lived longer in the 1990s.

Earlier periods are still important. Men aged 65 in 1992 could expect to live *only* 14 years longer on average then because they were born in 1927 and grew up through an economic slump. They came of age in 1945. In contrast, by 2007, 65-year-old men could expect to live for a further 17 years on average, largely because they were born in 1942 (the lucky war babies), coming of age (21 years old) in 1963. For women, the corresponding lengthening of life expectancies from age 65 are 18 and 20 years respectively. The improvements for women are less dramatic partly because fewer women smoked to begin with. And, if you are reading this book a few years after 2011, you might be tempted to add still more years to your life expectancy than 'just' three to account for the social progress of the past, or maybe even expected scientific progress to come.[31]

Use the correct column for your sex and correct row for your age and begin with the number below:

Male		Female	
Age	Life expectancy	Age	Life expectancy
0	74	0	79
1-35	75	1-40	80
35-49	76	41-54	81
50-59	77	55-64	82
60, 61	78	65	83
62, 63	79	66-69	84
64, 65	80	70-74	85
66-70	81	75	86
71, 72	82	76, 77	87
73, 74	83	78, 79	88
75	84	80-82	89
76, 77	85	83, 84	90
78, 79	86	85	91
80	87		
81	88		
82, 83	89		
84, 85	90		

FIGURE 2: Life Expectancy in Britain by Age
around the Year 1998[32]

Like all good modern quiz shows the updated version of
The Drop Dead Show would give you an easy initial win:
start with the number the table above gives you, and add
three years for being alive in 2011.

Now answer each of the following questions and keep
a tally of how your life expectancy changes. Just like the
numbers above, all the numbers that follow were derived

from published sources estimating the health effects of a particular condition when many other things had been taken into account ('all else being equal'). (The hard work behind all the numbers was mostly carried out by my friend and colleague Mary Shaw.)[33]

1. *When you were aged 14 did you know your father and was he in work and working in a non-manual occupation? If so add two years, otherwise subtract a year.*

I'm currently aged 43. I knew my father when I was 14 and he was working in a non-manual occupation so, I start off with 81 as a life expectancy (76+3+2). The reason for adding the two years or subtracting one is to include an estimate for the overall effects of growing up in a poorer or a more affluent household. This is a crude measure; more complex subdivisions of the population reveal a more nuanced continuum, and show that under certain social circumstances children brought up only by a mother can (on average) do better, and that it helps also to know your mother's social origins. Again there is a hidden geographical bias. Children growing up in the north of England, Wales and Scotland were far more likely to have a father in a manual occupation than were those in the South. But remember, these questions were designed to be asked in a TV game show.

2. *In what class category does your current occupation fall? If professional/semi-professional (for example nurse) then for men* <u>add three years</u> *and women* <u>add two</u>. *Non-professional but non-manual (secretary)* <u>add one</u> *for either sex. If manual-skilled (carpenter)* <u>no change</u>. *Manual-semi-skilled (machine operator)* <u>subtract two</u> *if male,* <u>subtract one</u> *if female.*

If manual-unskilled (cleaner) <u>subtract four</u> if male, <u>subtract two</u> if female.

I teach, so my 81 years jumps to 84. Again this is crude but, in addition, you should factor in that if you are out of work or retired you should use your last job as the marker of your occupation. If you are a student, or are young and have never worked, use your mother's or father's category, whichever is higher.

The effect of social status on life expectancy for men is a massive seven years' difference from top to bottom. Increasingly this is understood to be largely due to the psychological effects of being placed lower in a rank hierarchy, which is probably why men are more affected than women – how they compare to other members of their sex – when it comes to the chances of living a shorter life than others – matters more for them than for women.

Top civil servants who smoked and drank tended to live a little longer than bottom-grade, teetotal, non-smoking civil servants who sorted mail.[34] Again, when you think about where more professional jobs are located and where more of the (crudely described) semi-skilled and unskilled jobs are, you can see how these social divisions again have geographical boundaries.

3. How tall are you? If male and less than 5'8" *(173cm): <u>subtract a year</u>, more than 5'10" (178cm):* *<u>add a year</u>, if female and less than 5'3" (160 cm):* *<u>subtract a year</u>; more than 5'5" (165cm): <u>add a year</u>.*

I'm almost 6' tall, so it's 85 years for me; but why should height matter? All kinds of reasons, including status-anxiety again, but among these reasons height is indicative of how well-fed we were when young. The effects being described by these single-year adjustments are estimates of the independent effects of being shorter or taller, hence the presumption of receiving worse or better nutrition, independent of the correlations between height, class, and much else. We had an inkling then, but now know with more surety that what has *not* been measured are the effects of genetics.

More recent research than we had access to in 1998 has found that height is more socially than genetically determined, which is why Americans are no longer some of the tallest people in the world, as they were during the mid-nineteenth century. Now the far more equitable Dutch, Swedes and Norwegians are among the tallest.[35] The fact that height is mostly a matter of nutrition and care is why, if you attend a university graduation ceremony, you'll see that almost all of the students are taller than the older generation that has come to cheer them on.

Is there a North-South divide in height? Yes, but it's better described by anecdote than inches. I saw it most starkly when queuing to pay for a basket of groceries in a poor part of Glasgow. I was able to look all the way down the very long rows of tills, easily over the heads of every other customer in every other queue. As I said, I'm not quite six feet tall. The only other place in the world I've towered over so many people was in India.

4. *Have you been unemployed in the last three months? If this was not out of choice <u>deduct two years</u>.*

I stay at 85. Unemployment has an independent effect on our health when we live in a society where employment is the norm. If anything helps show how much our health is influenced by our social circumstances, it is this.

The two lost years this question threatens are caused by the debilitating effects of the social downgrading that comes from being cast out of work and deemed by the market as being a human not worthy of use. These debilitating effects are independent of falling income – and are far more likely to strike those from poorer backgrounds.

In Britain we have now had enough time to follow up some of the long-term sociological effects of unemployment during the early 1980s recession. Most strikingly, it was found that for young people, being offered and then accepting a place on what was called the Youth Training Scheme (YTS) was almost as bad as remaining unemployed in terms of later health outcome:[36] being *forced* on to the scheme was possibly worse; the enforcement was seen to be a form of slavery. In contrast, good quality training, such as apprenticeships, was associated with better health outcomes.

Is there a secondary geographical echo to the health-damaging effect of unemployment? In other words, does unemployment strike every town and city equally when recession hits? I think you've got the story by now. Much of the growing North-South health divide is attributable to the geographical fallout of economic, social and political factors, but not all of it.

5. *Where were you born? Caribbean: add two; England and Wales or other: no change; Indian sub-continent: subtract two; Africa, Ireland (all parts), or Scotland: subtract three.*

I was born in Oxford so I am still stuck on 85. Why should where you were born have an effect above and beyond all those we have already included? Well – geography matters. The Caribbean advantage may be due to older

27

people originally from the Caribbean sometimes returning there if ill, leaving a healthier population here; or due to the beneficial effects of sunlight and vitamin D. It might be due to the long-term benefits of financial reward – for example moving from a cheap area of London, where habitually immigrants would settle because this is what they could afford, to a better area once they were able to make their way. No one quite knows why. In contrast, the huge average penalties that are inflicted upon the UK's Celtic periphery, or the periphery of its former empire, in Africa, may be reflections of modern-day hardships, or less successful average migratory routes. We don't know. What we do know is that this has little to do with genes.

Migrants tend to be healthier than both the populations they leave and those they join. This is true even of forced migrants. Those millions of Africans who were enslaved and transported across the Atlantic tended to be healthier than those left behind. That is because healthier adults and children were selected to be slaves and only the healthiest of them survived the Atlantic passage and their subsequent life on plantations. Many were taken directly from West Africa to the Caribbean. Perhaps a small part of that explains why Caribbean-born people living in Britain tend even now to live longer than their peers. It is very complicated, but the simple effects of this on the North-South divide are to widen it further: more people of Caribbean origin live in the South.

6. *Where do you now live within the UK? In England south of or within Gloucestershire, Warwickshire, Leicestershire or Lincolnshire: add a year; otherwise subtract a year*.

Finally, my number moves, I'm back down to 84 as I live in

Sheffield. Irrespective of everything else so far measured, we are still left with a two-year difference depending on which side of the North-South line we currently reside. But what is it that makes me, as part of the group of Northerners I have joined, now live a shorter life? Is it the rain, the wind, the cold?

Look at that list of four counties in the last question. The mortality records reveal the line to slope up from the Severn to the Humber. So what is the reason for this dividing line? Our best guess is migration. Over time those people who leave the North to move South tend to be the ones who do a little better in life. People who are moving in the reverse direction tend, on average, to have fallen on harder times. These are generalizations, but so are life expectancy statistics.

In retirement, Southerners may move to Lincolnshire, just within the southern border, but much more rarely move across the divide. The housing is cheaper in the North, the cost of living is higher in the South; both these factors have an effect.[37] There may, of course, also be the effect of that cold and damp in the North but, before blaming the lack of warmth, ask why people live such longer lives in the north of Scandinavia and shorter lives in warmer but not excessively hot parts of Africa.

7. *What is your housing status? Owner-occupied: no change, renting: subtract a year; hostel for home-less: subtract twelve years, sleeping rough: subtract twenty-five years.*

I stay on 84. Should I find myself truly destitute that would shift rapidly to 59 but, what this twenty-five-year drop really means is that I would have a good chance of dying even earlier, possibly in my early forties. Thankfully, the majority of rough sleepers do survive their period of sleeping rough and so, if I'd been sleeping rough but didn't die soon, I'd probably live longer than 59, although 84 would be very lucky. All these chances average out at a net loss of an expected twenty-five years of life.

It was difficult to undertake the studies that would later find their way into *The Drop Dead Show* and uncover these statistics. We had to include this question, even though we assumed that few, if any of the people who would be asked it, would have been living in a hostel or would have only been able to watch the show on a TV set through a shop window.[38] But, given that more people sleep rough in the south of England than in the north, and that there are also more hostels in the south, this, finally, is one effect that should reduce the geographical divide a little – but only a little.

8. *Are you a smoker? Yes: <u>subtract four</u>; former: <u>no change</u>; never: <u>add three</u>.*

I stay on 84 because I smoked from the age of 16 to 36. What this question reveals (when you add four to three to get seven) is that someone who has never (or hardly ever) smoked will live, on average, a substantial seven years longer than a current smoker.[39] And, yes, statistics show that, for a wide variety of reasons, smoking is a little more common the further north you travel.

One of those reasons though is contagion: large numbers of the middle classes gave up smoking in the 1950s – and the South had a greater population of the middle classes than the North; thus, it was unusual to smoke in the South, this meant that, within a few decades, people of all classes in the South became less likely to smoke than did people in the North. At its simplest, there are fewer people to cadge a cigarette from where smoking is less common and more people to comment that you smell of smoke!

9. *How much alcohol do you drink? Abstain: sub-tract one; moderate: add one; heavy: subtract three. Any more than fourteen units a week for women or twenty-one units for men is heavy. A modern 250 ml-sized wine glass should be counted as two units).*

I'm down to 81. My consumption is more than twenty-one units a week, but not by much. It's nothing to be proud of. In fact drinking, even in moderation, is not necessarily that good for you, despite the implications of the answers to the question above. The main reason why abstainers tend on average to live slightly shorter lives than the rest of us is that they include former drinkers who have already been affected by the damage the alcohol has done.

Estimates have been made of how much alcohol is bought and drunk in each part of Britain, but the most efficient way to calculate this is simply by looking at the areas afflicted by the highest death rates from chronic liver disease. Between 1996 and 2000 the top twelve areas were, in descending order: Glasgow; West of Scotland; Central Scotland; London Central; London South Inner; Merseyside West; Lothian; Lancashire Central; Greater Manchester Central; Merseyside East and Wigan; Tyne and Wear; and South of Scotland.[40]

10. *Do you usually eat fruit daily (do not include juice)? Yes: add one; no: subtract one.*

Up to 82! It's the crudest possible question to ask about healthy eating. Of course it is far easier for some people to eat better than others. Income is a key factor. But everyone who is not a vegetarian could give up red meat, or give up a little of it once in a while and use the savings to buy more fruit. Trying to measure the independent effects of all these contributions to health is not an exact science and there are, again, great contagion effects within social categories – the over-exercising, fruit-eating, non-smoking, wine-glugging middle classes – as well as contagion effects by area.

It is far easier to be a vegetarian where it is more normal to be one, where cafes serve less meat, where it is strange *not* to feed your children fruit and vegetables. So with dieting, as in (almost) everything else, there is a geography as well as a season and, again, class-contagion effects have geographical implications: black pudding is stocked less frequently in deli counters in the South than in the North, and vice versa for guacamole (but guacamole is much better for you, in comparison).

11. *How much do you exercise? Regular vigorous, such as running at least twice a week: add two; regular moderate, such as at least two brisk walks a week: add one; less: subtract one.*

I'm back up to 84. I couldn't have said this back in 1998. Like many middle-aged men who are getting fatter, I now cycle to and from work (no longer smoking makes that easier); however, cycling used to be for the working classes and I can remember as a child waiting for ages for there to be a gap in the continuous lines of men cycling to work at the local car factory, so that I could cross the road to get to school. I got a shock recently: early one morning when I was visiting civil servants in Whitehall I had again to wait for a break in the continuous line of cyclists so that I could cross the road; on this occasion all the riders wore ties.

Among people aged 25 to 39 the bike is nowhere near the most common form of transport but it is the second most common in and around Cambridge, Oxford, near Ipswich and near to Portsmouth. In contrast, it never gets into even the second most favoured mode of transport in Wales or Scotland, and in England it is only second placed in places in and around Hull; in a couple of places on the flatter (colliery) edge of Sheffield, cycling is as common as in some parts of the South, but this is generally for reasons of finance and the lack of an adequate affordable bus or tram system rather than for fitness.[41]

12. *What is your weight? Underweight: <u>subtract two</u>; normal weight: <u>add one</u>; overweight: <u>subtract one</u>; very overweight (body mass index 30+): <u>subtract two</u>.*

Whoops, down to 82. I didn't say the cycling worked (and I blame getting fatter on no longer smoking). I could have just subtracted one but, like the drinking, that would not have been true for most weeks of the year. You really need a height-weight chart to know whether you are too fat or too thin, or indeed half an hour to have it explained to you how to square your weight and divide the result by your height and also to understand the different thresholds for what combination of imperial and metric measures are used.[42]

Obesity statistics are related to geography, although estimating this simply through the spatial prevalence of Type 2 diabetes is too crude. Some private companies are prone to do this when they want to get their company name in the press, for example by identifying the fattest town in Britain. The BBC quoted one company as claiming: 'Hull is the chubbiest town in Britain – while Kingston upon Thames is the leanest.' The BBC report continued by explaining that: 'Data analysts Experian compiled the tables based on hospital admission records for Type 2 diabetes. The most likely to be overweight were white, working-class families who have poor education and do little exercise.'[43]

Diagnosis of Type 2 diabetes is not a brilliant indicator of obesity. Although many people with Type 2 diabetes might have been obese when diagnosed with the illness, most obese people do not have Type 2 diabetes. The BBC reported Experian's spokesperson as suggesting that: 'These are white working-class people living in areas of council flats where diet is poor and exercise isn't taken regularly.' However, and as we've just discovered, Hull may not have much of a middle class but it is the town where more middle-aged people cycle than anywhere else in the North. Figure 3, overleaf, shows Experian's league table of places where you are most likely to suffer Type 2 diabetes. The BBC misleadingly titled it 'The Obesity League Table'.

13. *Are you an illegal-drug user who injects? If so subtract eight years. Otherwise no change.*

I stay on 82. The subtraction of eight years is, like the effects of homelessness, an averaging out of a few very young deaths against smaller, longer term ill-effects for the majority of people who have injected at some time. There are far more people who are injecting than you may think: the numbers are estimated regularly by testing small sections of hair taken from a random sample of the population. At any one time some 4 per cent of the population of Glasgow aged between 15 and 64 are using. Most of these will be towards the younger end and so the numbers who have injected at some time in their lives are now much

OBESITY LEAGUE TABLE			
The chubbiest areas .... and the slimmest			
1	Kingston upon Hull	1	Kingston upon Thames
2	Knowsley, Merseyside	2	Kensington and Chelsea
3	Blackburn, Lancs	3	Westminster
4	South Tyneside	4	Richmond upon Thames
5	Easington, C. Durham	5	Wandsworth
6	Merthyr Tydfil, Wales	6	Isles of Scilly
7	Blaenau Gwent, Wales	7	Hammersmith & Fulham
8	Stoke-on-Trent	8	Elmbridge, Surrey
9	Pendle, Lancs	9	Camden
10	Middlesborough	10	South Bucks
11	Hyndburn, Lancs	11	Barnet
12	Hartlepool	12	City of Glasgow
13	Corby, Northants	13	St. Albans, Herts
14	Sandwell, W. Midlands	14	Chiltern, Bucks
15	Burnley, Lancs	15	Mole Valley, Surrey
16	Sunderland	16	City of Edinburgh
17	Oldham, Lancs	17	Epsom & Ewell, Surrey
18	Halton, Cheshire	18	Tanbridge, Surrey
19	Rochdale, Lancs	19	Waverley, Surrey
20	Birmingham	20	Guildford

FIGURE 3: Type 2 Diabetes League Table

Source: http://news.bbc.co.uk/1/hi/health/3521551.stm BBC news online, 'Britain's Fattest Areas Revealed', 1 March 2004.

higher than they were in 1998 and, notably, even the overall figure of *current* users for Scotland rose by 30 per cent between 2003 and 2006.[44]

Why do more people inject, and then do so for more years of their lives in the North and especially to places such as the Clyde? It is partly because of what has happened to the North and especially to places such as the Clyde. It is largely because of the few consistent and long-term employment opportunities there. It is because you see everyone (who can) get out of the Clyde do exactly that, and if you can't, you might as well get out of your head.

14. *For men: do you have sex at least twice a week? If so, add a year. For women: do you enjoy sex at least twice a week? If so, add a year.*

I think now might be a good time for me to stop answering these questions. A life expectancy of 82 gets me to exactly 2050; at this point I'd be very happy with that – and this is a common phenomena. There is evidence that people put in a special effort to reach decennial and millennial dates, or to get just past their birthdays (and so on), and that very many also die within a short time of the death of a loved one.

The evidence that having sex appears to have an independent beneficial health effect comes from a paper that had been published a year before *The Drop Dead Show*. It was based on a study conducted in the Welsh town of Caerphilly and five villages adjacent to it, so it is, of course, possible that it is only here where sex matters. Should you ever feel the need to quote the result to a loved one, the key line from the paper is: 'Analysed in terms of actual frequency of orgasm, the odds ratio for total mortality associated with an increase in 100 orgasms per year was 0.64.'[45] (I'm not sure this has ever been used for chat-up purposes, and we don't know much about the geography of sex, although the British sex survey did imply that the nearer people lived to France, the more adventurous the British were in bed.)

36

15. *What is your marital status? Married, cohabiting or never married: <u>add one</u>; divorced, widowed or separated: <u>subtract one</u>.*

Maybe I really will get to see in New Year 2050. Note that when, in 1850 Alfred Lord Tennyson said 'better to have loved and lost than never to have loved at all'[46] he did not have access to modern-day cohort studies to test his assertion. For women the effects of marriage are not as beneficial as they are for men, but they are still there. Being happy with someone who is happy with you has a great deal to be said for it, beyond the net effect of two more years of life.

I was once told by a very kindly academic from Cambridge that what really matters in life is not how long you might expect to live, but how much time you might get to share with those you love. He then rather spoiled the effect by trying to teach me how to calculate the relevant joint probability functions.

As ever, there is a geography associated to relationship success or failure: the divorce capital of Britain is Blackpool; remarriage is most common along the south coast.[47] But I'll say more about that in some of the following chapters.

That is the end of the quiz. Since the show was first aired, the North-South divide has become deeper and deeper. On Thursday, 2 December 1999, the BBC announced that the 'North-South health divide [was] "widening"'[48] with Professor George Davey Smith of the University of Bristol explaining that: 'The difference between the better off and the worse off has increased absolutely dramatically . . . Even in the last couple of years under a new government there has been rather little relative to what has happened over the last twenty years to reduce that.'

The Prime Minister's response inspired the BBC news headline: 'Blair: North-South Divide "a myth"'.[49] It wasn't that I believed him, but I did leave Bristol shortly afterwards and took a job at the University of Leeds in early 2000. Leeds was big, commercial and felt like a little London in the North. I moved again, to Sheffield in 2003, and there, a few years later in 2007, received that phone call from the man who worked at the Lowry art gallery. 'Why does this age-old [dividing] line persist?' he asked. I told him that I spent a lot of time on trains, and from the train window you can see at what point the style of house-building changes as you 'go northern' (as I put it).

There are lots of dividing lines, I said, 'Inner and outer London, north and south of the river. Where the Home Counties start and end is another question. Is the Welsh border really the border of Wales? And where exactly is the "top" we are told exists as we go over the Pennines? Nonetheless, this particular North-South line fascinates us more than any other.' He asked me to define the line for him, and part of the result is drawn at the start of this chapter.

The North-South divide matters today because it is now a very different line in terms of meaning. It is now the furthest extent north many southerners would consider retiring to, if they could not make it out of the UK. It is also the furthest north and west where many London commuters would imagine living, or be able to live given commuting times. The South is almost becoming a separate country: Gainsborough is included, but not Grimsby; Cheltenham but not Cinderford. The really 'adventurous' Southerners live just over the southern border in Hay-on-Wye or York.

I'll end this chapter by telling you a secret, but please don't pass it on too widely. There is a city in the North, a third of which is national park. This city has uncrowded trains that arrive in London in just over two hours. Unlike in Manchester it doesn't rain much and people still say thanks to their bus drivers. There are traffic jams on only one road and only then for part of the year. You wouldn't want it becoming like Hay or York so I shouldn't really be telling you this but it is the place where, despite hard times, more people decided to stay and call it home during the last recession than any other badly hit northern town. It is the city of *The Full Monty*; it is the nearest metropolis to the colliery village used for the basis of the film *Brassed Off*; it is the city that received more government spending cuts over the summer of 2010 than any other – in a cruel test of Deputy Prime Minister, Nick Clegg's, loyalty. It is the kind of place that a less cut-throat, less depressed, less divided Britain could well emulate: it is Sheffield, where a higher proportion of children grow up to attend university each year than do children from Britain's most affluent large city, Bristol. This is because education in Sheffield is more equally distributed and, in a less divided country, what is commonplace in places like Sheffield would be nearer the centre of our thinking everywhere else.[50]

CHAPTER 2

WHERE HAVE ALL THE GOOD MEN GONE?

'The only thing worse than smug married couple; lots of smug married couples.'

Bridget Jones's Diary[1]

Bridget Jones's Diary began as a newspaper column written by Helen Fielding in 1995; the novel that followed became a bestseller in 1997. Rumours spread among young women in London that their life story was out. The diary won the British Book of the Year in 1998 and adaptation to film quickly followed, opening in 2001. The sequel, *Edge of Reason* (2004) was based on the follow-up book of the same name. Fielding celebrated her fifty-second birthday in February 2010. And in 2011 the *Bridget Jones* musical goes on stage in London's West End. Lily Allen, who turned 25 in May 2010, and whose age was not even in double digits when the column first appeared, is rumoured to have been writing the score.[2]

Bridget Jones was a fictional thirtysomething 1990s singleton Londoner, created by an *actual* thirtysomething

1990s singleton Yorkshire lass living in London, who found it difficult to find a man. It struck a chord – there really was a shortage of men at this time, especially in London. But what the column, the book, the film and (I expect) the musical do not explain is why this was so. Where had all the good men gone? What were they doing? Would they ever return? Could part of the reason be that fewer boys than girls had been born thirty-odd years ago? Well, in an attempt to answer these vital questions I spent some time in the 1990s, and the early years of the last decade, pondering over this puzzle. Here's what I came up with (in brief): many of these men had gone abroad to work and they might never come back. Also, starting from around thirty years ago, an unusually low number of boys were born in Britain in comparison to girls, and the trend continued after that. So, yes, the *Bridget Jones* phenomenon is here to stay. And it will hit Lily Allen's generation far harder than it hit Helen Fielding's.

The stories of a lack of men are not going away. For the first time since the loss of so many young male lives in the First World War, young women in Britain are finding that there are fewer young men to go round. Indeed, in 2003 the newspaper that started the Bridget Jones column, the *Independent*, ran the headline: 'Speed-Dating Boom Hit by Shortage of Men'.[3]

What has changed most recently is the advent of newspaper stories written by women in their thirties who accept that they may be single for life and so talk up the advantages of never again being in a relationship. One such report in 2010 ended: 'The planet's overpopulated anyway.'[4] The 34-year-old who wrote those words appeared to have consigned herself to never having children or a long-term relationship and that, despite other people telling her, 'Don't worry, there's someone out there for everyone', she had learnt that there wasn't.

Surely there are enough men around, aren't there? (There must be enough unscrupulous cads to take part in speed dating – or at least that's what I thought – who would slip their wedding ring off and add a bit of artificial tan to their ring fingers.) But, if there weren't enough, perhaps it would make life easier for men if they were in greater demand than ever? And what about the situation for gay men? Are there more gay men now than there were thirty years ago? And are there more homosexual men than women? Why is it so hard to find a man nowadays – a good man? Why are most single young people either women with degrees or men with no qualifications? So many questions!

Yes, so many questions, and a multitude of answers, which may have little to do with female emancipation or male inability to impress but, maybe, if you removed the paternalistic image from the breadwinner society, you also remove some of the attractiveness of the benefits of a longer-term relationship with a man. If you earn your own crust, you no longer have to put up with the man you might have put up with in the past. And, anyway, he may no longer be quite good enough for your standards, so you set your sights a little higher. The problem is that you are not the only one setting your sights higher. Your female friends are doing the same, and apart from that are working at the same jobs that in the past were 'men-only'. Could this be the problem?

As I said earlier, I've been pondering this problem, on and off, for quite a few years now, but I had forgotten about it recently, until summer 2010 when a particular news story caught my attention. A study had been undertaken of babies born in recent years in the city of Fallujah in Iraq. This was the place where fighting had been most intense during the recent war. Nobody is sure what [weapons] the Americans used in the streets of that city and there were claims made of war crimes being committed against the civilian population. War crimes in Fallujah may appear a million miles away from speed dating in London, but what has happened there not only has a great deal to do with decisions we make in the UK, it also gives us clues about the problems of an apparent shortage of males in what should be far easier lives in Britain today.

The study found that after 2005 the proportion of girls born in Fallujah increased sharply; that prior to the war the birth ratio was usually around 105 boys to 100 girls. However, in Fallujah in the four years after the US assault, the birth ratio was reduced to 86 boys to 100 girls, an alteration last found in Hiroshima after the atomic bomb was dropped in 1945. Again, the blame might be the toxicity of US weapons, such as those that use depleted uranium. Additionally there may be clues in our evolution, in the robustness of our design. Male foetuses have one X-chromosome; females have a spare/additional X-chromosome, which gives them a little more leeway to cope with genetic damage and continue to develop rather than miscarry. If this were true, then at least an extra 10 per cent of foetuses would have been miscarried in Fallujah since 2005; however, and in addition, many of the babies that were born would have been damaged and would have soon died. As those reporting the story put it:

The assault on Fallujah, a city located forty-three miles west of Baghdad, was one of the most horrific war crimes of our time . . . "collective" punishment is, according to the laws of war, illegal.

. . . In September 2009, Fallujah General Hospital had 170 newborn babies, 24 per cent of whom were dead within the first seven days [and] a staggering 75 per cent of the dead babies were classified as deformed.[5]

Perhaps I should have been more shocked, but in recent years we have become used to stories of war crimes. What did shock me, though, was the realization that sex ratios could be altered so dramatically. I wondered if the ratios, which were altered so much by damaging chemical and radioactive exposure and/or physiological stress, could also be affected over time by other factors such as pollution. A look back at the records shows how many boys were born for every 100 girls each year in Britain since 1970:

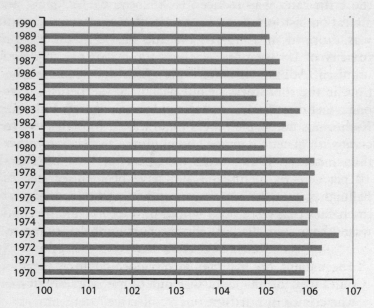

FIGURE 4: Male/Female Birth Ratio in Britain 1970–90

Boys Born in Britain for Every 100 Girls Born Each Year. Source ONS and GRO(S)[6]

The year most boys were born in Britain, relative to girls, was 1973, when 7 extra boys were born for every 100 girls.[7] Just 7 per 100 may not appear to be much of a variation, but it could make all the difference in the world if that seventh extra boy grew up to be the man who would become your future partner. Think of dating as a game of musical chairs: when the music stops each boy has to sit on a girl's lap. A couple of pairs of boys will excuse themselves from the game to instead play football or video games; a pair of girls will do the same. A few more exit because they don't want to play at all, a lot of people just want to be on their own most of the time – and a few more boys than girls opt for solitude: more hermits are male, and there have always been more monks than nuns.[8] Suddenly you find you have fewer boys than girls, and that as a result some girls are missing out. Not too many – but every time that birth excess of 7 is reduced by 1, another chance for 1 girl in 100 to be partnered with a male disappears forever.

The year 1973 was a good one, 1974 less so – two elections and the inflationary fall-out from oil shocks and rising job losses, helped to reduce the ratio to 6 extra boys for every 100 girls. Yet no one would really notice until a couple of decades later: *Bridget Jones's Diary* was published in 1996, when the missing boys would have been aged 22. Things picked up a bit during the rest of the 1970s, but then came the recession of 1980 and we lost another boy, never born, for every 100 girls. He would have been 21 years old when Renée Zellweger starred as the eponymous Bridget Jones, the girl trying to choose between the staid Colin Firth and the caddish Hugh Grant, while both men had many alternative options.

The graph also shows that a little later in the 1980s there was again a small bounce back, with a few extra boys born; but then came the misery of the miners' strike in 1984 and we were back to only five extra boys, a level to which we dipped again in the recession around 1990.

In 2006, one of the most prestigious academic journals, *The Proceedings of the United State's National Academy of Sciences*, reported that 'the odds of a newborn's being male . . . declines when populations cope with shocks such as natural and human-made disasters, economic and political disruption, and terror attacks'.[9] All kinds of reasons have been posited as to why this happens, but among researchers there seems little argument against it. So, if you are trying for a boy, think happy thoughts, and if you want a girl, daydream a little about redundancy and your credit card bills.

There's nowhere like Fallujah in Britain, you might say, where only 86 boys are born for every 100 girls; but, actually, there is. It is a place where there are only 87 males for every 100 females. It is about as far away from Fallujah as you can get, in all kinds of ways, a quiet and peaceful place just fifty-three miles from London: Eastbourne, that East Sussex town sitting sleepily on the south coast.[10]

Eastbourne has more women because it is a place people retire to and, among these retirees, the women tend to live longer than the men. It is at precisely the age of 75 that there tend to be only 86 men left for every 100 women.[11] In areas with many people aged over 75 and with many young women caring for older people, it is not hard to achieve the same sex-ratio as found in Fallujah, but for opposite reasons, such as: a strong welfare state, the security of equal rights for women and, crucially, good maternity services that reduce childbirth mortality. But Eastbourne is atypical – if you look at the table below you'll see that, of the ten districts of Britain where there are the most women relative to men, only a few of them are retirement destinations, which tend to gain folk over time as the population ages. And now, as more men live longer, the sex ratio is equalizing.

Four locations stand out, and include those where the population as a whole has fallen greatly in recent years, alongside falling male-female sex ratios. This is not because the population is elderly, nor because of the long-term success of the welfare state and human advancement; rather, it is because so many of the young men have left and, of those young men who have remained, quite a few have died, many before reaching retirement age, which is roughly where life expectancy lies for men in the poorest of the four areas shaded darker in the table – Glasgow.[12]

2001 census	Males	Females	ratio 2001	ratio 1991	change (from 1991)
Eastbourne	41,650	48,017	87	82	4,786
Rother LA	39,880	45,548	88	84	2,362
Worthing LA	45,764	51,804	88	84	-498
Arun LA	66,212	74,547	89	87	9,442
Christchurch LA	21,130	23,735	89	87	3,625
Glasgow City LA	272,309	305,560	89	90	-53,143
Wirral MB	147,182	165,111	89	91	-23,812
East Devon LA	59,203	66,317	89	88	7,423
Sefton MB	133,489	149,469	89	91	-12,246
Knowsley MB	71,064	79,395	90	93	-6,343

FIGURE 5: Districts in Britain with the Most Women per Men in 2001 and Change since 1991.

Males, Females, Ratios and Population Change 2001/1991. Source ONS and GRO(S)

Glasgow is no Fallujah, but it was shocking to find that in 2001 there were only 89 males for every 100 females living there. In the Wirral, Sefton and Knowsley there are different mixtures of sociological factors that impact on the ratio including retirement, new and predominately female university accommodation and also a little more relative deprivation than experienced before. As a result, the towns that feature in this top-ten list are areas that have experienced rapid population change that ends up being female dominated. It is in Glasgow that the trends are most stark.

In recent years Glasgow has been compared to Gaza because life expectancies were similarly short, despite the many cultural and economic differences between the two places. So how is this similarity explained? One reason is that there is no wall around Glasgow and as emigration from the city is positively encouraged, those with better health are more likely to leave; in contrast, there is a restrictive wall around Gaza preventing or inhibiting emigration or, indeed, return. Really, to compare Glasgow with Gaza is both as sensible and as ridiculous as is comparing Eastbourne and Fallujah; however, when it comes to understanding how we have ended up with so few men in some of our cities, such comparisons help. It helps to ask why the life expectancies of two such different places can be so similar, or how male-female ratios overall, and at birth, can equate in a sleepy, middle-class retirement town and a third-world town that has been ravaged by war.

Variations in fertility and mortality are just two small factors of the reason why some places are home to fewer (or more) boys than girls. However, over time I've found that related to these facts is *migration*, which helps us understand the North-South divide, as well as the fluctuations in the male-female population ratios. And, again, we have to go back a few years to study the historical statistics.

What follows is a story to try to explain the numbers. The characters are fictional, the numbers are real.

It was spring 1991 and twenty-five young men and women were partying in a flat in Islington, north London. To be precise there were thirteen men and twelve women, a ratio typical in all of London at that time. Remember how many more boys had been born in the early 1970s? Boys also tended to do better than girls at school back in the 1980s, more went to university then than did young women, and so more young men than women moved to London for graduate jobs. One such young man, born in 1968 and who graduated from university in the summer of 1989 is Kevin. At age 23 Kevin was qualified, working, single and lonely – and at a party.

At the party, Chesney Hawkes is playing on a tape deck.[13] Chesney was number one in the charts that spring and the chorus to 'I Am the One and Only' was reverberating through Kevin's head as he cursed his bad luck at being the odd man out at the party (again). The flat was normally shared by one couple, whose engagement they were now celebrating.

On the floor of the flat is a discarded census form. In 1991 the recent introduction of the poll tax had led to unprecedented numbers of young people in Britain refusing to fill in their census forms. These young people had more important things to think about, though this particular couple *did* fill in their form, unlike Kevin who, when he got back to his flat just couldn't be bothered and, eventually, threw the form in the bin.

Nevertheless, and luckily, the powers-that-be had worked out how many people were living in Islington. Academics carried out a project called 'Estimating with Confidence' to work out just how many people there really were living in each part of the country.[14] They knew how many had been born, how many had died, and had estimates of how many had left these shores and how many had arrived but, most importantly, they had an idea of how many people tended not to fill in forms in each place, according to the characteristics of that place and of the inhabitants.

There are some places where people tend not to fill in forms – inner cities. There are some people who tend not to fill in forms – single young men in particular. There are also particular times when people tend not to fill in forms. You need to account for such trends and characteristics so that you will understand the odds of how such actions, or inactions, affect your estimate of how many young men and women there are living in a certain place at a certain time.

The methods used by the academics to estimate the numbers were enhanced at the next census by the census authorities themselves. With the help of a few boffins, the authorities employed a technique called 'capture-recapture' to estimate how many people living in each area did not fill in their census form. Capture-recapture is the same method used for estimating how many whales are still living in the oceans after extensive overfishing. Because it was used in 1991 in a crude way, and in 2001 in a more sophisticated manner, we now have a better idea of population statistics and so can construct fictitious stories based on firm facts – at least in relation to how many young men and women there are, or were.

Roll forward ten years to 2001 and yet another group of twenty-five young people are partying in the same flat in London, but now there are more women (thirteen) than men (twelve), the odd one out being Kate, who is pondering the deeper meaning hidden within the lyrics of S Club 7's number-one hit 'Don't Stop Moving', which is being played on CD.[15]

Again, the census form is on the floor and many of the guests will leave their own copies uncompleted but, as before with the 1991 census, their numbers will be estimated by other means. The poll tax had gone by 2001 but despite this there was even greater apathy among the young when it came to answering to authority. During 2001, proportionately, just as many youngsters, when provoked by the police, rioted against the World Trade Organization as had ever rioted against the now-defunct poll tax.[16] Protestors were becoming more sophisticated; but so were people-counters.

A few weeks after the party two men called at the door to ask who was staying in the flat that night. Kate, 25, single, and now the tenant of the original [couple] (who had since moved to leafy Surrey), answered the door. She filled in the special 2001 census coverage survey form, which was issued to hundreds of thousands of households in Britain between May and June 2001.[17] And it is only because of such tedious and meticulous exercises of pounding the pavements and knocking on doors that we know with even greater confidence just how many young men and women there were in Britain, and where they are now. We can only be sure of these numbers at census dates, but successive censuses give us some idea of the direction of trend. The figures shown above were representative of all of London, not just Islington.

By 2001 there were 13 young women for every 12 young men living in London, 8 per cent more women than men in the 25 to 29 age-group. Nationally, there were by then 4 per cent more women of this age range than men; outside of London there were only 1 per cent more women than men in their late twenties. A decade ago it had been a different story: nationally, but especially in the capital, there had been more men than women of these ages. London had lost many young men and gained a great many young women. But why, and with what effect?

To understand how and why the balance of the sexes in London had changed so abruptly, almost every other aspect of changing lives in this country needs to be considered. This is a story of sex, love and rejection but first, please, a few more numbers are needed. Although anecdote matters, it is the aggregation of some thousands and then some millions of very personal stories that leads us to where we are today.

In 1991 there were 366,000 women and 386,000 men aged 25 to 29 in London; in 2001 there were approximately 360,000 women and 332,000 men aged 25 to 29. These figures altered a little when revised estimates of the population were published for Southwark, Wandsworth and Westminster (following the threat of legal challenges to the census estimates). But they did not alter greatly. Therefore, a deficit of roughly 20,000 women turned into a similarly sized surplus in just 10 years.[18]

In 2001, of the 10 districts in Britain with the highest proportions of women to men aged 25 to 29, 5 districts were found in London: Barking and Dagenham; Hackney; Hillingdon; Islington; and Kensington & Chelsea. The 10 areas with the fastest increases in women as a proportion of the population of any area in Britain included 4 of these 5 boroughs. What was occurring in recent years in London is also happening elsewhere today, but nowhere to the same extent and with the same importance, and for no other age group has this change been so clear.

To begin to understand why the population of London in particular is becoming more female we have to understand what is happening nationwide – both in the present and more than forty years ago. Between 1962 and 1966 a majority of the baby-boom generation (those born just after the Second World War) had given birth to their own children. These were the children of Philip Larkin's 'Annus Mirabilis', conceived (the children, not the poem) around the time of the Beatles' first LP, *Please, Please Me*. In those years some 2,464,000 boys and 2,326,000 girls were born in Britain. Larkin's 'Annus Mirabilis' poem was the one about sexual intercourse, beginning around 1963, a bit late for Mr Larkin, being after the end of the Chatterley ban, but (thankfully for him at least) before the Beatles' first LP.[19]

By 1991 there were 2,375,000 men and 2,290,000 women aged 25 to 29 alive and kicking in Britain. Young deaths and no great gains of immigration over emigration accounted for the slight declines as compared to the 1960s. The surplus of men that was the result of 5.9 per cent more boys being born than girls had been reduced, but not eliminated, mostly by premature deaths. Boys, who are generally more accident prone, were a little more likely to die than girls. Young men were also slightly more likely to leave the country than young women. Was this possibly the result of greater wanderlust and fewer job opportunities at home?

One of the factors could have been the differences in the birth cohort size of boys compared to girls. Add to that increasing differential migration and there has been a growing geographical mismatch in terms of where young men and women end up living in Britain. We might find our soulmates on the Internet but we'd then have to be ready to perhaps do a fair bit of travelling in order to meet up regularly. Nobody ever told us in geography lessons that one day we might have to commute for love.

And speaking of travelling, when all those young men went abroad in the 1980s and 1990s looking for work, some found more than they were looking for – they found a partner. When it came to deciding where to settle down, especially if it's a choice between two countries, nowadays being nearer to the woman's mother tends to rank slightly higher than being near her mother-in-law – one final reason why the men are missing: women, when they settle down, have a tendency to settle near mum, especially when they become a mum themselves. Yet, despite all that, by the start of the 1990s there were still more young men than women in the country.

A decade after the baby boomers started having their own children we saw a slight decrease in the birth rate: between 1972 and 1976 1,846,000 boys and 1,738,000 girls were born in Britain, 6.2 per cent more boys than girls. Why? Well, the early 1970s were 'the never had it so good years', even better than the early 1960s and even better than could have been expected when, on 20 July 1957, Prime Minister Harold Macmillan told the population that they had never had it so good.[20] After Macmillan's party lost power in 1964 things suddenly got much better. They carried on getting better when the Conservatives got back into government for a few years in the early 1970s, despite the issues of oil shock and inflation (and some awful glamrock).[21] For people who did not usually drive very far by car and were not wealthy (and did not know any better about music), the early 1970s were a wonderful time to grow up and live in Britain. National happiness peaked (under Labour) in 1976.[22] It was only for the very rich that times were bad, but the rich have a disproportionate influence on how our recent history is told, not least through their control of newspapers. In 1976, three years after the highest ever wage rates were recorded, and in the midst of a heat wave, there was a bumper crop of males born, destined to be 25 years old in 2001.

By 2001 there were 1,839,000 men and 1,913,000 women aged 25 to 29 living in Britain. Almost as many men had died as had entered the country (net), but fewer young women died each year, and net migration had boosted women's numbers by 10 per cent by the start of the 1990s. By 2001 over a third of the roughly 75,000 excess of 25- to 29-year-old women were living in London.

Many of these women had moved to the capital for skilled work; they had degrees, often postgraduate degrees. But women's success also brought in many other young women, partly to care for the professional women's children. These other young women came from all over the world. At first the au pairs were disproportionately from Finland, but that little monopoly did not last long.

When I first saw data on birthplace, sex and age from the 1991 census I thought some mistake had been made regarding how many young women born in Finland lived in London. The majority of the 5,285 Finns in the UK were living in or near London and were female. Similarly 1.09 per cent of the population of Kensington & Chelsea had been born in the Philippines. Almost (but not quite all) of these were not former dictators fleeing prosecution, instead many were modern-day Mary Poppinses.[23]

Although the influx appeared to start with childcare, it quickly extended to young women coming in to do other work needed to free up the time of the increasingly affluent couples they usually came to work for. Their lot was cleaning, cooking, arranging birthday parties (not just for the children) and providing help in general to those who increasingly liked to talk about their lives as busy, but who rarely appeared to be in a flap, probably because of the hired help busying around for them. For every Bridget Jones there was another woman who had met the man of her dreams (and sometimes her financial aspirations). These women – both the employers and their domestic employees – tipped the balance of London's population towards the feminine. Yet their financial disparity also began to create a more economically divided society.

More university students arrived in London and other large cities during the 1990s and with every year that passed a larger proportion of them were young women. A few years later their numbers swelled, as each year more women took graduate jobs in the capital: starter jobs on career ladders that looked as if they reached the clouds. As the number of university graduates increased, year on year, an ever higher proportion of that growing number ended up in London, and an ever higher proportion of that higher proportion were female.[24]

Meanwhile where had all the men gone? Many had remained outside of the cities, going to their local university rather than an elite one, or being more likely to not go at all, but many others were simply no longer in Britain. If they were hiding they had done a very good job of it – as described above, the census authorities had massaged the figures (in a necessary way) by accounting for large numbers of young men who had failed to fill in the forms.[25]

The authorities' use of 'capture-recapture'[26] to estimate the actual population in 2001, one of the most sophisticated techniques employed worldwide, is what allows us to be so sure today that the young men have gone. The census authorities used this consistently, even when threatened with court action by local councils, but did negotiate, under duress, to increase the count by an extra 0.1 per cent of the population. A few extra tens of thousands of people were created in places such as Manchester and Westminster in order to placate those more litigious locals. It is the hard work of government demographers that makes it possible to know about Britain, but academics don't assume the figures are infallible.

When the census figures were first released my colleagues and I spent several months trying to prove the figures wrong, and failed. What convinced me that there were not 'enough' young men in the country was that mortality rates had not risen for this group. Escaping the census enumerator, the electoral roll, doctors' lists and numerous other ways in which you can be counted is one thing, escaping the grim reaper (and avoiding receiving a death certificate – the ultimate 'capture-recapture' survey) is rather more difficult.

Almost as many men born in the early 1970s have left Britain as have entered the country. Men came here – mainly to the south of England – often for a better life; and men left here – mainly from the north of England and from Scotland – often for a better life. British men were not doing the jobs the extra young women immigrants were undertaking, because the men had not been brought up to think of childcare as a career option (and hardly any of the affluent London families who offered such work would have thought in the 1990s of employing a young man from the north as their nanny). But that world is changing – sometimes so much within a single generation that it is hard to comprehend. You can easily begin to believe that what you yourself know is what is 'normal'; however, if you think back to just a few years ago you'll see that what's deemed to be normal now is not the same as it was then.

When the Beatles were at the height of their popularity, most young men left school to walk into jobs that would see them through to retirement. At that time, the few young people who went to university were mostly male. Immigration from overseas saw more men coming into the country than women; and women had their children young, largely regardless of class. But soon, by the time of Chesney

Hawkes's solitary hit, young men's domination of almost everything, from the music charts to university places to making up the bulk of immigrants, was on the wane.[27]

By the turn of the twenty-first century a large number of young men found themselves to be ill-equipped to compete for jobs with women of the same age. They had been brought up assuming they would take their fathers' roles and occupations. The occupation that saw the greatest growth in 1990s Britain was hairdressing, but all the growth occupations, high paid and low paid, were in service industries. For poorer men these were jobs that started to be very different from those of their fathers; many had trouble finding work and were thinking of looking overseas.

As S Club 7 (a group made up of four women and three men) came to the fore, the majority of university graduates were female, and the majority of new graduate jobs were opening up in and around London. Even today, and despite the economic slump of 1991 and the crash of 2008, London now offers 40 per cent of all graduate jobs in the country.[28] Less than a tenth of the population lives there but almost four out of ten graduate jobs are found there! And these graduate jobs are increasingly being taken up by women.

Women in Britain started doing better in school at the point at which they were allowed to attend in as great a number as boys were. For example, grammar schools had disqualified many women from doing better by limiting the places available to girls; thus, the 11 plus exam in many areas set a higher pass threshold for girls than for boys. The legacy of this exclusion extended into the era of mass comprehensive education, when, initially in the late 1970s, and during most of the 1980s, girls were simply not expected to do as well as boys. It was a shock when they started to do so in large numbers.

Replacing the apartheid distinction between O-level students and those destined to take CSEs with the single GCSE helped greatly to reduce discrimination against the success of girls. Most important was the amount of coursework involved in GCSEs as compared to the coursework necessary for the old-style exams. At ages 14 and 15 the girls got their heads down and worked; the boys were more often still working their way through puberty. In the last couple of years the coursework element of many GCSEs has been removed due to recent fears of cheating (ironically, more often by boys than by girls). One result of the coursework ban has been a revival in the exam fortunes of boys as they are assessed not during their studies but more towards the end, when most boys are through puberty.

By the mid-1990s the women who went to university in greater numbers than men were those who had done better at GCSEs and A levels and, by 2008–9, some 51 per cent of young women in England were embarking on university studies.[29] In the 1990s, Oxford and Cambridge were the two districts (outside of London), which saw the greatest increase in university attendance for women aged 25 to 29 – average increases of 4 per cent and 3 per cent, respectively. Many of these women will have been postgraduate students.

A surplus of women in London has occurred in the past: in the nineteenth century due to the predominance of female domestic servants; in the 1920s due to the large number of male casualties in the First World War. After this, and for the six decades that followed, the number of men in London increased but, by the 1990s, when the balance was again in favour of females, the capital made sense as the location where Bridget Jones should find searching for a lover so hard. What made little sense, statistically speaking, was that she should have a choice of two.

At the start of the noughties many commentators asked if London was moving towards the New York scenario, with a shortage of eligible bachelors. Would London, too, be a place where overt consumption of Manolo Blahnik shoes and other luxury goods (à la *Sex in the City*) became the predominant concern of young women? It was thought at the time that, unlike Bridget Jones, young women seemed to be happily single, concentrating more on their careers and enjoying a fast-paced, high-consumption lifestyle rather than concentrating on finding a permanent partner.

Later we discovered that it was the young women in their late twenties who were by far the most likely to get into debt in Britain. Young men were less profligate. Women in their twenties had borrowed most heavily, with median borrowing of £3,700. It was more likely for women to use credit and charge cards as 'the most commonly used form of non-mortgage credit' and to not settle their accounts in full each month.[30]

Almost nothing was known of the story of youthful mounting debt as I was writing about the early results of the 2001 census in the summer of 2004. Back then, Rachel Stevens (formerly of S Club) came out with a new single, 'Some Girls', which was climbing the charts. Some girls might always get what they wanna wanna, but others, especially in London would be forced to make do with the never never. Debt appeared to be substituting for companionship. But the cards that take the waiting out of wanting also encourage you to think that what you really wanted was to spend more.[31]

We will not know for sure how many men and women of particular ages there are now in Britain (or even of all ages) until sometime in 2013 when the first of the 2011 census results are released. Any guessing about a change in trend before then is purely speculative. Without a census it is not possible to know.

In July 2010 the new government announced it would scrap the 2021 census in order to save money.[32] The real reason for the ending of 200 years of census taking was that the Con-Dems are opposed to planning and, instead, see the free market as the ideal solution to almost everything: 'Why count people when the market will sort everything out', was the extreme philosophy of the new times.

Around the world other governments are drawn to this suggestion that they can abandon the census. In Canada in 2010 it was reported that the law was being changed to make much of the census voluntary;[33] and in the United States the Republicans have been trying for decades to reduce the numbers of people eligible to be counted, and continue to resist attempts to estimate the under-enumerated populations: if no census is taken then the government cannot easily be held responsible for what happens to its population.

But look at the United Nations and you'll hear a different story. Its '2010 World Population and Housing Census Programme' celebrates the number of countries that are now organized enough to take a census, just at the time when mavericks in some rich countries talk of abandoning such record-keeping.[34] Most people in the world never receive a birth certificate and their deaths are not documented either. Even fewer have the chance for their existence during life to be noted every decade for the public record.

Censuses, in the main, have only been taken in affluent countries since the onset of industrialization. Only in places such as Britain can the population have the apparent luxury of being able to query why there appear to be so few young men now living in the country, and to realize that the reason for this is that women are doing so well: only in places like Britain do so few young women die in childbirth; only in wealthy nations are girls not neglected in favour of boys when there is not enough to go round; only in places as rich as Britain can we afford to be stupid enough to suggest that there is suddenly now no need to accurately count people. But in other, poorer countries, female foetuses are still disproportionately aborted and more females than males are killed or neglected as infants.

Times though are changing, everywhere. In almost every country in the world women finally live longer than men.[35] And more boys than girls continue to be born, except under the most dire of conditions. Globally, there are more men than women, but only just. The latest demographic yearbook of the United Nations, with figures verified up to 2007, suggests that in 2007 there were 3,363 million men and 3,308 million women alive worldwide – just 55 million more men than women, which is a figure within the margin of error for such estimates.[36] Fifty-five million is about the size of the population of England and Wales combined. And this 55 million excess of men was due entirely to numbers of young men in parts of Asia where women remain so much less valued. However, by the time you read this, there are probably slightly more women than men in the world, perhaps for the first time ever.

As I say – times are changing. In Fallujah, the war goes on: a policeman, his wife, and their 4-year-old son were blown apart on 2 August 2010, on the day when President Obama said that the withdrawal of US troops from Iraq would take place by the end of that month.[37] This was just four days before the President sent the first ever US envoy to attend the annual ceremony of remembrance in Hiroshima, on the sixty-fifth anniversary of the dropping of the first atomic bomb.

And what has happened to speed dating, the craze that hit London in 2003 when the shortage of men first became so acutely obvious, when the first results of the 2001 census were released? Speed dating was short-lived. It was killed off by the Internet, by online dating and by people interacting on social networking sites instead of in bars. Why speed-date thirty people in one night when you could leisurely browse through thirty-thousand faces online? However, in July 2010, a speed-dating revival was reported in New York, where the phenomena was being tried again for old times' sake, as a quaint distraction for twentysomethings bored of living in a virtual universe.[38]

It still does work out OK in the end for most young people. However, the end for many will be quite different to what their parents experienced. Most young people will find partners, but at current rates about a quarter may never be parents themselves, and that is new. Those who do become parents will mostly have only one or two children. And many of those will be the only grandchildren of two sets of grandparents. Great expectations are being heaped upon fewer shoulders; that pressure is heavier now than it ever was. There is no need for us to experience the levels of communal stress last felt in the 1930s – but we may soon find that those years were the last time that as few boys were born as now.

We know from the historic record that the last time there were regularly fewer than 4 extra boys born for every 100 girls was before the First World War, and we know from recent records that in two of the three years, from 2006–8, we saw the excess dip below five extra, back towards the minimum last reached more than a century ago.[39] And, if sex ratios at birth are the measure you use, then life is now stressful, but not as stressful as it was between 1900 and 1919, which was even more stressful than the period that covers the Great Depression. And by that same marker we are becoming greatly stressed again.

The last year of the First World War was a peak for the birth of excess boys, as was 1944, the penultimate year of the Second World War. Many women had children younger at these times, as they did during the 1960s boom, and that might have had an impact. We do not yet know what precise mechanism might operate that recognizes wartime slaughter, or the easing of wartime fear, in differential survival rates during gestation. We can now see that the early 1920s were clearly a time for social relaxation as compared to the period of war that had preceded it and that the years 1926 through to 1930 were particularly (economically) traumatic. Fewer boys were born then, too, but more than five extra every year from 1934 onwards.

By 2008 we were not yet back to just 4 extra boys being born for every 100 baby girls. But the longer record suggests that 1944 through 1976 were golden years. The one exception was 1958, which implies that Macmillan was wrong about people having had it so good nine months earlier.

Back in the early 1930s we really didn't have enough to go round. Now we have enough for everyone's needs, but not for the greed of a few, for the bankers with their bonuses and the super-rich with their mansions – and that stresses the rest of us. Is it possible that so many men are missing because we allowed our society to become so selfish? From *Auf Wiedersehen Pet* in 1983, to the lack of men available for speed dating in 2003, we have had many warnings.[40] When things get really bad we humans produce far more girls than boys in order to ensure survival of the species. Even when things get just *a bit* bad the signs of that old evolutionary trait may well, again, become evident.

CHAPTER 3

WHEN ENOUGH IS ENOUGH – OPTIMUM POPULATION

'UK is the second most congested nation in EU'

Sun, 27 August 2010[1]

It's getting worse isn't it? Your commute is taking longer; there are more cars on the roads because there are more people, too many people. Can't they just go somewhere else? Your exhaust is pumping out fumes into the lungs of pedestrians, especially young children who are at exhaust height.[2] You jostle to move forward a few metres and cyclists weave dangerously around you. Where did they come from? It's not your fault: we passed optimum population long ago. But at least in the privacy of your own car you can decide who you sit next to, when you come and go (to a certain extent) and what you listen to on the radio or iPod.

The idea of an optimum population comes from biology. It is the concept that there is a tipping point for any particular species living on any particular land mass, or in any volume of the ocean; in other words, there is a perfect population number, which is neither so small as to risk further depletion and an inability to work together efficiently, nor so large as to overgraze on the resources available and so deplete them, or to be too many to work together efficiently.

When too many are crowded together in an area of a particular size then they are said to be congested. The phrase 'optimum population' was first used in its current sense less than ninety years ago.[3] Since then there have been a steady stream of warnings, shouted around the world, suggesting that in one place or another we have reached the limits of sustainability. In 1927 it was suggested that 'at 104 million, the United States has exceeded "optimum" population'.[4] In 1934 it was declared that India, too, had a population 'very nearly up to the possible limit'.[5] In 1968 it was (wrongly we now suspect) predicted that the population of the United States would double in 63 years, of Britain in 140 years, of Turkey and Kenya in 24, of the Philippines, Mexico and El Salvador in 19 or 20. There was a small baby boom around 1965, but that really is no excuse for all this overexaggeration and fear of other baby booms and immigration.[6]

Today, what we do know is how much we really don't know, and how wrong we have been before. In 1971 a House of Commons committee called on the government 'to prevent the consequences of population growth becoming intolerable for the everyday conditions of life'.[7] The government panel of experts set up in response to this outcry reported in March 1973 that the problem was not so much numbers of people, but how those people were behaving: 'Over the last six years population in this country has increased by less than 3 per cent but the number of cars by over 30 per cent. Restrictions on private cars will need to be imposed in the future regardless of the growth of population.'[8]

The geographical range of the population is the area over which it makes sense to measure their numbers in relation to the resources they require. The range for fish in a pond is the size of pond – for flightless birds on an island it is the island – and for humans it is the planet. It is so commonly proclaimed that human population is beyond some optimum that it has become a cliché: 'population explosion'; 'full-up'; 'swamped', 'time to emigrate'. Yet this is to miss the point. Migration often alleviates overcrowding. People move to where they are needed and away from where they are not. Bear this in mind the next time you read something negative about immigrants in Britain.

In August 2010, in the very brief honeymoon months of the new coalition government, the authorities announced – and the news media spun – that: 'an extra 196,000 people flooded into Britain last year'. The *Sun* newspaper ran the front-page headline, in bold capitals, that this was a '20 PER CENT' increase on 2008. 'What?' the reader might respond. 'The population of Britain has risen by a fifth overnight because of immigrants? Where are we going to house them all? There simply isn't enough space. Send them all home. Now!'

To be fair, the authorities did *not* announce a 'flood' – it was the *Sun* newspaper that chose to use that word and to present the numbers in this way. The statisticians did not say there had been a 20 per cent increase. All they did was to release two new figures: their estimates of the numbers of people leaving the country and the numbers arriving, in the latest twelve-month period. The difference between those numbers happened to be 196,000 more coming in than leaving, which, yes, happened to be 20 per cent higher than the equivalent difference estimated the year before.

What the *Sun* decided to leave out, however, was that the government's statistical agency had emphasized the *absolute* numbers, which were falling as migration rates shrank across the board with the economic recession. Tabloid newspaper reporters and editors chose to emphasize instead the change in *net* migrants, because net migration was rising.

Net migration is the difference between two flows. It is the number of people entering a place in a particular year, less the number leaving that same place over the course of that year. Net migration is akin to the difference between the water running out of the taps and the water running down the plughole. Net migration is the surplus or deficit of water in the bath resulting from the balance of inflow and outflow.[9] And net migration is scary if you think of Britain as rather like a bathtub – where the water level is high and rising and the taps have been left on.

Imagine it. There is just *so* much water coming into the tub, *so* much, that even though the level has risen above the overflow, enough can't get out through that pipe, and the water is beginning to lap over the edge of the bath. This is what happens if you don't control the taps, if you are just lying back in the tub and thinking of England, nibbling on that *Flake*, or doing whatever it is you do in the bath. The bath gets too full, then disaster: the water overflows, the electrics blow and your ceiling caves in.

However much this may be true for water and a bathtub, it is not entirely true for people and a country – or at least for the migration statistics. I've spent a long time counting people and the things they have in this country and I have come to see that there is no such thing as optimum population. I am convinced that there is no line to be drawn six inches below the overflow.[10] Or rather, that we cannot say that we know what the optimum population of the country is. And to announce or declare how many people should or shouldn't be around you is – I believe – akin to playing a fool's game. You wouldn't like to be talked of as surplus to requirements, so why talk of other people like that?[11]

You can never meet a net migrant, never shake their hand or wave goodbye to them. A net migrant will never take your job or sleep with your daughter. Furthermore you will never *be* a net migrant, no matter how hard you try. Net migrants don't exist, at least not in the real world. They are the creation of a form of demographic accounting and are shadows, not solid. But people can be taught to fear shadows.

British tabloid newspapers swing widely between announcing that there will soon be far too many inhabitants of these islands and announcing that soon there will be far too few. 'Can the last one to leave turn out the light?!' is a much repeated headline above stories of the allegedly inevitable depopulation resulting from whatever any even mildly left-leaning government might do. It was a story most famously about to happen had Old Labour won the 1992 general election. A picture of Neil Kinnock was memorably placed within a light bulb on the pre-election cover of the *Sun*. The same was done using Gordon Brown's image and the visual metaphor reapplied to New Labour in the run-up to the election of 2010.[12] British tabloids yo-yo between announcing that the country will soon be depopulated or, instead, will quickly fill up beyond any possible capacity. Either the plug has been pulled out too early, or the taps have been left on for too long.

How congested is the UK today? In a recent news story, the country was named the second most congested in the

European Union (EU).[13] It came only behind Malta. After some investigation I discovered that the instigation of the story was the work of the lobby group 'Migration Watch', and after a quick read of their report I discovered the news story had distorted the facts so that the story was only tangentially related to them.

In Appendix 1 of their 'Inquiry into Economic Migration to the EU',[14] Migration Watch ranked the UK fourth, not second, in terms of population density, still behind Malta but also behind the Netherlands and Belgium – the UK is simply *not* the second most congested nation after Malta. However, and to confuse things, the report noted that:

> England has a population density of over 3 times the EU average and second only to the Netherlands and Malta in the 25-nation EU ... Congestion is therefore a much more significant factor in the UK than elsewhere and points to a very clear need for the UK to be able to limit immigration by controlling its own borders and having its own immigration policy.[15]

Note that Belgium was omitted from this list, even though it appears in the Migration Watch graph, reproduced overleaf, and note also that England has been substituted for the UK as a whole. Further, you'll see that while both England and the UK are listed, Scotland, Wales, Northern Ireland, Catalonia, the other sixteen autonomous communities of Spain, the sixteen Länder of Germany, the ten provinces of two regions of Belgium (and Brussels), the twenty regions of Italy (many of which were former states themselves), or any of the hundreds of other parts of Europe that could be included likewise, are not.

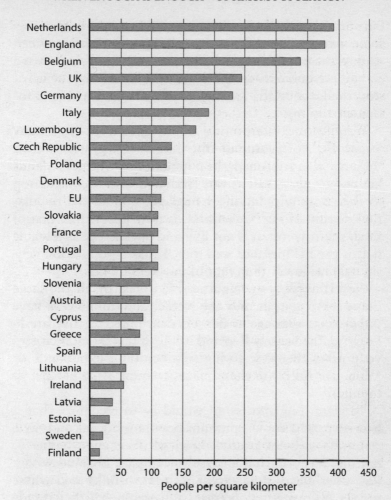

FIGURE 6: Population Densities of the EU Member States (excluding Malta) and England

Note: figures are people per kilometre square. Places shown are States, or the EU or England. Source: Redrawn from diagram originally produced by Migration Watch and attributed to Sir Andrew Green: Briefing Paper 1.7 'Inquiry into economic migration to the EU' http:// www.migrationwatchuk.org/briefingPaper/document/9

The *Sun*'s headline cited on page 67 most probably came from information gleaned from Migration Watch, which ranked the population density of England as being second to the Netherlands in the graph shown above, which it said excluded Malta (but which did not give a reason for that exclusion).

Reading and interpreting graphs has rarely been many journalists' forte. Admittedly, since the Migration Watch 'Inquiry' was published, the population of the Netherlands has not grown as fast as was estimated, and in comparison to the rising population of England, and so the population density of the Netherlands is now lower than that of England; however, it is not England but the UK as a whole that is the EU member, and the UK has a population density still far lower than that of the Netherlands.[16]

Nevertheless, you might say, if today, of all the large European countries only the Netherlands and Malta have populations that are as densely distributed as they are in England, then surely England is full? If this thought crosses your mind then try asking whether the Netherlands or Malta are full? Are these places teeming with people, fit to burst?

To claim England is full would be to recognize that it had surpassed some optimum population level and, as a result, has become overly congested. To gauge whether or not that has occurred it helps to compare England with a few other places that appear to be even fuller and where people are living in conditions so terrible that they decide to emigrate.

Surprisingly, news reports from Malta don't tend to concentrate on how terrible life is on the island, nor do they tell us how civil society has broken down due to population density. In fact, in 2010, it was announced that of all the countries of the world, the Maltese were the most generous, with 83 per cent of their population giving to charity each year, some 25 per cent more compared to the United States or Switzerland, and 10 per cent more giving as compared to the very charitable British.[17] And all those Dutch folk crowded into the Netherlands? They rank second in the charitable league-table, giving more even than the British. Higher-density living does not make people less charitable, and is one indication that we, or they, have not yet reached optimum population.

The population density of Malta is around 1,282 people per kilometre squared. Immigration plays a part in this, yet despite Malta being the nearest part of Europe to Africa, the largest immigrant minority living on the island are British ex-pats, mostly retired.[18] And most of these British retirees are English. It is odd to think that if England itself were so congested, so many English people should choose to retire somewhere even more congested. Odd, that is, until you look a little more closely at the numbers.

The square root of 1,282 is just under 36. You might ask 'why should that matter?' Well, to figure out population density you need to visualize the number of people on the land, and to do that you need to know how to work out a square root. Take 18 pairs of people and space out each pair in a line with some 27 metres between them. Your line will be 972 metres long – almost a kilometre. Then, at right angles to the initial line, draw another line from each person, which would create 36 new lines, each made up by adding 35 new people, with each new pairing spaced some 27 metres apart. That is what the population density of Malta would look like if everyone on the island were equally spaced out. Everyone would have about 27 by 27 metres of land, or some 780 square metres.[19]

How much is 780 square metres? Well, think of a large

detached house with a decent garden and a road outside it. That is what a population density of 1,282 looks like because that is the footprint of 780 square metres. If people are willing to share, on average, two to a house, then half the island can be agricultural land, mountain, parks and beaches. If not everyone lives in bungalows then you can double the amount of open land again. If most people live in apartments double it again and so on. Build an airport and what you get, with a little maths, is . . . Malta. The most congested country in Europe is hardly congested at all. Thus, without panic and bluster, one can quickly conclude that national population densities have almost nothing to do with congestion. What matters is how people are spatially organized.

Congestion means to be overfilled and overcrowded: jammed, clogged full. The extent to which a group of people might be suffering from congestion depends on their local population densities but also, and more importantly, on how well they have arranged their infrastructure to allow them to move about. It is possible to have a far greater population than can be found in Britain living at far greater local densities and suffering far less congestion. For example, Japan is home to twice the population of the UK, has far less flat land available but it also has a far superior transport system that in turn allows its populace greater ease of movement. Conversely, if you want to see people suffering terrible congestion despite having a huge amount of land then try driving in rush hour in Auckland in New Zealand, where there are only fourteen people per square kilometre, which makes New Zealand some twenty-five times less densely populated than Japan; or consider many congested cities in car-bound Australia, a country with only 2.5 people per square kilometre – some 138 times less densely populated than Japan – but most

Australians are concentrated in a few cities and they often drive (and then queue) for miles to get to and from home.

It seems ironic that, with all that space in Australia and New Zealand, and after centuries of colonizing some of the most remote and spacious areas of the planet, British emigrants tend today to sniff out places of relatively high population density. Often these are places they can more easily travel to or retire to – and so increase the density even further. The Mediterranean coast of Spain is one such spot.

Catalonia, the most north-eastern autonomous community of Spain, is home to 7.5 million people living on 32,000 square kilometres, 234 people per square kilometre. If you did not have a sense for what these numbers meant you might be tempted to suggest that Catalan living is done at a more civilized density of occupation when compared to England's 395 people per square kilometre. After all, the capital of Catalonia is Barcelona, one of the favourite short-haul holiday destinations of the English. Is Barcelona such a nice place to visit because the Catalans have so much more space?

If the English were spaced evenly across England in a square grid, each resident would have four neighbours, each positioned exactly fifty metres away. You can just about shout to someone that far away and be heard. In Catalonia the distance would be sixty-five metres between people, a very antisocial distance. So why is Catalonia such a social place? It is perhaps because almost no one there chooses to live at such low density.

In the urban region of Barcelona the population density is 2,300 people per square kilometre, almost six times that of England's population density. In the city of Barcelona itself, density is 16,000 people per square kilometre, and in the most densely populated 30 neighbourhoods of that city the concentration is 40,300 people per square kilometre, over 100 times denser than in England, almost 10 times denser than in London and 4 times denser than the borough of Westminster![20] No one in these parts of Barcelona has a garden and, as a result, there are some great public spaces and children's playgrounds. There isn't a borough in London that could rival the densities at which most people live in downtown Barcelona, which could be re-created if you were to space out people at 5-metre intervals, and give them each 25 square metres (compared to Malta's 780 square metres).

But where to find space for the roads, pavements, parks and cafes? The latter tend to be on the ground floors of high-rise buildings, which are more common than large houses. Few people live on these ground floors in Barcelona, which instead house the city's shops and cafes. In contrast, in Westminster, where each resident has on average 100 square metres to themselves, much of that space is unavailable at night as it is empty office blocks. Most of the time the residents of Westminster only have 100 square metres to themselves at night or, more correctly, at about 5 a.m., when Westminster's population density is at its lowest at just under a quarter of a million souls. At 10 a.m., five hours later, most estimates have the borough's human body-count numbered at well over a million, a figure closer in density to that of Barcelona at night.

In cities such as Barcelona, Paris, Madrid and Berlin – in fact in most cities in Europe – people tend to live much nearer to where they work than we do in the UK. City centres are places to inhabit and have fun in, as much as to labour within. London is different in that most people live outside the city limits, or live in places further away from work than do their European counterparts. London is a city of sprawling suburbs using up a huge area, 1,572 square metres, excluding dormitory towns, just within its built-up boundary.[21] Land is consumed inefficiently within London, and this creates problems, not least that almost everywhere is too far to walk.

But when it comes to sleep-time population densities, Britain is certainly not full. It is when people wake up and try to get to school, or shop, or to work that we suddenly have a 'congestion' problem. Is it our inefficient use of land that is the problem? Or not? What are the real causes of congestion in Britain?

Could Britain be overpopulated because it has too few roads and the railway network doesn't work? If we built a better infrastructure could we better house more people? I thought we could, and I thought this was something worth looking into, so I did something very crude but roughly indicative. I had a go at working out how many kilometres of road there were for every square kilometre of land in every country in the world.[22] The highest ratio happens to be in Monaco, with twenty-six kilometres of road per square kilometre of land.

Monaco is more a city than a state, and has the highest population density of any country in the world: 17,400 people per square kilometre. In fact, with a land area of only 1.95 square kilometres per person they have just 1.5 metres worth of road per person.[23] If every Monégasque were to lay down on the road, then their country's population could connect every road to every other through their bodies![24] But does Monaco have too many roads or too few?

Affluent countries have the greatest length of roads per square kilometre, but usually the least kilometres of road per person. For example, if you looked at a road atlas of Britain, you would see that London has the most roads but if you looked at a 'stretched' map, that made area proportional to population – a population cartogram – you'd see that London seemed to have the sparsest network of roads per person.

Roads are unevenly distributed over both land and people. They are an inefficient way of moving goods and folk about. They make sense locally, but not globally. In contrast, on a population cartogram, the lines that appear evenly spaced out between people when people are evenly spaced out on the map – are railways. Roads increase congestion whereas rail networks decrease the problem, and can help to solve our needs to travel further and efficiently.

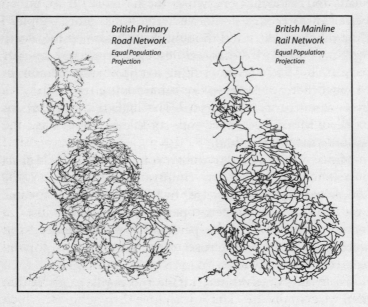

FIGURE 7: The British Mainland Rail and Road Networks on an Equal-Population Projection

Source: I drew these in 1990 as part of my PhD dissertation. A few extra roads have been built within London since then but the city remains, inevitably, poorly served by road.[25]

78

In order to know if Britain really were full we would need to widen our points of reference to the thirty-five countries that are more densely populated than the UK.[26] These include richer countries than us, poorer countries, larger countries and much smaller ones – the likes of Barbados, India, Japan and Rwanda.

After Monaco, and ranking by road density, the highest densities are found in Malta (7 km/km²), Belgium (5 km/ km²) and the Netherlands (3 km/ km²). Where have we seen that list before? Oh yes, the 'Migration Watch' list in their statistical appendix of countries supposedly more overpopulated even than the UK (see the graph on page 71).

The figure for tarmac roadway in the UK is two kilometres of road per square kilometre, or six metres per person, four times the length available per person in Monaco. It's not that we don't have roads in Britain, it's that we are using them too much. Roads are useful for local journeys, but collectively they make less sense the further you drive. Of course driving often makes sense if there are few alternatives; however, in a country such as ours that is well served by rail, trams, buses, cycle paths and pavements (unlike the USA), the main reason for our overuse of roads is the fact that so many of us now live too far from where we work, from where we study and from where we shop – and that so many of us insist on driving between all these places.

We make ourselves feel far more congested in Britain than we actually are. The British love their suburbs, which sprang up in the 1840s with the construction of the railway and the concerted effort to entice people away from the hearts of Victorian cities. And so this suburbanization provided local transport solutions associated with rail – for example buses and trams that would take the population to and from the train station. Car parks next to train stations didn't arrive until later, and were not planned for at the outset.

What makes sense for each individual often makes little sense for the collective, as every personal decision can, in effect, hack a little freedom off the choices of everyone else.[27] If you get into your car in the morning, in order to drive to work and minimize any walking, you may think that you are slightly freer than your neighbour who uses public transport, but when you crowd on to the road along with everyone else who has made the same decision as you then, you slow down, and so have a part of your freedom curtailed. It is when the aggregate of those thousands of curtailments is greater than your added benefit that you have physical and social gridlock. Then you start to curse the other 'idiots' on the road, just as they are cursing you back from within their isolated glass and steel one-ton shells on wheels.

Why do we overuse our road network when railways are largely more efficient? Why are mainland Europe and Japan better provided for in terms of rail transport, which has been better planned than ours here in Britain? Because they learned from our mistakes – we built our railway before almost anyone else in the world; we have more rail per square kilometre than anywhere else. But then we closed huge amounts of it in the 1960s.[28] As a result, Belgium and Germany now have 50 per cent more rail per square kilometre of land than we do in the UK; the Netherlands and Switzerland, about 16 per cent more (at least). However, we still have a lot of track left and still in use, it's just that it's pretty old and inefficiently used.

But, apart from using the trains more, what would help reduce congestion is for people to live closer to work, or to work from home, even for just part of the week. This would rapidly reduce congestion, and if people lived closer to work they could more easily walk or cycle or use the buses, which again would reduce congestion.

Cities are places where people gather to perform and enjoy communal activities – both work and play related, with a concentration of appropriate facilities available. Some industries require a high density of people working in a very small amount of space, such as coal mining, which saw terraced houses built densely around old pit heads. When the mines closed there were few other industries that could fit overground (especially in narrow Welsh valleys) to employ as many men as used to work underground.

Today banking and finance are the industries requiring the greatest number of people working within a small area of space. The offices that tower above Canary Wharf in London allow as many people to be employed in that one small area as were employed in the deepest and busiest of mines. Number 1 Canada Square, the tallest building in the capital, has been built in or near places that many who work in the offices would consider uninhabitable – Poplar, Bow, All Saints. It is only at night when the cleaners, who often live locally in Poplar, Bow and All Saints, arrive in the tower blocks to work through the hours of darkness to earn less than a living wage. And it is the income and wealth inequality between those who clean the offices at night and those who work in them by day that results in employees living across so large an area of London and even further afield, thus necessitating so many long commutes. Every reduction in the income gap results in a slightly more functional city on the ground.

Recently, when publicly shamed, some of the banks began to pay their cleaners the London living wage. There are now many calls for the top-to-bottom income ratio of all companies to be published on the front page of their annual accounts, to attempt to ensure that in future that ratio becomes more equalized. It is possible to imagine a more equally distributed wealth and consequently a more sane future for commuters in Britain in general; for it is not so much the number of people living in Britain that makes these islands seem congested, but how the people live and work. Congestion would be far lower if the British behaved a little more like other Europeans, not just in terms of pay disparity (or lack thereof) but in other aspects of life. If the British were more like the Europeans, we'd be able to allow more people to study, or retire early, or look after their own children or their own elderly relatives; more could clean their own homes. More men could, too.

Take, for example, the issue of childcare and how our arrangement of that creates congestion. More men could undertake childcare if taking a break from the corporate career were not so damaging to their finances. We could even set an example to the Japanese for once! In Scandinavia and other northern European countries, where income inequalities are lower, far more men care for children. Each person, whether man or woman, who stays home to look after their child is one less commuter and so one less person adding to the perceived sense of congestion.

For every 1-year-old infant in Britain transported to day care, an adult must travel with them (usually one of their parents who then travels on to work); another adult must also travel: the person who works at the day-care centre. The more we privatize caring that used to take place within the family, the more congestion we create. I'm not advocating going back to the time when women were chained to the kitchen sink; instead, I think we could free both men and women from believing that to ensure a financially secure future for their children they must continually seek promotion at work and endure long hours at the office.

What is most unusual about the English in Britain, when compared with other communities within European countries, is not the population densities at which they live, but how very inefficiently they use the space and time they have to live in. The Scots, Welsh and Irish do better. It is because the English have gone much further along the individualist route than have most people in Europe (or even in the rest of the UK) that we have so many problems of congestion. The English seem to accept that congestion is a consequence of the generation of money and the division of household and workplace labour, almost regardless of how many extra car journeys that creates.

British roads, pavements and railway carriages could be far more comfortable places to travel on (and in) if we did not so often judge an activity as worthy only if it makes a profit. We don't always do this, we don't always seek only profit, otherwise none of us would have children. If the middle classes could do a decent or simply a good job, rather than endlessly being told they must be excellent at work, we could be far more honest with each other. We choose the extent to which we let the market dominate our lives. In Britain we have gone way beyond the optimum in this, not in how many people there are, but in how much greed we tolerate. We shouldn't be questioning if we have too many people, but rather, we should question the ways in which we live, with too much commuting, too much selfish use of space, too many small and wasted gardens and too few adults living above the ground floor.

If you are lucky enough to have visited a few other cities in other countries and then ever wondered why most European or Japanese cities were so much nicer places to be in, as compared to British cities, have a think about their lives in general, about how different they are to us culturally and sociologically – look at the way they live as families; compare their priorities to ours.

If you've been to cities in the United States and have been told which part of town not to walk in, or have been told not to walk at all – always drive – and you have wondered how people can bear to live in such places, think what people in mainland Europe might be thinking about us. If you wonder why the countryside is so idolized in the UK, think about how our urban space isn't used to its optimum and why so many of us dream of escaping from our dysfunctional cities. But only a few escape. Why? The answer is partly planning restrictions, which keep population density low in rural areas, and ensure that there is not enough space for all.

But there has to be an optimum population, not just an optimum way of using the space for the population you have, doesn't there? An optimum population sounds such a sensible thing, so apparently reasonable, that someone set up an eponymous charitable trust – the Optimum Population Trust – in 1991.[29] The patrons (as of 2010) include luminaries, environmentalists and academics such as Sir David Attenborough, Lady Kulukundis (Susan Hampshire), Sir James Lovelock, Sir Jonathon Porritt and Sir Crispin Tickell.[30]

In July 2010 the Optimum Population Trust claimed that the United Kingdom was 'overpopulated by forty-five million people'[31] and advocated that couples should only have two children, that immigration should never exceed emigration, and that the population should be reduced by at least a quarter of a per cent per year. But, even with such a decline, it would take 555 years to get to their optimum of 15 million people based on current levels of consumption per capita and assuming that one quarter of a percentage reduction was achieved each year.[32]

There is an alternative that neither the Trust nor Migration Watch mention, which is for people who live in Britain to live *differently* to how they live at the moment, instead of in much the same ways but in much smaller numbers. It would be far better, greener and more sociable if we used our motorways less frequently, rather than have them used by fewer people overall. The same goes for our housing stock and railway systems, for the shops and the offices. We would have enough for everyone if only we did not each try to use our infrastructure so frequently and if only we shared out our resources a little more evenly. Could someone start up a 'Consumption Watch' or 'Optimum Living Trust' to work out where we are going wrong? Do far too many people own two or three or four homes? How many people have more than one job; hence, more than one workplace to travel to? In which areas are many people travelling too far to work? Are there many people who don't want to do paid work, who would rather be retired, or studying, or be caring for others for free – who are forced into paid work to avoid poverty? Do far too many of us shop too often? Do we need so much retail space or so many trips to the mall?

Britain is home to 1 per cent of the world's adults, but only half a per cent of the planet's children[33] – so, would a fair share in the future be a population of 120 million? After all, as is obvious, we already have far more infrastructure already built and serviceable than exists on most of the rest of the planet. Why are we so unwilling to share what we see as our land?[34] There may not be an optimum population, but there is an optimal way of behaving – share and share alike.[35]

My work on housing estimates over the last couple of

decades has convinced me that it is not a question of how many or how few people you can fit in.[36] Interestingly, I found that the numbers of households we form, our marriage and divorce rates, even how many children we have, are strongly influenced by how many physical dwellings we build. When we had too few dwellings, especially after the war, people had to delay getting married – thus overcrowding was rife.

Now, after massive post-war council-house construction and much greater private speculative building, we have huge numbers of homes in Britain. And now, for various reasons such as the acceptability and ease of divorce and partly because of available housing, women no longer have to stay with their husbands to secure a roof over their heads. We now only have shortages of housing in Britain because we share out our stock so badly – we have never had as many bedrooms per person as we have now. It is not easy to estimate how many rooms in Britain are actually used as bedrooms.[37] It depends partly on how much space you think you need to fit a bed in. But if you're liberal with your ideas of what a bedroom could be it would work out that we have about two bedrooms available per each person.

It is also far from easy to estimate how many homes are second homes. In 1973, a time of acute housing shortage, it was estimated that there were 200,000 second homes in Britain.[38] That number will be far higher now, but we are more unsure as to what exactly a second home is: if he has a home and she has a home, but they mostly live together, which one is the second home?

Even MPs claimed their second homes were their first and vice versa and admitted to having the second home only to secure expenses. Hardly anyone calls their second or third homes by those names. More than three homes and people often lose count, just as David Cameron did. He and his wife owned at least four in 2009, maybe more. The then future Prime Minister asked the reporter who revealed this to please 'not make me sound like a prat for not knowing how many houses I've got'.[39] Some people have many homes; some have many rooms in one home: studies, dens, playrooms, guestrooms.

The number of people who can fit in a particular space can be calculated as the product of looking at technology and sociology combined. There will be an optimal human population for the planet because it is from the space of the whole planet that we now gather resources – just look at where the food you eat at breakfast comes from, or where the clothes you put on were made. However, that planetary human optimum is dependent on how we use technology. The planet can support a low density of hunter-and-gatherer humans, it can support a much greater number of farmers, but the most efficient way to live is for most of us to reside, most of the time, in densely populated towns and cities. These need not be megacities, they can be ecotowns, for example, but we cannot all live in a cottage sitting in a half-acre garden.

People are reducing, collectively, the numbers of children they have, and with fertility speedily falling worldwide, our planet's population will only grow to around nine billion[40] (that number will stop rising just within my lifetime if you believe the projections for my lifespan referred to at the end of chapter one and those for world population given towards the end of chapter seven, on page 207). Until the population stops growing, some parts of the world will be better equipped to absorb more of that global increase. Some parts already have millions of spare bedrooms, a falling birth rate and an aging population in need of an influx of younger people.

Some parts of the world grew rich largely on the labours of people living in other parts: people transported from Africa to pick cotton as slaves in the Americas, and people in India forced to buy the goods made from that cotton, rather than weave their own. Britain grew rich largely at the expense of people from places whose descendants we try now to bar entry to. Our Victorian and Edwardian roads, railways, sewers, banks, homes, schools, museums and universities were built largely by using the profit we extracted from our interests across the rest of the world.[41] Now, other places are poor partly because we are rich.

There may not be an optimum population for Britain but we – as well as Europe, Japan and North America – could all play a much better part in ensuring the optimal distribution of people in the world, in ensuring a greener world, if all these regions would reduce their barriers to human movement. We, in Britain, are where the population is aging.

Humans are exceptionally good at working out where they need to be. Enough of us move around in a state of agitation to ensure that we quickly leave places we over-occupy and colonize the parts that have the potential to bring us benefit. We flee war zones, we rush to new gold mines, we leave decaying cities, we move to where the work is. Such rapid movement is how the Americas came to be occupied so quickly both prehistorically (when the ice melted) and in recent history in terms of colonization and western expansion and exploration. Such movement is why we are now such a successful species, occupying more geographical niches than any other mammal.[42]

There is an optimum number to the population of any group of animals living in a particular territory. Some animals organize themselves collectively in order to maximize that optimum. Most of those animals whose populations fluctuate around some optimum have had much longer to reach those steady optimal numbers than we have. Our numbers have only been in the billions for a few generations, only in the hundreds of millions for a couple of thousand years. We humans are a new species of animal to have grown to these numbers worldwide. We still occupy much the same parts of the planet as we occupied a millennia ago, in river valleys and flat plains, and we are still working out how best to arrange ourselves and to occupy ourselves, geographically.[43]

CHAPTER 4

OVERKEEN, UNDERPAID AND OVER HERE – IMMIGRATION

> Duffy: But all these Eastern Europeans coming in, where are they flocking from?
>
> Brown: A million people come in from Europe, but a million British people have gone into Europe, you do know there's [sic] a lot of British people staying in Europe as well. So education, health and helping people, that's what I'm about.
>
> *The Times*, 28 April 2010[1]

Within a few seconds of this exchange Gordon Brown had muttered the sentence he may possibly most regret: 'She's just the sort of bigoted woman who said she used to be a Labour voter.' If you remember anything about this you'll know that Brown was in the privacy of his own car when he uttered those words but he was also still wearing his radio microphone, switched on. What you might not know is that Gillian Duffy did not object to being called bigoted, she objected to being called a 'woman' rather than a 'lady', as she later told the *Daily Mail*. The three *Mail* journalists who interviewed her were polite enough not to ask her if she knew what bigoted meant. She said, 'I'm not "that woman". It's no way to talk of someone, that, is it? As if I'm to be brushed away. Why couldn't he have said "that lady"?'[2]

Three days after Duffy complained of not being called 'that bigoted lady', the general election was held. Perhaps a few seats would have stayed Labour if Gordon had kept his mouth shut in the car. Just a few thousand extra Labour voters might not have stayed at home that night and instead gone out to elect a dozen extra Labour MPs, who might have been enough to change the political arithmetic during those post-election negotiations. However, in the long run I don't think it would have made much difference. In the short run Gordon sat in that radio studio with his head in his hands listening to his words being played back to him. I doubt he was thinking: 'Why didn't I say "lady"?'

Immigration played a key role in the 2010 election; it was the second most important issue as far as voters were concerned, and the most important issue for one voter in seven although three times as many as this cited the economy as most important. Significantly, for those who voted Labour in 2005 – and apart from some wobbling over Afghanistan – immigration was the only major political issue thought to have been badly handled. Past Labour voters thought their party was dealing well with the economic crisis and, like that lady (Mrs Duffy), if they were not going to vote Labour it was immigration they would cite.[3]

The newspapers that had been stoking up anti-immigrant sentiment had succeeded in making many people believe that immigration was a great evil. Migration Watch had succeeded in getting over its message: the floodgates were open. The Optimum Population Trust had succeeded in adding its piece to the ire, helping to justify anger, strengthen emotions and reinforce supposed grievances. And of the three main political parties the one that had most strongly opposed immigration, the Conservatives, gained the most seats and formed a coalition with the Liberal Democrat party, the one that had presented itself as least anti-immigration.

Just two weeks into power, on 20 May 2010, the new coalition government published an official document committing to the introduction of an annual limit on the number of non-EU migrants to be admitted into the UK to live and work.[4] The limit could only apply to people coming in from outside of the EU because of European law, which permits the free movement of people within Europe and which, as Gordon Brown fatally tried to explain to Mrs Duffy, and as Nick Clegg endlessly repeated prior to the election, allows roughly as many Brits to live outside of Britain (in the rest of Europe) as there are other Europeans living in Britain.

Part of the politicians' problem was that in recent years the kinds of people from Britain who settle in the rest of Europe tend to be affluent. At the time of the election Nick Clegg's parents were settled in France, in a 'ten-bedroom château',[5] and David Cameron's parents were often found holidaying in France. His father would die there later in the summer while staying at an exclusive resort on the Mediterranean near Cavalière.[6] And these affluent Brits upset the balance – the 'million-in-million out' transfer had not been a fair exchange – it was more often affluent Brits out, and poorer Europeans in, those who (by definition, because they were poorer) could generally only afford to live in poor areas.

One reason for the housing shortage in Britain is that affluent people leave their homes here empty when they go to another of their properties elsewhere or overseas. But it is not the affluent who are blamed for the shortage, instead the finger is pointed at the immigrants, who are used as scapegoats for a raft of other social problems – not only for using up too much housing but also for taking jobs, school places and benefits; thus, it seemed politically popular to suggest capping immigration to the UK and, because by law this cap could only apply to those outside the EU, the government had to appear to be cracking down particularly hard on those non-EU émigrés.

On Thursday, 15 July 2010 the government published yet more changes to their immigration policy in a document titled 'The Explanatory Memorandum to the Statement of Changes in Immigration Rules',[7] which expressed 'regret' for the haste in which the rules were being changed: 'The Government regrets that it has not been possible to comply with the convention that changes should be laid before Parliament no less than twenty-one days before they will come into force.'[8] The new rules were to be applied from Monday, 19 July, just four days after they were announced; thus, someone arriving on that Monday morning could be in breach of the new laws if they did not satisfy entry requirements that were stricter than they had been on the previous Friday.

The coalition government were tightening up all avenues of entry prior to the setting of an annual limit with the 'objective of reducing net migration to the tens of thousands over the lifetime of this Parliament'[9] and stated that there would only be a few weeks, mostly in August, which would be used for a so-called consultation period, when these amendments could be discussed. In addition, all written comments had to be in by 7 September, with the results announced at the end of that month. But why the need for such breakneck speed?[10]

Every time we have had a recession – in the 1880s, 1930s, 1970s, 1980s and even in the early 1990s – more people have left British shores than have arrived here. And those who were born between 1876 and 1920 left in droves, with some two million more leaving England and Wales than arriving, due mainly to the Great Depression. The numbers of births in Britain fell, first with our discovery of the wonders of condoms in the 1870s, then again with economic disincentives to procreate in the 1930s,[11] next with the discovery of the wonders of the birth-control pill in the 1960s and then the fear of AIDS in the 1980s. Each time the birth rate fell fewer people left and more were needed to replace the children we did not have.

Between 1880 and 1890, in the decade of Lowry's Manchester childhood, a 795,000 (net) left Britain. In contrast, 732,000 (net) entered during the period of the 1955–64 Conservative government, which led to the infamy of Enoch Powell's 1968 'Rivers of Blood' speech, in which the then shadow Tory Defence Minister claimed that what he called the 'tragic and intractable phenomenon which we watch with horror on the other side of the Atlantic' would soon be seen here.[12]

Partly as a result of that speech, and despite a Labour administration, immigration rules were tightened in 1968 with the short-term effect that some 104,000 (net) left during the six years of Labour government (1964–70) and despite the mini economic boom. That exodus was reversed at the start of Ted Heath's tenure (in 1971–2), but then it flip-flopped back to a net migration of (-112,000) under Labour from 1973–9, then again at -105,000 (net) in the three key Thatcher years of 1980–2 and yet again a figure of -76,000 (net) during John Major's 1990–3 recession.[13] I point all this out in case you thought that usually more people tended to arrive than leave. In most years since 1840 that has not been the case.

More people leave this country during economic recessions than come in. However, when I put this to the Migration Advisory Committee the only response was – well, this recession might be different. The very latest figures from the International Passenger Survey suggested a slowdown in emigration from Britain, with fewer leaving in 2008 (some 87,000) than in 2007; figures which were themselves less than the estimates of emigration for 2006 (a high point). Again, though, the Advisory Committee claimed that the International Passenger Survey was extremely unreliable even though, according to the Committee Chair, the 'government have set the limit according to that survey'.

The Migration Advisory Committee is made up largely of economists, who are themselves largely in favour of migration; they see it as helping oil the wheels of commerce. And as we discussed previously, given the freedom and the resources, people tend to travel to where they are needed and leave places where they are not. Economists generally consider migration controls to be inefficient; however, the Advisory Committee's problem was that even though immigration and net inflow from non-EU countries had been falling since 2006, the corresponding estimated rates of outflow, or emigration, were not rising quickly enough.

The 2008 'net inflow of non-EU' immigrants (the most recent figure available in September 2010), was of 187,000 more people coming in than leaving within twelve months. This was the figure that had to be seen to be cut down to the 'tens of thousands'. The total net inflow of all people during 2008 was 163,000, which is lower than the 'net inflow of non-EU' figure because more EU-residents were leaving the UK than entering. Despite this, those 163,000, just 0.3 per cent of the population (rounded up), were seen as a step too far into Britain.

I and others consulted on these figures pointed out that the numbers included poor estimates of emigration. A professor (of German origin) put his head in his hands at one point as he tried very hard not to ask why all these English people were being so stupid and not using more decent estimates. We also explained how emigration lags behind unemployment rises: people leave after the shock of redundancy and lay-offs, rather than before it. In the International Passenger Survey a tiny percentage of people are asked, often while they approach or leave customs (mostly at Heathrow), if they would be willing to answer a few questions, including how long they intend to be out of the country, and whether or not they are emigrating.

An exit survey is, of course, a stupid way to try to measure emigration as so many people do not know what their futures hold: they may be travelling to spend a few months studying abroad, which is what they tell the interviewer. But then later they find a job, then a partner and then they stay away. Other people might be reluctant to tell someone official that they are thinking of leaving for good. Others might not see themselves as emigrants, just ex-pats with a home in more than one country and reasons to stay away from the UK, such as to reduce their taxation liability (the so-called non-doms). Others plan to visit an elderly relative but then realize soon after arrival that they need to stay a while longer to help. People do not have crystal balls and as a result emigration statistics are almost always underestimated.

If we really wanted to know how many people emigrate from Britain we should do what the Dutch do and register people living abroad, though the benefits of registration would have to be great enough to ensure British citizens would participate in the process, just as Dutch citizens do. Short of that, the next best method we have for estimating how many people really do leave these shores is the decadal population census, which brings to light a discrepancy between its figures and the figures from the International Passenger Survey and which was the reason I was so sceptical of the Migration Advisory Committee's findings. The last two decadal censuses have indicated that up to a million more people had left the country than were counted by the International Passenger Survey.

However, the next – and if the coalition government has its way – final, decadal population census is to be held on 27 March 2011, with the results released by 2013. The data should tell us just how many people we really have left, and how many have come in since the last survey. It will also reveal how incorrect the passenger survey had been, again. But the government will not wait for that figure, which is due to be released well within what they intend to be their tenure of office. Why? Because they know what I know: that immigration would naturally likely fall below emigration, regardless of their crackdowns. But they were acting fast in order to claim credit for the drop. Within policy circles the stories of the 1991 and 2001 census corrections are well known. Outside those circles far too much certainty concerning migration estimates is declared. So here follow a few details of what the last two censuses revealed about immigration. And then what the last sixteen censuses combined show us about Britain's immigrant history.

Censuses are far from perfect. The 1991 census estimated that some one million people had avoided filling in their form, mainly because they were concerned they would be made to pay the poll tax.[14] Due to widespread and popular protest the poll tax was abolished soon after it was introduced, but not before it could influence the census taking. British subjects were right to be concerned that filling in a census form could result in them being identified as non-tax paying criminals. This was not because the census forms were passed to the local councils (that would be illegal), but because the census results told the local councils how many people in every small area should be paying tax, but were not. It told the authorities where to look.

A further 200,000 people did not complete the 1991 census form because they were transient, sleeping on others' sofas or otherwise homeless. Analysis of these and other factors allowed us to then estimate the population of mainly young men who were living abroad at this time.[15] It was this estimate that first helped show that the International Passenger Survey had a systematic bias.

After all the adjustments were made, including those for the poll tax, some 974,000 people who had been thought to be living in Britain were found not to be living here. These were people who were known to have been born in Britain and who were thought to have been mostly in their late teens or twenties, members of existing British households and more often male than female. Where were they living? Abroad, with their emigration previously undetected, sometime between 1981–91.[16] Why were they living abroad? Well, it's obvious, in retrospect – in 1984 more than a million people between the ages of 16 to 24 were claiming the dole. Many hundreds of thousands of others had left Britain to find work elsewhere and avoid this fate.

As a result of all that was learnt after the debacle of 1991, when 899,000 people could not be accounted for even by the post-census validation survey (established to check the census), the 2001 census was undertaken assuming that people would, again, be harder to count. This was despite the abolition of the poll tax and a change of government in 1997 to one which was still in its 'things can only get better' honeymoon. The 2001 census was taken very carefully and, most importantly, a massive post-enumeration-coverage survey was carried out to allow capture-recapture techniques to be employed (discussed in chapter two).[17] Although the early 1990s recession had not been as bad as that of the early 1980s, hundreds of thousands of people still left to work overseas, many thinking, incorrectly, that the move was temporary.

Outside of Britain – on the European continent, in Australia, Canada and New Zealand, in almost every other affluent country in the world – it was easier to be average. In Britain, where social polarization was growing despite things allegedly only getting better, it was gradually becoming the case that if you could not be one of life's winners you were destined for a loser's job (or no job). The phrase 'McJobs'[18] was imported from the United States at this time. Many of those McJobs jobs served the new rich of the late 1990s (and early 2000s) boom and included businesses such as car valeting, house-cleaning and hotel-staffing. Increasingly, many of these businesses were run, and staffed, by immigrants.

When the 2001 census results were first published, and despite the careful attention to the information-gathering process and the influx of immigrants willing to take low-paying jobs that were sometimes dirty and low-skilled, almost a million people who the authorities had thought were here, were found to be missing. And this was after the additional estimated adjustments to account for those missing hundreds of thousands, including people living here without the proper papers; as with the 1991 census results, the authorities concluded that the International Passenger Survey had hugely underestimated British emigrants, yet again.

The population of Britain had grown, yet by half as much as our officials had thought: by a million in the ten years to the millennium, rather than by more than two million. Again, until the release of census numbers in 2003, we had thought far more people were living here than actually were; the census proved that national estimates of population *change* in a decade were 105 per cent awry. And we British are supposed to be so good at queuing and counting! It was a bit of a mess, and it took some explaining.

Many local authorities complained and some even threatened to take the national authorities to court. Manchester local council cannily put its fraud department on to the case. Why bother chasing up people about not paying council tax if central government is going to take away millions from your budgets, billions over decades, by claiming that you are servicing a smaller population than you thought you were? The national authorities caved in to some of these local threats and adjusted the overall estimates upwards by just under a third of a million people but only in proportion to how effectively particular areas complained. In an attempt to summarize all this I wrote:

> Until the new census results were released we believed that international migration had led to a net additional 2,092,574 people coming to live in the United Kingdom between April 1991 and January 2001. After the release of the census, that change was revised down to an increase of 1,018,968 people between April 1991 and April 2001. The census also cast doubt on the 1991 estimate, and the 2001 census result was similarly questioned and subsequently the mid-year estimate for the UK population in 2001 was revised up to 59,113,500 people when an additional 324,300 souls were later added to the population removing a third of the discrepancy.[19]

100

Having twice had to work out how we miscalculated the figures after 1991 and 2001, I don't believe there to be reason to believe people won't be writing such things again in a few years when the 2011 results are released. To give you an idea of how little we really accurately know about migration, hence our overall population total, I've included below a few quotes from newspaper stories taken from 2001, 2004 and 2006, with each breathlessly announcing that the population had just passed sixty million when, in at least the first two cases, it had not.

The misrepresentation is not the fault of the journalists or their newspapers but of the errors in International Passenger Survey estimates, resulting in the Office for National Statistics at least twice prematurely announcing that the sixty-million milestone had been passed. These extracts are followed below by a few headlines and the summaries from more recent reports that have too quickly announced that the sixty-one- and sixty-two-million mark had been passed, with one even claiming that a seventy-eight-million total will soon be attained!

The population of the United Kingdom has passed 60 million, fuelled by record immigration and increasing life expectancy. It is growing at the fastest rate since the baby boom of the sixties. Almost all the growth is in the South of England. The number of people living in the North and Scotland is declining. The latest government estimates say the UK population rose from 59,755,700 on 30 June last year to 59,862,800 on 1 January 2001. If that growth rate continued, this country's sixty millionth resident was born last Tuesday.

'UK Population Soars Above 60 Million',
Observer, 26 August 2001[20]

My first child was born shortly before this announcement. There is a small chance he was the fifty-nine-millionth resident of Britain, as the national authorities added on too many people when local authorities complained in 2003. There is almost no chance he was the sixty-millionth, although I did wonder that August . . . Here's an extract from 2004:

> The United Kingdom population looks set to top 60 million before the end of this summer, following figures yesterday from the Office for National Statistics showing it climbed to a record high in 2003. After adjusting the totals for the past three years to take account of people missed during the 2001 census, the population reached 59.6 million in June 2003 – 400,000 more than the year before. The increase was the same as in 2002 and one more step of this magnitude would have taken the total past 60 million by June this year.

> 'UK Population is Poised to Pass 60m',
> *Guardian*, 10 September 2004[21]

My second child was just six months old in the June of the year in which this story was published. Had she missed out on her chance to claim the rights to be the sixty-millionth resident of the UK? As it turns out she would be around a year older before that point was reached (at least if what we currently think we know of what the population totals have been is right). When she was aged two, this report came out:

> The UK's population has passed 60 million for the first time, according to new Government figures. The

population grew by 375,000 to 60.2 million in the year to June 2005, the biggest annual rise since 1962, the Office for National Statistics (ONS) said.

'UK Population Passes 60m for First Time',
Telegraph, 24 August 2006[22]

Damn, I thought, reading this. My third child was born in August 2006. I was beginning to get a bit obsessed by the milestone and thought we had timed it perfectly this time, but no. It turns out that we had waited a year too long to be able to claim that sixty-millionth-prize-child status. But then, not long after, another milestone was reached:

Population growth at 47-year high – the UK population is now growing by 0.7% every year. The UK population grew by 408,000 in 2008 – the biggest increase for almost 50 years, according to the Office for National Statistics. The total number of people passed 61m for the first time, with changes in birth and death rates now a bigger cause of growth than immigration.

'The Total Number of People Passed 61m for
the First Time', BBC, 27 August 2009[23]

I was on a fool's mission thinking that any of my children might be 'the one'. The sixty-millionth resident of the UK almost certainly would have entered this country via Heathrow Terminal Three; however, it is probable that they were born in Britain, and were now returning after spending many years abroad.

At least a million people come in and out of Heathrow every three days. Most are tourists or short-term visitors but many are coming or going for longer periods.

In contrast, just over 2,000 babies are born each day in Britain, during what we call a baby boom. But just as I was pondering all this, and trying to work out our chances of having been out of the country long enough in 2005 to count as immigrants at exactly the right point[24] – another milestone passed:

> The great election TV debate last Thursday night was launched with a question on the vexed issue of immigration, a subject that until then had been barely touched on by the three party leaders. But in the ten minutes allocated to the subject, there was one figure conspicuous by its absence from the lips of Messrs Brown, Cameron and Clegg: 70 million. That's the number of people who our national statisticians expect will populate the UK by mid-2029.
>
> 'The UK's population is currently estimated to be just over 62 million', *Daily Mail*, picture caption, 21 April 2010[25]

What? We finally reach sixty million in summer 2005, sixty-one million in summer 2008 (reported when figures were collated in August 2009), but within just over another year we are up to sixty-two million, with projections being announced that were topping seventy million in just nineteen years? Was this demographics or politics?

It was exactly a week after the *Daily Mail* printed the '62 million' story that Gillian Duffy asked the then Prime Minister Gordon Brown why 'all these Eastern Europeans [were] coming in; where are they flocking from?'[26] He should have replied, 'Eastern Europe', and perhaps added, with a flourish, 'Dear Lady'. But it's easy to be wise after the event. And then, three months later, and in a run-up to the Migration Advisory Committee's consultation phase, the BBC itself began playing the same game as the *Daily Mail*:

> A new survey predicts the UK population will reach 78m by 2051. What will that mean for the UK? The study by the University of Leeds says [that] by 2051 a growing birth rate, coupled with high levels of immigration from Europe, Australasia and the US, as well as India, Pakistan and Bangladesh, will take the UK population to 78m. One of the authors, Professor Philip Rees, says the UK's ethnic make-up is "evolving significantly". The report predicts ethnic minorities will make up 20% of a 78m population.
>
> 'Can the UK Cope with a 78m Population?'
> BBC, 13 July 2010[27]

The 'new survey' was simply the same old Office for National Statistics (ONS) estimates of future population growth based on the 2001 census and assuming that current rates of births, death, immigration and emigration would continue. Although I say 'same old', the estimating process, and the government's actuaries department that carried it out, had recently been brought into ONS to curtail its consistent record on overestimating the population growth rate. This was overestimation that could only be corrected when the census revealed the cumulative effects of its systematic errors.

Gordon Brown might have had more success if he had tried to explain to Gillian Duffy that even though we knew where most Eastern Europeans were coming from, we could not be too sure of how many were here, of how many of those who had come had now left, of how many other people were leaving Britain for good (even before those people knew this themselves), of how many of us there might be in the first place and of whether more people were coming than going or not. But even a little demographic small-talk would have been unlikely to secure victory for Gordon because, despite all the uncertainty surrounding these numbers, despite entering the worst recession for more than seventy years – with fewer people coming in than usual, and more people leaving than usual – the British became convinced that the barbarians were at the gates and were flooding in.

It is perhaps time for a little calm, and a few more numbers.

The estimate of UK population reaching seventy-eight million by 2051 assumes an average net growth of around 391,000 people a year. This is the kind of growth only experienced with a rapidly aging but not yet dying population, further fuelled by high levels of net immigration and above-average fertility, all factors that are the results of living through a sustained economic boom. In future we might be lucky enough to achieve seventy-eight million, but only if we trusted in those who are likely to start families. The alternative would be a repeat of history – what has happened following *every single* major recession: emigration and the consequent slump in fertility that comes with economic distress. Fewer people start families when their jobs are at risk, as so many fear being unable to set up home.

I hope we reach seventy-eight million by 2051 (the year I am estimated to die). I worry about what kind of country Britain would be to die in if we don't. Who will be inserting a catheter into my body as I lie in that hospital bed? Or should I try to get to France? Where will my children be living? Will there have been enough opportunities for them in this country or will they have gone abroad, not because of immigrants displacing their opportunities but because

Britain has not been growing sustainably and developing socially enough to be a welcoming place. Perhaps they might have wanted to go to university but could not afford it here; perhaps they might travel abroad and then never come back?

World population is rising, but that rise is slowing down rapidly. Some nine billion people can comfortably fit on this planet, but not if countries such as the UK and international bodies such as the EU put up walls around themselves. Life would become much harder to live within those walls, as well as outside them, if this attempt at a global apartheid of the world's peoples were allowed to continue. The reasons the Conservative party want to curtail immigration in 2010 are the same reasons their Shadow Defence Minister gave in 1968, and have nothing to do with overall population numbers and everything to do with who might be coming and what political advantage can be gained.

Is apartheid too strong a word? Lying under the surface of every debate on immigration are questions about race. The University of Leeds study used by the newspapers to raise the spectre of seventy-eight million was actually a study of the changing racial nature of the population of Britain over the next forty years. Often with migration it is not the immigration that is of actual concern to some of our newspaper editors, it is the question of *who* the potential immigrants may be.

One of the largest groups of immigrants in Britain, and the group responsible for the greatest concentrations of immigrant children found within London neighbourhoods – 32,700 children in all – are non-EU immigrants who were born in the United States of America.[28] Often these are the offspring of wealthy individuals, who, as a consequence of that affluence, take up far more housing space than do most British residents. Their parents also take many of the very best paid jobs in London. The cost of educating their children is disproportionately high, yet I have never read a single newspaper story complaining about the unfairness of this. More than one in seven[29] of all the pre-school children you might meet in Kensington & Chelsea (by far the richest borough in Britain) have been born in the USA.[30]

Not all migrants are the same. Migration to the USA was a significant route out for those 795,000 migrants who fled the famine and the factories and mills (or who could not find work there) in the 1880s, never to return. And though migration from the USA has been a much smaller stream into Britain, it is now significant and growing rapidly. It is shown in the figure overleaf as the second thin line at the top of the recently growing wedge, just under migration from South America. Note also that migration from South Africa also increased after the abolition of apartheid.

The figure below gives the migratory history of Britain from when we first systematically recorded everyone's geographical origins, to as recently as we can now reliably count. Until the 2011 census is released, 'recently' refers to about 2006; after then – as the stories above illustrate – population estimates, let alone estimates of who has come from where, are much more speculation than fact.

The figure below tells the story of who came to Britain and settled here, yet it has never been published before. It is not part of our national culture or understanding. This is odd. Almost everyone living in Britain will have a great or great-great grandparent who was one of these immigrants, who overall left far more often than they arrived. And as the figure shows at its end, by 2006 at least 10 per cent of us were not born in Britain. There is no good reason why that should not rise to 20 per cent by 2050.

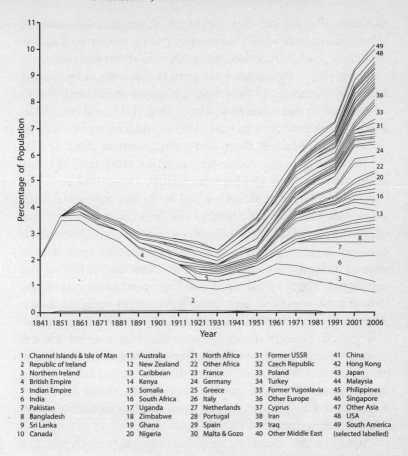

FIGURE 8: **People Born Abroad but Living in Britain, by Country of Birth, 1841–2006**

Source: Population censuses, interpolation in 1941 and LFS in 2006 (originally drawn, and statistical research, by Bethan Thomas)

Around 1841 the great bulk of immigration to Britain was from Ireland (which increased as the English allowed the potato famine of the 1840s to ravage the population without offering any significant relief, despite the riches of the Empire).[31] By 1861 some 4 per cent of the population of Britain had been born overseas, mostly in Ireland.

Long-term immigration rates fell after the 1860s once the Irish determined they had far better prospects if they emigrated to the Americas. Those that did come to the UK during that time had trouble finding decent work and, up until 1931, they left more often than settled. That is why there is a dip in the above figure, from 1861 to 1931, but showing that after 1931 came change.

By the 1930s the British were no longer replacing their own numbers through births, the lack of which sparked scare stories that the country would be depopulated by the end of the century, although no one in that decade was as infantile to suggest that the 'last one out turn out the light'. As a result of the falling birth rate, immigration was encouraged, particularly of adults from what was then called the Indian Empire; not least by an inconsistent Enoch Powell when he was the Minister of Health (1960–3). The results of this influx can be seen in the graph. In the early 1960s the largest inflows were still from the Irish Republic, then from the rest of the (then) European Economic Community, then from India (including what are now Bangladesh and Pakistan).

Next, more people were encouraged in from the Caribbean,[32] and immigration from there surpassed flows from India by 1965, then subsided and was surpassed in 1975 by the East African influx after the emergency orchastrated by Idi Amin. After that came the German inflow, which stands out most prominently and that grew even greater in the 1990s, before the most recent 'other Europe' band becomes more prominent, including the distinct Polish-born bands, but this is just one group amid a spreading rainbow of lines.

Read the list above again. The Irish, Indians, Caribbeans, East Africans and Poles you will have heard of, before them maybe Jews and Huguenots, but had you heard of the recent influx of Germans? In the 1990s, and earlier, we had a huge German inflow.[33] More than twice as many German-born people (well over a quarter of a million of them), live in Britain as do the French-born or Italian-born. What are they doing here? Does the government know?

Many of these German-born immigrants were the children of British soldiers who served in the army of the Rhine during the Cold War. They were born in Germany but then travelled back with their parents when the tour of duty was complete. You might say, 'they're not German, then', but what is German? These folk were born in the 'fatherland'.

Immigration is about moving between countries of residence, not so much about nationality or citizenship and, ultimately, an international migrant is someone who is born in one country and dies in another. Birthplace is only a part of identity, not all of it. And most of those who came to Britain from East Africa during the emergency orchestrated by Idi Amin were Indians, born in Africa. Their origins, but also their expectations and education made their later average social trajectories different to those from the Indian subcontinent arriving in Britain, or to other people born in Africa moving to live here. Every migration stream is unique, and remarkably useful for telling us more about ourselves.

Where people were born does provide us with clues about the places they live now, and why. For example, one of the clearest indicators of poor economic development in an area is the high ratio of Germany-born children to the total overseas-born population and these are often places where recruitment to the army had been and remains high because there are few other jobs on offer. The Germany-born-English-ex-forces-children had different average life trajectories than that of the average Britain-born child and so, like certain elements in a chemical spectrum, their high presence in an area is often an indicator of economic woe.

Conversely, the arrival of many of the most recent migrants from countries that make up much of the rainbow of bands at the end of the graph are often indicators of economic success: areas that are home to high numbers of people who are newly arrived are usually areas where there are job opportunities. The reverse of this can be even more telling.

People born in countries from which high numbers of refugees come – Somalia, Afghanistan, Iraq – through their concentration in particular areas of the country, indicate where housing is cheapest and where groups have been deliberately relocated into neighbourhoods with the least opportunities, perhaps because the authorities imagine somehow that getting to know that you might end up in Sighthill in Glasgow might deter you from fleeing for your life. More likely it is because there is no great surplus of well educated local advocates living nearby such poor areas who might assist those trying to claim asylum.[34]

Many of the population-flows into Britain, from rich and poor places alike, are made up of the children or grandchildren of people who left earlier, descendants who often have a wider mixture of ancestors as a result of emigration. People have moved around so much, and to and from Britain, that there simply is no 'stock'[35] of true-born English in contrast to a group of foreigners who are from another 'stock'. Increasingly, and especially in the case of migrants, people are of mixed origins, the only question being how far back you have to go to locate the origin of the mix. The mixing is further complicated as older emigrants become folded back into the dough.

Often British emigrants return with their tails between their legs or are soon at loose ends, such as soldiers returning from overseas tours of duty. Many of these soldiers find it difficult to resettle, reacclimatize and find civilian jobs once they're back in Britain; hence, they often end up in poorer areas. More British soldiers are serving time in British prisons now than were serving in Afghanistan, even at the heights of 2009 deployment.[36]

Again, there are clues in the statistical record. Returning emigrants who bring back their overseas-born children probably account for the fact that there are more Canadian-born people than USA-born now living in Barrow in Furness, the Highlands of Scotland, Castlereagh in Northern Ireland, Oldham in the north-west of England and North Tyneside in the north-east of England. They are often the children of people who emigrated in the 1950s and 1960s but returned when things went wrong,[37] or when they simply felt homesick.

From the 1950s to the 1970s Canada tried harder than the US to attract British emigrants, just as Mr Powell was trying to attract India's doctors and nurses! All this, decades later, left a 'trace' that we can now use to reconstruct their histories through the birthplace patterns created by their children who returned with them. And the net result is that millions of individual stories of great courage and adventure can be discovered within the few percentage figures created from a computerized analysis of a census. While easier than trying to reconstruct migratory stories from the chemical analysis of the teeth of pre-historical peoples, modern human geography is still a form of archaeology: part science, part art.

Emigration from Britain was so high in the past, and so

relatively high in the recent present, that there might well be twice as many grandchildren of Britain-born people living overseas as there are people living in Britain who have grandparents who were themselves born abroad. You might need to read that sentence again. What I'm trying to say is that we British are as much an emigrant nation as we are an immigrant one. We are not, despite being an island, insular.

Nevertheless, the headlines continue to blare on about the flood that is drowning the country. The last decade did see high net numbers of entries and one could argue that we did not need all this immigration. That surely it would be better if youngsters here could find work in Britain rather than travelling abroad in search of jobs? Well, it would be better, yes, but usually those youngsters do not want to do the kind of work on offer in Britain, and for good reason.

Would you want to make up two dozen hotel rooms each morning, clean all those toilets, arrange everything 'just so', serve at tables over lunch, take insults and hope for tips? Or would you rather go and look for something a little more rewarding to do abroad? The same goes for picking vegetables in Lincolnshire fields, or sorting through rubbish put out for recycling (who do you think does that?). We have created a lot of jobs in recent years that offer unattractively low pay and that are mostly filled by young people coming in from other countries for whom the experience of Britain is at least interesting at first, and for whom the money, until recently, used to be good, if spent back home.

Rather like the Icelanders who could be heard complaining at the height of their economic boom that they had to speak English at supermarket tills in Reykjavik because the Poles who worked there could not speak Icelandic, we will continue to complain about the people who do our dirty, dangerous and tedious work – until the moment they are no longer here. However, we are unlikely to read many more headlines in the near future that suggest 'Supermarket Supplier Demands Workers Speak Polish', as the *Telegraph* newspaper misleadingly splashed upon its pages in March 2010, in the run-up to the general election. In fact, the supplier had not demanded Polish be spoken, he was offering to allow workers to use it in the workplace.[38]

In the run-up to the general election the *Telegraph* was helping to stoke the flames of prejudice by disparaging workers who had the skill of speaking Polish. The final lines of the paper's own story revealed that the employers would not discriminate against workers who could only speak English.

Nevertheless, it would unarguably be better to have more jobs in Britain paying average decent wages[39] and leading to careers that people born and brought up here could aspire to, but we will still require more people coming in than leaving if we are simply to replace the children we choose not to have.

It has been decades since we last had, on average, two children per couple. So what we have as a result is an aging population that cannot out-source care abroad (other than by emigrating to Spain to retire). Who will care for them?

Even these facts do not seem to quell the scary myths about migration, and there are many myths. One is that immigrants take housing. But without immigration, much current housing would no longer be standing in many cities. Many immigrants in recent decades came to towns and cities in the north of England that otherwise would have suffered depopulation. The poorest immigrants consume the least housing because they pack themselves so tightly in.

Others claim that immigrants are a drain on the health service and there are moves to make it even harder than it is already for people from outside of the EU to be treated here. Yet without these immigrants the National Health Service would not work. There are more nurses from Malawi working in Manchester alone than there are nurses in all of Malawi.[40] Immigrants and the offspring of immigrants make up a vastly disproportionate share of the staff of the National Health Service.

A third myth concerns the perception that immigration means some white children becoming isolated at school. Recently I took a phone call at work. Someone had read something I'd written about segregation. The man on the line said 'My boy's the only white boy in his school – I can't leave him there can I?'[41] He thought his boy might be bullied. We talked, emailed, and I later wrote something along these lines: In every class one child will be tallest, shortest, fattest, thinnest, have the most spots; however, if your child is being bullied because he is white, that is different from being bullied for having spots. For instance, being bullied for being the only child playing the violin is unlikely to follow a child into the job market, or lead to a more racist society. Whether you leave your child in a school, or demand that the school act, depends on what is happening to your child in that school.

If all children went to their nearest school there would be slightly fewer schools in which only one lone child was white, or from any other category. There would still be a great number of schools that had only one child in a class who was not white: most children in Britain who are the only child of their ethnicity in a schoolroom are not white. However, far too many schools are near majority-white, and a few are near-majority non-white. This is because children are not quite as well mixed by school as they are by neighbourhood.

It is a myth that immigration encourages schools to become more segregated, that over time particular schools become more strongly identified with particular groups. In reality there is no evidence that schools in Britain are becoming more segregated by ethnicity; however, they are more segregated than are the neighbourhoods they draw from. This is because large numbers of children do not attend their nearest school. It is likely, though, that schools will become less segregated over time: trends show us that the areas that particular schools are in are becoming less segregated, despite high rates of immigration into those areas.[42]

A fourth myth of immigration can be summarized by asking 'Multiculturalism or Nationalism: I have to choose sides don't I?' No, you don't: British society is a multicultural society so, really, it would be difficult to see the difference between your choices, if you were forced to choose. Britain is a state made from an amalgam of foreigners and the importation of peoples from a large and former empire. Multiculturalism – the acceptance of multiple ethnic cultures – is one of the things that is special about Britain, and which sets it apart from other countries.

The major social splits within Britain are by wealth, not by race, religion or birthplace. Those children who never mix at normal school are often at private schools, or are misbehaving children excluded from any school. These are on the one hand very rich and on the other very poor; not black, Asian or white. In fact, in the schools for the affluent and for the poor there is more often now a mix of children from a wide variety of ethnic, religious and birthplace backgrounds. Children within the state sector are similarly very divided. Middle-class children tend to attend comprehensive schools in middle-class areas, which can be as different from comprehensives in poor areas as they are different from the lower end of private schooling.

A fifth myth is that immigration means a fragmented society. We all 'live separately' and we all have links outside of where we live, even if that means just outside in the street. What is of concern is the misperception that people of certain faiths, for example, tend not to mix, shop, play, attend school or work with other people as much as they might if we were not so segregated. However, such ideas of isolation and fragmentation are indeed misperceptions, at least when it concerns Muslims, for example, according to the census, a greater proportion of Muslims marry non-Muslims than white Christians marry outside 'their' group.

Most white Christians live in areas where there are far fewer people of other faiths to meet. It is much easier for white people to segregate than it is for other people to keep to themselves. White Christians appear, through census records, to be a little less open to socializing outside their groups – or perhaps they are just not led into temptation as much as those belonging to smaller groups more often are. London is partly so racially and religiously mixed because of a glut of free will: imagine if young adults were told to pair up only with someone who had similar skin or hair colour or beliefs to those of their own parents. Such a dictate would be easier to enforce in New York, perhaps, where there is less variety of ethnicity and so it is easier to remain in and among your own group.

A sixth myth is that immigrants are holding themselves back if they don't speak English; however, you'd think that if the government wanted everyone to speak English fluently, they wouldn't cut funding for English-language classes. Our government encourages us to learn more foreign languages yet at the same time criticizes foreign-language speakers for not speaking English. (The administration in Wales wants more people to speak, read and write Welsh, but the British government often forgets this.) Indeed, there are people who live here who cannot speak English but there are also many people in Britain who can *only* speak English.

Incidentally, if the British had not lost the Battle of Catraeth, which took place near what is now Catterick around 1,410 years ago, then we could all still be speaking British, or to give it its common name: Welsh, rather than the language brought in by those immigrant Anglos. The Battle of Catraeth was far more of a defining moment in British history than was that skirmish between Vikings at Hastings, or the 'Glorious' revolution, or even the most recent Battle of Britain, but it does not fit the English version of who Britons were and who the British are, so if you are English you were almost certainly not told about the battle of Catraeth at school.[43]

A seventh myth is that immigration results in white flight – from urban centres. This is also false. Researchers recently showed in exacting detail[44] how people almost always move when they can get better housing and a better environment; when they can no longer afford the house they are living in; or when they grow up and leave home. Some areas are becoming 'more Asian' and 'less white' but this isn't because white people are moving out and more Asians are moving in. If there is an area of Britain suffering from an influx of immigrants to such an extent as to have a detrimental effect on the locals it is in areas where large numbers of English retire: Devon, Cornwall, rural Wales and rural Scotland.

Which leads me to my final, eighth myth, concerning those who really are the most intrusive immigrants. Who actually 'swamps' areas, disrespects the local culture, refuses to speak or learn the local languages? Who are so much better-off, on average, compared to the indigenous population that they can buy up the best housing and price-out locals from the land? Well, other than in some very affluent parts of London, it isn't the Americans, nor those caviar-munching, champagne-sipping Russians, and other such people – there simply aren't enough of these people to make the kind of adverse impact I'm talking about.

And apart from 'who?', the question is also 'where?' have these immigrants had the greatest impact? Where do they now make up often more than a third of the entire population of local authorities, where in 1971 there were hardly any such immigrants, born in another country but now landed in a place where they usually know little of the local customs? To find the answer look to the most scenic parts of Scotland, Wales and the South West. Ask a few locals what they think of the many tens of thousands of southern-England-born who now retire to these places each year. Ask the locals how they are treated by the English, and what they think the English immigrants think of them.

Immigration has the potential to be less give and more take when immigrants come simply to retire, not to set down roots, or come just to work or study for a few years, to extract a profit and then go home. Places are enriched by immigration only if the immigrants stay, and contribute. The immigrants who have most disrupted formerly stable communities in Britain have been the English themselves, buying retirement or holiday homes in places they like to visit, but where they choose not to belong.

In order to thrive a country requires immigration, and if you have more get up and go than most folk, a little more about you, you will consider emigration. A century ago, after California took first place in the migration sweep-stakes (with gold), South Wales was the second greatest world centre of attraction for immigrants. They came from all across Europe and even further afield to dig for black gold. The problems of the Valleys began when those immigrants stopped coming. We should not be afraid of immigrants, but we should be wary of some immigrants who don't intend to stay: they are only after the good times, or the views.

Winston Churchill's grandson, Nicholas Soames, recently called for a change in the law to:

> [B]reak the link between people coming to work here and people being able to settle here. That is key. Of course, they should come here; we welcome them and recognise that they have very important work to do. It is that link between coming to work here and settle here that needs to be broken.

In contrast, many people like me would argue that intro-ducing a German style 'guest-worker' system to Britain would not be a very British thing to do, and would not make the country a better place. What you want is for people living in an area to be committed to that area, not be labelled as "guests".[45]

Britain is both an immigrant and an emigrant nation. And the exodus of young people from our shores is almost certainly a current problem: they are leaving because there are too few opportunities here. Many will never come back.

The British are so mistrustful of their government that the country has no way of accurately counting its residents other than in a decadal census, but to save money and because of a fear of snooping, even that British tradition

121

is set to be abolished after 2011. Before we all get too old it would help greatly if we stopped thinking that some of us are more British than others, accept that the only truly true Brits are the few who can still speak Welsh, and that we need not all speak Welsh (or fluent English even), but that we should all start respecting each other more than we currently do. That's how you mix well.

CHAPTER 5

THE HUMAN MOSAIC – NEIGHBOURS AND NEIGHBOURHOODS

'Britain is "sleepwalking into New Orleans-style segregation"'

Independent, 19 September 2005[1]

Around midday on 1 September 2005 I was sitting in London in the BBC News 24 studio and seven words kept repeating in my mind: 'They've not been killed by a hurricane.' On the screens in front of me I watched the first live images of bodies floating in the flood waters of New Orleans. The US voice-over reported the deaths as attributable to the hurricane, and eventually a BBC reporter explained:

We've just heard that the evacuation operation that has been taking place at the Dome – the football stadium where up to 20,000 people have been staying – has been suspended because shots were fired within the dome. Apparently shots were also fired at a rescue helicopter that was passing overhead. There really is an edgy feeling about the city, it is no longer comfortable and it doesn't seem as if the emergency services are dealing with this very well.[2]

That reporter was based in Los Angeles.

One BBC correspondent who got into New Orleans that day chose his words with a distinct lack of tact: 'The battle between nature and man is almost over, but the battle between man and man is just beginning. The scene here is more Africa than America.'[3] Almost all the faces on the screen as he said that were black. One white woman he did show, in hysterics, shouted to him: 'It's not about low income, it's not about rich people and poor people, it's about people! Nobody wants to hurt anybody in this city, nobody wants to hurt these people who have these businesses.' The National Guard were training their gun sights on those whose hunger was driving them to consider looting for food.

The BBC presenter sitting next to me was clearly very shocked by the images but started reading professionally from the autocue to ask me why, over here in the UK, in work with the Joseph Rowntree Foundation, we were reporting that Britain was becoming more divided and unequal. Immediately the camera was on me. I didn't say the seven words that were going through my mind, or try to explain, then, why we should not be reporting those New Orleans deaths as some act of God. Instead, and almost certainly for the better, I tried to answer the question I had been asked about Britain.

But then, and ever since then, I knew that what people had just seen on the screen and what I was about to say were related. I just didn't know how to say it. I'll try and say it now, the way I wished I could have said it then.

What I said, as if I too were reading a script, was that with colleagues from the universities of Bristol and Edinburgh, we had just issued a series of ten reports analysing how the most recent population censuses revealed that life in Britain was unfair and often becoming more unfair; meaning that those in greatest need were often being least well served. I argued that more imaginative policies would be required if health inequalities were to be reduced. What I didn't say was that if we carried on the way we were, we would become more like the US, which although one of the largest and richest nations in the world was the most unequal of all significant rich countries in the world. Even today I wish I had been brave enough, and quick-thinking enough, to say that the way it needed to be said, on air, in 2005.

Try to imagine that, in the aftermath of a natural disaster in Britain, the government compounded the suffering by sending in the Territorial Army to prevent looting, instead of to ensure there was enough food for all. Is it hard to imagine? As hard as you might have found it a decade ago? Britain is not as socially divided as the United States, but we have become more like them, reflecting their high inequalities – more than any other country in Western Europe in recent decades.

The woman in New Orleans had said to the reporter: 'It's about people'. But increasingly it is about rich people and poor people, about rules that differ between one group and the next. A parking fine is a very minor inconvenience to someone who is affluent, but a significant problem to someone who is poor. It is about low income and high income. It should not be – most people do not want to hurt other people or see them suffer – but when those with the most take even more, those with least become increasingly vulnerable: cities divide into income-specific quarters and then people begin to fear mixing with those in other quarters, and sometimes begin to describe parts of their towns as 'more like Africa', even if they have never been to Africa.

My BBC questioner's mind was clearly still taking in the images from New Orleans and I was allowed to talk at length to fill the gaps. I described how divided the population was between poor and affluent areas. How, for instance, there were now more households in Britain with spare cars – three or more – than there were car-less households with dependant children to care for. I pointed out that there were hundreds of thousands of empty homes that could be used by families in need if we allocated our housing better. The BBC helpfully put up one of their very simple graphics to illustrate the point about cars:

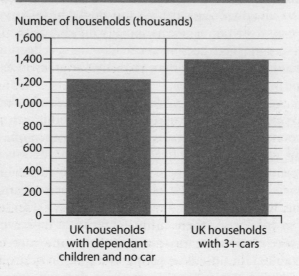

FIGURE 9: BBC online graphic, 1 September 2005

Redrawn from BBC website, which in turn was redrawn from our report[4]

126

Because I was reporting mainly on British census results, I failed to mention the hurricane, or the connection between those without cars and their corresponding inability to flee New Orleans and the strengthening concentrations of carless households within the poorest parts of British cities.

What I also didn't say was that other, more recent data was beginning to uncover a disturbing truth. In 2005, eight years into a New Labour government, social inequalities in Britain were all too often still rising. Britain was becoming a little more unequal each year – again, a place ever so slightly more like the US, more like that city where people died because they were too poor to get out when the winds and rain came. At the beginning of the twenty-first century, Britain had become a country with enough to go around but one that chose instead to distribute our resources far less evenly than *ever* before. More people in Britain owned cars they could not find the time to drive, than there were people with young children who could not afford to run a car.

We did not own so many cars because poverty was falling but because avarice was rising. If a New Orleans-type disaster were to hit a British city, we too would find that we had tens of thousands of people who could not afford to flee, who would have to wait for buses that might never turn up.

To tourists, New Orleans is famous for being the city of Mardi Gras, jazz and the blues. To social scientists, New Orleans is famous as one of the most socially segregated cities to be found in any affluent nation.[5] It is a city so segregated that when the levee broke at the very end of August 2005, hundreds of people lost their lives trapped in a place their poverty would not allow them to escape; in a nation with more cars than any other in the world, the poor of New Orleans had no means of escape.[6] 'They also had precious little help from the authorities, who were ordered to be more concerned with shooting potential looters and protecting the property of the affluent, than with preserving lives. Almost all who died in September 2005 in that city were killed because they lived in a country where so many of the rich had stopped caring for others.

The claim that Britain is 'sleepwalking into New Orleans-style segregation' came from a speech given by the former Constitutional Affairs Minister, Harriet Harman, just a fortnight after the hurricane. She echoed the words of Trevor Phillips, the then chairman of the Commission for Racial Equality who, to quote the newspaper that printed her words: 'believes the UK must heed the lessons of the Louisiana catastrophe, which highlighted the economic disparity and racial division in parts of the US.' And, on Thursday of that week, 'Mr Phillips [told] Manchester Council for Community Relations [that]: "We are a society which, almost without noticing it, is becoming more divided by race and religion".'

Harriet Harman was also reported to have said: 'We don't want to get into a situation like America, but if you look at the figures, we are already looking like America – in London, poor, young and black people don't register to vote.'[7] She then made the promise that she would fund a campaign that would encourage these same people to participate in the electoral process. However, it would have been better if she had funded research into the reasons why we have concentrations of poverty in particular areas; or if she had asked why increasing numbers of poorer people of all ethnicities didn't vote and why they found the choices offered to them irrelevant to their own financial and social circumstances.

Since 1997, in an attempt to stop Britain becoming too much like the United States, the Labour government began to invest in (US-style) New Deals – large-scale pro-grammes that would help to rebuild and refurbish housing and schools and rejuvenate the health service. Educational provision was improved to the point that, in 2010, we learnt that *extra* university places were filled for the first time by more working-class students than by those com-ing from the middle classes.[8] But while Labour achieved so much in education, they had little notion of where they were falling down elsewhere.

In 2009 Ludi Simpson's and Nissa Finney's book *Sleepwalking to Segregation?: Challenging Myths About Race and Migration*, explained in great detail why Harriet Harman and Trevor Phillips were wrong.[9] Simpson and Finney's research, using successive censuses and more recent school and other records, showed that over time minority groups in the UK had become more integrated into the rest of the population. People had begun to mix more by race and religion with the result that we have no ghettos in Britain. So when Trevor Phillips told the *Independent* in 2005 that: 'The number of people of Pakistani heritage in ghettos, defined as areas with more than two-thirds of any one ethnic group, trebled between 1991 and 2001',[10] he was telling them something that was simply not true.

Phillips had been badly advised.[11] Why? Because those of us lucky enough to be able to see all the numbers had done a poor job of explaining what we saw when the census was first released. Phillips' definition of a ghetto contrasts with the precise definition understood by academics: 'a residential district which is almost exclusively the pre-serve of one ethnic or cultural group [and where] most members of that group are found in such areas.'[12] Other than white people in remote rural areas and in a few poor, almost all-white estates, Britain does not even have small

residential districts that satisfy the first half of this definition, let alone the second half. This definition applied to
the original ghetto in Venice and to the African-American
ghetto in Chicago in the 1930s. Again, nowhere now in
Britain even approaches such extremes yet,[13] although we
do not have ghettos, we are nonetheless moving towards
a situation where one day we too could mistakenly blame
deaths in the event of a catastrophe as 'acts of God', when
instead they were results of our own social and economic
divisions.

The census reveals a different kind of segregation than
ghettoization: racial concentrations of the kind that rightly
worry Trevor Phillips but that are not found on the ground,
but in the sky. The majority of children who live above
the fourth floor of tower blocks, in England, are black or
Asian.[14] This concentration is only possible because prejudice, poverty and locality are so closely linked – especially
in London, where the richest tenth[15] are now 271 times
better off than the poorest tenth of the population. This
is the statistic politicians should have used to make their
point about racial segregation in contemporary Britain.
These tower blocks are not ghettos, because below the fifth
floor (and in the low-rise properties adjacent), a majority
of children and their parents are white. As a whole, the
neighbourhoods are racially mixed, but are nonetheless
divided by income levels, which are evident when we look
at who lives where – lower or higher (and cheaper).

Again, rather than encouraging young adults to vote, our
politicians should have asked why mostly black and Asian
children are housed in this way, so high up and far from
street level. Why would these people vote for mostly white
politicians, who usually come from more affluent households than they do, and who don't know as much about
disadvantaged Britain. Politicians from average-income

backgrounds now often talk as if they grew up in poverty but, in truth, almost no one who did grow up impoverished becomes a politician today.[16]

It was when more of our politicians did come from more representative backgrounds that issues such as slum clearance and the provision of universal benefits for all were better championed. No child should be housed many floors above the street – when the lift breaks, struggling with shopping and a toddler up multiple flights of stairs is exhausting and dangerous.

So, if racial segregation and ghettoization is not one of the defining characteristics of a divided Britain, what is it that splits up our cities so neatly? Perhaps we need a new way to look at society, a new set of questions that would help us understand how our communities are established – how, where and why – what makes them work? As a student of human cartography, of drawing the maps of people's lives, I was influenced by a man from Hungary who lived most of his life in Sweden: Janos Szegö. Janos drew some of the earliest computer-aided maps of people's lives and used to talk about how it might be possible one day to draw maps as if you could see into all the houses in a street and know what everyone wanted and hoped for, as if you could see happiness and sadness, fear and fun, chart movement, flows and even the collective fascination with plans for a better world. He wrote of how, in his maps, he could see older people talk with muted voices of 'their joy in their children and of their hopes on their behalf'.[17]

Later, after a few years of teaching human geography, I wrote of the subway I had cycled through every day to school and home again. When, as an adult, I returned to the subway, I found this graffiti on its wall: '<– good puppies this way – lost puppies this way –>', identifying where the most and least affluent residents lived in relation to the many subway exits. The arrows woke me up. I had been getting tired of listening to academic rhetoric about things called 'neighbourhood effects', discussions about whether it mattered where children grew up and whether this influenced their outcomes in life beyond the effects of family, school and chance.

I decided to publish my thoughts in an academic journal:

For me, given my past and my places, I am unlikely ever to be impressed by an A-level grade on its own (or even a string of As) – to believe [that] it is much more than a signpost to your street, school, and socialisation. I am unlikely to think that if you do not have a job it is because of your personal failing rather than the choices of the employers in your area, and what in turn affects them and your luck and status when you enter that market. I am unlikely to be convinced that people in Britain do not know these things themselves – that when they choose and are forced where to live they are not expressing their intimate knowledge that place matters.[18]

Writing those words had an effect: I wasn't asked to be a university admissions officer again.

I had learnt at school, but mostly outside of school, that it mattered where you grew up within a city, from which quarter you came. I learnt from going to university that almost no matter where they came from many people felt that the divisions were especially acute in the place they called home. From studying those divisions I found that they tended to be most acute in towns, and that these differences between neighbourhoods were now generally accepted as unfortunate, but not unusual.

The records show that the divisions between our neigh-bourhoods have not always been as bad as they are now. In fact we have to go a long time back to find divisions as bad as we find today. Therefore, at particular times in particular places the mosaic of social differences must have gone back and forth in importance – at one time more and at another time less.

In nineteenth-century Britain this mosaic, the dif-ferentiation of space by class, was exposed by popular writers such as Charles Dickens and campaigners such as Edwin Chadwick. The mosaic was made visible when the philanthropist Charles Booth, with help from a young Beatrix Potter[19] (later Webb), drew his poverty maps of 1880s London. Booth labelled the rookeries – the poorest enclosed back streets – as 'vicious semi-criminal' places. He coloured them black, while not very far away, in golden yellow, he painted the streets of the homes of the servant-keeping households. The maps made the people in power think about what makes up a cohesive society and what maintains the persistence of poverty.

A little earlier, Charles Ansell's 1874 survey of child-hood mortality had revealed that, among the professional and well-to-do classes, one in ten of their children died within the first year of life, a figure confirmed by Seebohm Rowntree's survey of York in 1899. For children born within the families of tradesmen, some one in six died within that first year of life; among the vast mass of work-ing-class families it was often one in four who did not live a year. These survival rates, just over a century old, are today matched only in the very poorest of landlocked African countries (sometimes where we now import our nurses from).[20]

Today the very best-off babies born in Britain are almost 100 times more likely to survive their first year of life than the worst-off a century ago. Even the worst-off today are almost ten times better off than the best-off a century ago. However, because improvements in survival have been greatest in recent decades among those who have the most, a child born into poverty is now two, or three, or four times more likely to die within its first year if born in some parts of London as compared to others, and outside of London the differentials can be even greater.

Every generation has poverty and inequality described anew to them in the terms of their times. Often those creating the descriptions are seen as agitators, a little unreasonable, complaining too much. Edwin Chadwick was a 'romantic', Robert Tressell a 'troublemaker', George Orwell a 'socialist', Emmeline Pankhurst (that other Salford native) a 'militant'; a few decades after their deaths such people are almost always seen as reasonable, visionary, forward thinking and relatively lone voices in a sea of indifference and apathy.[21]

Absolute conditions of material well-being have improved beyond what could have been envisaged in the wildest of our grandparents' imaginations. But relative deprivation remains and the relative gaps are widening. In 1899 a young adult was seen as poor if he could not afford to buy a postage stamp to send a letter to a loved one. In 2009 a young adult was seen as poor if she could not afford a top-up to send a text to a loved one. It was the Young Foundation, in their major study of contemporary unmet needs, which discovered that some of our poorest teenagers now often go without food in order to keep their phones working.[22]

Right-wing politicians have recently caught on to the idea of describing poverty and inequality as unjust. The Conservative party coined the phrase 'Broken Britain', which became one of the battle cries of their long electoral campaign from 2005 to 2010. The first sound of Britain breaking came in that early autumn of 2005, with the sudden onslaught of stories about the country sleepwalking into segregation, the stories with which this chapter began. Muslims were said to be living separately, sticking with their own kind, building their mosques with minarets in the areas they were 'taking over'. Islamaphobia was rife.

Next the white working-class were wheeled out in debates held around middle-class dinner tables, and on both BBC Radio 4 and BBC2. We were told that the white working-class were becoming segregated, too – away from jobs, away from private housing, away from the good schools, squeezed out by the immigrants and the rich. While some parts of our cities were becoming bohemian or gentrified or on 'the up' as places to invest in, other parts were slowly going 'downhill', without any hope of investment buyers or job-creating industry. A new mosaic was forming.

Commentators did recognize that the times were changing, it was just that most, following the wrong-headed lead of a few, were describing changes that were far more complex than the real thing; however, one commentator got it spot on, but his observations went largely unnoticed and left little impact due to the fact that his book was published first in the US and came too late to change the racial segregation angle the British press had swallowed and which academic researchers were scrambling so hard to dismiss.[23] The commentator was Robert Frank and it was his masterpiece *Falling Behind: How Rising Inequality Harms the Middle Class*[24] that, although published in 2007, had been written many years earlier and based on a lecture given to the Seventh Aaron Wildavsky Forum for Public Policy at the Richard and Rhoda Goldman School of Public Policy, University of California, Berkeley, way back in October

2001. Had the book appeared a little earlier, or if a version had been written for the UK . . . things may have been different. We may have begun to look at the world in a different way.

Frank is the H. J. Louis Professor of Management and Professor of Economics at the Johnson School of Management, Cornell University.[25] Towards the end of New Labour's years of power he was invited to present his theories at Number 11 Downing Street, the official home of the Chancellor of the Exchequer. But, as I've said – it was too late.

It was on a junket along those corridors of power that I first heard Frank talk about how American men always want a bigger barbecue. He explained that what had been happening in America, right through the 1980s and 1990s, was that as inequalities in incomes were rising, it became ever more important where folk lived, for all kinds of outcomes: for school results, for crime levels, even for house-price rises. People began to spend more and more on housing in order to get away from living near those who were becoming relatively poorer than them. They had to spend more and more just to be able to afford an average home in an increasingly unequal society. And that continued through the next decade, too. All the way through to the crash, possibly even beyond.

Why should you take Frank seriously? Well, apart from his other books he is also co-author of what has become a popular textbook, *Principals of Economics*, with someone called Ben Bernanke.[26] They followed that up with *Principals of Macroeconomics* in 2006.[27] Frank's co-author could, of course, be another Ben Bernanke, but I suspect it is the same person who is currently the chairman of the United States Federal Reserve, and who previously had been chair of George W. Bush's Council of Economic Advisors. So Frank (who advertises his sons' bands on his website) writes textbooks with the world's most powerful economist, the man who in turn advised President Obama on how to help the world emerge through economic Armageddon. You have to take Robert Frank seriously.

The earliest version of Frank's book was beautifully illustrated. It contained many cartoons – the floor plans of houses, comparing them in size to the cabins of luxury yachts, and then to 6,000 square-foot homes. He had pictures of moose competing to mate, cars of various shapes and sizes, babies kissing and looking neglected, women wearing diamond-studded bras, and a diagram of an experiment using orange juice that you could perform on your 5- and 7-year-old sons.[28] But here I'll reproduce just the second diagram from his book *Falling Behind*. On the face of it the diagram looks like a boring graph; it isn't. It explains why we now have such a geographical mosaic of different neighbourhoods in our cities, in both the US and the UK.

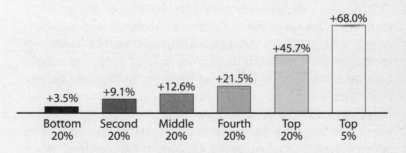

FIGURE 10: Changes in before-tax Incomes by quintile and top 5 per cent group, 1979–2003

Note: These changes are for the United States and are measured between before-tax incomes at both points in time. Source: R. H. Frank (2007) [29]

137

A couple of pages later Frank shows how the top 1 per cent of Americans saw their incomes rise by a massive 201 per cent between just 1979 and 2000. The figures for the UK are similar, although more extreme in the initial 1979–90 Margaret Thatcher period, when, to the nearest half per cent, the annual incomes of quintile groups in Britain rose by 0.5 per cent, 1 per cent, 2 per cent, 3 per cent and 4 per cent respectively from poorest to richest.

When compared to those for the USA and from poorest to richest quintiles, the UK rises equate to 6 per cent, 12 per cent, 24 per cent, 38 per cent and 54 per cent overall income increases over the eleven years that Margaret Thatcher was in power.[30] Those increases all slowed under John Major, and so became even more like the American figures shown above. There was no noticeable redistribution under Tony Blair. Gordon Brown left office so recently that we are still assessing his record, which may be similar to John Major's.[31] Essentially, you can read the graph above as representative of societal changes in both the US and the UK, and of comparing similar income groups.

It is when the already well-off top fifth of the population see their incomes increase at thirteen times (USA) or eight times (UK) the rate of increase of the worst-off (bottom) fifth's income that a mosaic of differing neighbourhoods in US or UK cities becomes ever more clearly apparent. In the poorer areas of cities, in former pit villages, in old towns that have lost their purpose, there is no real increase in monies, and relative to the rest of society these areas are going downhill. In contrast, when the highest of all income rises are enjoyed by the richest fifth, and that group now secures most of the income anyway, the majority of additional monies ends up going into the top fifth of neighbourhoods. This is what happened during the 1980s, 1990s and for most of the 2000s: the richest areas of cities became even better off and then even more exclusive.

In between the extremes, strung out like show homes to our national inequality parades, are neighbourhoods which, although 'modest', have usually enjoyed two to three times the income growth of the poorest. Up from this are the 'average' neighbourhoods, where people who have a much narrower range of incomes now concentrate and where previously there was a greater social mix. Next comes the 'affluent' fifth of neighbourhoods, with incomes growing by twice as much as the average and, as a result, with the people who can afford to live in this affluent fifth becoming even more segregated themselves. Finally, there are the 'richest' fifth of neighbourhoods, which saw the incomes of their residents grow by twice as much again as the high growth that even the affluent enjoyed.

If you compare all quintile groups to the median, the changes become far easier to understand. Incomes in the poorest fifth of the population have only grown by *a quarter* of average income growth between 1979–2000, those in the richest fifth by almost *four times* the average; incomes in the modest second quintile by only 70 per cent of the average, and those in the affluent but not richest fifth saw growth of 170 per cent of the average.[32]

Everything you can buy: cars, phones, homes, clothes, dental treatment, cosmetic surgery, servants, holidays, food, style, culture, class – everything – distinguishes one group of people from another, especially in our cities where the inhabitants choose more carefully where to live (if they are able to choose); thus, their choices, dependent on income, make the differences more distinct, more clear.

In many ways, though, the mosaic of our cities is no more, and in some ways a bit less, distinctive today than it has been in the past. It is less distinctive in that we no

139

longer have any ghettos (which still exist in the United States), with our last ghetto a Jewish one in Whitechapel, which was at the peak of its minority concentration in around 1905.[33]

There was a time when our surnames betrayed our occupations, when streets were named by the work done in them. Today we are becoming again more occupationally segregated, our futures depending more and more once again on the jobs our parents hold, rather than on our own motivations and interests. But in terms of ethnicity and religion we are mixing socially, economically and geographically more than ever. We are just mixing less and less according to our incomes and wealth, and so minority groups are also polarizing: between rich and poor Asians, between rich and poor blacks.

Social polarization is the contemporary root of any so-called breaking of Britain, in terms of the mosaic being more widely spaced. Only a minority of us are rich enough to have a multitude of choices such as where to live, thus where to send our children to school and then, as a result, who to mix with. Few societies with our kind of division in it are not in some way broken, are not sleepwalking into segregation – the real New Orleans-style segregation, which was between the haves (who could get out) and the have-nots (who had no way out). And we should be aware that social segregation in the UK almost certainly accelerated greatly after May 2010, gathering even greater momentum after October 2010.[34]

Should you not believe how socially segregated we have become, take a walk through our large municipal cemeteries, the saddest parts, where they tend to place the recent graves of children, often infants. This is very recent 'data'. We are most likely to die in our first year, and especially within our first few weeks of life. Take this walk in a northern cemetery, and then take the same walk in a cemetery or crematorium in the south. Cemeteries and crematoria are a little like model villages of the recent past. Their spatial arrangements indicate who is to be remembered, and how.

If you walk among the recent graves in Bradford's Undercliffe cemetery you will find eight times as many teddy-bear shaped gravestones as in the equivalent cemetery near Hampstead, London.[35] I've done this. You are drawn to do this if mortality statistics are the kind of numbers you look at, and the graves of children are places to think about what matters. Unfortunately, we will always suffer from child mortality, but there is no good reason, other than because of our greed and ignorance, for those mortality rates to be higher for children from poor families.[36]

When we look back at the past we ask why health inequalities were great and why more was not done to relieve the situation, especially as we were aware of the disparity. In his 1875 annual report, the great Victorian demographer, and Queen Victoria's Registrar General, William Farr, explained that:

> the agencies which destroy infant life are many, and they vary in different localities. Some of the principal causes are improper and insufficient food, bad management, use of opiates, neglect, early marriages, and debility of mothers . . . it must also be borne in mind that a high death rate is in a great measure also due to bad sanitary arrangements.[37]

Despite this knowledge the Victorians failed to enact adequate legislation to reduce infant mortality. It wasn't until after 1901 that sanitary conditions and workers' rights (especially for women) were improved. It took a while for these improvements to be implemented, and to take effect: infant mortality remained as high in 1905 as in 1875.

A few years before Farr was writing, women had been laid off from Manchester's mills in huge numbers during the cotton famine,[38] and it was noticed that infant mortality then fell. One of the observations that led to William Farr's conclusions was that the women stopped using opiates to sedate their babies and keep them quiet during the day – a practice that resulted in so many babies dying. People had thought it was God who took away so many infant lives and, unlike the graves of infants today, you do not see the many infant graves in Victorian cemeteries, which left almost all of these tens of thousands of plots in each large graveyard unmarked. Such were the numbers that there was not space to mark them.

It was through statistics as well as maps and novels that the staggering death rates and inequalities of Victorian Britain became understood, and it was then that it began to become evident that if it was God who was taking these lives, he had a method to his slaughter. Today we rely on doctors to help protect the lives of our infants. But who gets to study and practise medicine? Here, too, we find that access to this profession is affected by social inequality and these disparities in who gets to care also show us how minority groups are becoming polarized both within their own group and outside it.

Almost all groups associated with immigration to Britain do well economically in later generations as the get-up-and-go advantage of immigrant heritage (grandmothers telling you how hard it was and the sacrifices they've made), outweighs the disadvantages of prejudice. The immigration and economic history of each particular minority group does affect the advantage or disadvantage of that group and it is the census that underpins our ability to predict who is most likely to succeed or not in life. It is the census, combined with university admission records, which allows us to calculate how your chances of, say, going to medical school, may range greatly. From the data, we see that, after taking into account the size of each young minority group in Britain, young Asians are almost *ten times* more likely to study medicine than are white youngsters.

The census also allows us to work out that children from the top socio-economic class are *thirty times* more likely to become doctors than are those from the lowest class. And, when we calculated the ratios by ethnicity and social class combined, we found they varied *600-fold*. The most over-represented group studying medicine a few years ago consisted of Asians from the highest class, which is known as Social Class I – those having parents working in the professions or who own substantial businesses. Compared to an average young person such school students were *forty-two times* more likely to attend medical school.

In contrast, the most under-represented group, those with fewest admissions, were black people from Social Class IV – those with the second lowest classification of occupation: semi-skilled. Only 7 children from such a background attended medical school for each 100 who attended from the population as a whole and, notably, only 1 for every 600 affluent Asian students.

In case you are wondering why the worst-off group was Class IV and not Class V (the offspring of unskilled parents), the answer is that we could not calculate a ratio for Class V when we carried out this research in 2004. Back then we found that no black people from social class V had been admitted to medical school between the years 1996 to 2000.[39] Since then educational divides have reduced a little. But income and wealth divides have continued to widen. So even if affluent doctors may now be more likely to come from a wider range of minority backgrounds, you can predict with increasing accuracy where, from a narrow range of neighbourhoods in the city, they most likely lived as children.

The huge chasm between who can and cannot become a doctor is a great cause for concern. The fact that many poorer children are trapped so high in the sky is a fact worth getting angry about, as are the myths of growing residential ethnic segregation and ghettos – myths that stoke the fears that groups such as Muslims are separating from the rest of British society, myths that divert attention from the actual growing divides in our society that matter most. These myths also divert attention from improvements such as the growth in educational opportunities despite the great socio-economic inequalities and helped by the fact that most people in Britain are still kind and caring.

Segregation of another type, not by race but by health, has been growing in Britain in recent years. In poorer neighbourhoods in poorer parts of the country mortality rates have hardly fallen in the most recent decade and the numbers of people reporting they are suffering from a debilitating illness have risen quickly. In contrast, in the most affluent areas of the country, life expectancy has in some years been rising by more than a year per year, a rate that is impossible to achieve for long without securing immortality, and rates of reported illness and disability in such places have been falling rapidly.[40]

Behind these statistics we know that it is differences in the 'migratory trajectories' of different groups in a polarizing society that are to blame. As the gap between rich and poor grows, people are forced far more rigidly to move between areas according to their circumstances, much more so than their parents were. The government accelerated this process greatly in the Comprehensive Spending Review of 20 October 2010, when it announced measures to clear at least 82,000 poor families out of London.[41] This will accelerate the process whereby people are divided geographically: by education, income, employment, wealth and health.[42] As affluent areas become richer only the healthiest can now afford to live in them: when ill-fortune strikes, those falling ill have to leave. This is business-as-usual in societies becoming more unequal. But underneath the growing polarization in health there are signs of hope.

One of the most remarkable and least commented upon finding revealed by the last census was the fact of just how much people in Britain do care, and how predictably they do so. This was what I was trying to explain on the TV news that September day in 2005, the day with which I began this chapter, just after the first pictures of the death and destruction floating in New Orleans had been shown.

For a long time we have known that we suffered in Britain from what has been called 'the inverse-care law': those areas where people are most in need of care, usually containing the most ill and least healthy adults (and children), have traditionally been least well served by care services, even sixty years after the establishment of the NHS. In addition, our doctors tend to live and work in areas where the fewest people are ill (which is in no small part caused by drawing almost all young medics from such a narrow set of privileged backgrounds and then paying them so highly for their services).

It is hardly surprising that doctors don't want to live and work in the places that are most unfamiliar to them. The 'inverse-care law' was confirmed by work undertaken jointly by Mary Shaw and myself on the last census, which revealed that there was a correlation[43] by area of -0.22 between where people were most unwell and where medical practitioners most often lived and worked in Britain. A negative correlation means that where there were fewer medical practitioners in an area, more people tended to be suffering illness. In fact, of all the medical professions, only nurses were employed in greater numbers where more people suffered more ill health; a positive correlation of +0.31.[44]

The National Health Service's budgetary arrangements do allocate slightly more funds to areas where there is more ill health, but it would appear that this is mainly spent on more nurses, than on other better paid NHS staff in such areas. It will become harder still as we corral the poor even further into such towns and cities where the costs of housing are lowest. It would be nice to think there were more doctors where fewer people are ill because the doctors have cured them, but it doesn't quite work out like that.

It was when Mary Shaw checked, almost by chance, what the relationship was between those who provided unpaid care and those in need, that the statistics gave us a shock and revealed what appeared to be a 'positive-care law': the correlation between the locations of the population with health needs and those providing many hours of unpaid care a week. The correlation was an almost perfect 0.97 (the highest correlation possible is 1.00). Initially we wondered whether this was because most care was concentrated within the family, but what we found was that many of the carers and many of the sick were living on their own, separate from one another even. Our study showed that one group of people, the carers, often visited others' homes simply to help, for no monetary reward, and often for reasons other than family ties.

This was proof of an extensive network of care within the community, administered by people other than the officials whose job it was to try to ensure that the health needs of all were met. This was reinforced by our finding that there are many physicians being paid to work where people are not very ill. For example, some plastic surgeons specialize in 'beauty' treatments. These doctors tend to be employed where people are affluent and do not suffer much ill health by comparison. The private health sector as a whole is concentrated in those parts of the country where illness rates are lowest; the large majority of people in Britain who are actually ill cannot afford to pay for a private doctor. Also, many of the procedures carried out by private doctors are undertaken when the clients have the cash to pay for them, rather than when the physicians believe they are necessary. However, perhaps surprisingly, NHS doctors are also more commonly found working in areas where health needs are less.

In contrast to these doctors usually working up to fifty hours a week, thousands of other people are providing the same number of hours (or more) of unpaid care a week and do so in almost perfect proportion to the numbers of people who tick the two boxes on the census form to say they have both poor health *and* limiting long-term illness. It was these two groups of people, those who provide and those who need the highest amount of care, who gave Mary that 0.97 correlation.

Sometimes you see things that change what you believe. The positive-care graph set out below changed what I believed about people. I know that many of us are kind, but I was shocked to find that so many were so kind and caring as to give care when it was needed in almost perfect proportion to that need, free not just at the time of delivery but, apparently, for ever.

147

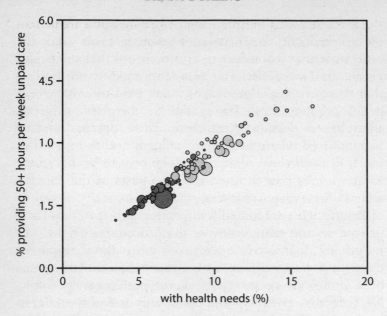

FIGURE 11: People with Health Needs and
Those Providing Unpaid Care, %, Britain 2001

Note: the light circles are areas (towns, cities and counties) in the North.[45]

But, of course, caregiving is never truly free. In areas where more than 15 per cent of the population is in poor health, such as in some parts of the Welsh Valleys and the East End of Glasgow, almost 5 per cent of the population is providing fifty or more hours a week of unpaid care to one or more of those 15 per cent, and many others are providing fewer, but still much needed, hours. It may seem to be a contradiction but paid care work is much less common where there are greater rates of illness. Instead, we have David Cameron's big society – one that is staffed by volunteers and that existed long before he put a name to it. It just took until 2001 for us to ask people in a national census how they volunteered, and then a little longer for us to figure out that they were doing it in such perfect proportion to need. You don't waste your own time when you are not being paid by the hour. However, most of these volunteers are dependant on government support to feed and clothe them, through state pensions, carers' allowances, or even child allowance so they can care more, instead of having to work another paid hour more. Often kindness alone is not enough.

Even though we have so many carers looking after the ill, there are still many who are in need of such care who will not get to see anyone at all who is willing and able to give up time for them. Caring, thoughtful friends and neighbours do not know enough to spot medical conditions they have never been trained to recognize or to deal with issues that even a professional would find taxing. We still need doctors to work and live mainly where people are most likely to be ill. The numbers are rising of people who are dying alone, whose bodies are only found later, who were without a carer of any kind.[46] It is easier to slip through the cracks when we live in a society that is increasingly unequal both socially and economically.

In many ways, the last time we were as unequal as we are in 2010 was around 1918. Since then we have mostly followed the trajectory of the United States, rather than the rest of Europe. Between 1918 and 1973 economic *equality* rose in both the UK and the US but since then it steadily, and then rapidly, fell.[47] And now the right-wing politicians in the US are starting to look to our coalition government's spending cuts as a model of how they might implement similar policies themselves. Conversely, I think it is often worth looking to the US to see just how wrong things can get, and so we should be very concerned when right-wing Americans start admiring us.

Hurricane Katrina was not the most deadly storm ever to visit the States; more than 2,500 people died in Florida in 1928 when Lake Okeechobee breeched its dike in the middle of a hurricane. 'Most survivors and bodies were washed out into the Everglades where many of the bodies were never found.'[48] Most of those bodies washed away were of poorer black Americans; only the whites were buried. There were not enough coffins to go round.

In the aftermath of the hurricane, a campaign of public works began to divert the waters and the US Army Corps of Engineers built a forty-foot high dike to replace the basic earthen dike that had failed so catastrophically. Building and planning controls were introduced to ensure future winds could be resisted. The poverty of the families of most of those who died was slowly alleviated as the New Deal – and then post-war settlement, and then civil rights – ushered in an era when Americans would no longer allow so many to live in such poverty at such risk.

And then people began to forget when the lake was last breeched and the bloated bodies of adults and children floated into the Everglades. Instead, Ronald Reagan (while Governor of California) talked of black 'welfare queens' living it up on the largesse of the public purse. There are uncanny echoes of this in the *Daily Mail* in Britain today, with its feckless 'welfare cheats', who are more often white than black.

A year after Thatcher became Prime Minister of Great Britain and Northern Ireland, Reagan became President of the United States of America. Public spending in the US was cut severely, millions were pushed into poverty, the levees were left untended and the Herbert Hoover Dike around Lake Okeechobee began to fall into disrepair.[49]

And, since Americans are often far better at plain speaking than we are, I'll let their Army Corps of Engineers describe what forty years of neglect does to a project built eighty-odd years earlier: 'For the layman, the problem with the Herbert Hoover Dike when the lake reaches high water levels can be summed up in two words: "It leaks".'[50]

CHAPTER 6

A NATION EVER MORE DIVIDED BETWEEN TOWN AND COUNTRY

'The perfect rural idyll',

BBC, 21 May 2009[1]

Back in our Camberwick Green past, in that 1960s children's TV series of rural life, all was simple. Windy Miller stood happily outside his windmill as the corn arrived to be milled, and somehow the sails always missed him when he bobbed in and out to check the workings inside. Mr Robinson carried his ladder around so that he could clean windows and Mr Rumpling spent lazy days on his barge. Almost all the characters were men, not least the fire brigade that consisted of Pugh, Pugh and Barney McGrew (as well as Cuthbert, Dibble and Grubb). Everyone knew their place and, for the few women, that place was largely in the home.

The windmill in Camberwick Green has long since been converted into a holiday let.[2] There is no window cleaner any longer. Who could afford to live in the village on the meagre wages that job would pay? The canal is now only for tourists too, and the fire station has had to be shut in the last round of cuts.[3] The building insurance for anyone with a thatched roof has gone sky high, but the executives from London who retreat to their country cottages in this village at the weekend can afford it. There are still 102 children attending the local school. Enough to ensure its viability for a little while yet, but many are driven in from nearby villages that long ago lost their own schools.

The fate that I imagine for Camberwick Green has not been the fate of most villages in Britain, just those that happen to have been especially picturesque and within weekday or even just weekend commuting distance of London or other prosperous cities. But why do so many of us still crave the chocolate-box, country-cottage idyll? Especially as we age? Is it the image of the roses around the door that attracts us, or is it something else? Is it that we know we've 'made it' if we get there – we are safe – we've risen above the rest, above the humdrum. Is it really true that you know you have finally succeeded if the ceilings are so low that you bump your head on the original timber beams, and if your roof is made of thatch?

What is so great about country living? What is it about the mud, the smells, the cold and the wet? Maybe it isn't as much about where you are, as where you are not? Live in the country and you have escaped the concrete jungle; no tower block, tenement, or pokey terrace for you. You are not destined to while away your days in the ubiquitous semi found elsewhere in Britain. You live in a village. You are part of a real community. Is that why you retired so far away from the city?[4]

Many people have hopes as they grow old of moving to the country to rekindle a little of what they wished their own childhoods could have been. If that is the case, we should not continue to segregate the poor and the young into cities and away from fields. We should have more children in the country, not so many children looking down from high tower-block windows at the ground far below. But we do, and we are still closing rural schools and, in their place, building retirement settlements sometimes even in those old school buildings. We are letting many homes in the countryside become holiday lets or second homes and then lamenting the death of community there.

British rural depopulation began a long time ago with the Enclosure Acts of Parliament. The first Act was in 1604, enclosing land in Radipole, Dorset.[5] This practice, even before the first official Act, was identified over half a millennium ago as the cause of destitution among the people who lost their right to the land and who were then often forced to tramp to cities.[6] The arrival of the destitute in towns and cities swelled the population of these places and this, combined with a breakdown of social customs there and in nearby villages, led to the economist Thomas Malthus in 1798 suggesting that people's fertility was burgeoning out of control.

Thomas Malthus was the world's first academic economist but his presumptions and hypotheses were incorrect. He assumed enclosure was necessary but that we still had a shortfall of agricultural land to feed what he believed to be an uncontrollable increase in population. Many people still believe this to be true; others disagree and think that, should we wish to, we could still be self-sustaining if we ate little or no meat. Ironically, the Enclosure Acts and the forced evictions that followed them are responsible for what we now recognize as the pretty village, the rural idyll.

The statistics tell another story. The idyllic village of Fringford in Oxfordshire saw its population almost double in the century during which much of its land was enclosed.

Enclosure came to Fringford in 1762 and by 1871 its residential population had almost doubled – to 479. But then during the lean 1880s and 1890s,[7] and with rural poverty on the rise, out-migration to the rapidly growing cities and further abroad caused the population in Fringford to fall to 335 by 1901.

Since the 1960s Fringford has seen a revival in its resident numbers. It is now home to around 600 souls and according to its local website has 'a church, a pub and a school but no shops'.[8] However, as in many villages located not too far from London, the people living in Fringford today are mostly very different to those who lived there just a couple of generations ago. It is as if the enclosures have occurred all over again, but far faster this time and with a far greater turnover of people.

The countryside isn't what it used to be and neither is life in our towns. Villages used to be far more mixed places, where you could shop locally for basics and you'd venture into town only on market days. Villages used to serve a far wider cross-section of society far better than most do today, especially given that the country's social range as a whole encompassed less variety, when farm labourers were not so badly off in comparison to the local bobby and the local bobby's income was not that far below the man who liked to think of himself as 'in business'.

I like to think of the Camberwick Green fiction (that I watched as a child) as being based on the adult fiction of Candleford Green, the village made real in the novel *Lark Rise to Candleford*. Candleford, hence Camberwick in my mind, was itself based on the actual village of Fringford, a place which mains electricity did not reach until after the Second World War and mains water not until 1960.[9] The place that now has a church, a pub and a school, but no shops.

The book *Lark Rise to Candleford* was made famous in Britain in 2008 and in the United States in 2009 when the BBC TV adaptation was aired. When I heard it was showing in the States I wondered how many affluent Americans would be interested in buying property in Fringford. In autumn 2010 there were 341 properties for sale in and around Fringford. A three-bedroom stone cottage was available for £390,000. The particulars noted that 'Fringford is a good-sized and sought-after village which lies just three miles to the north of Bicester and some seven miles from Junction 9 of the M40, while Oxford is easily accessible to the south. Village amenities include historic church, public house with a restaurant, village hall, primary school and cricket club, while various equestrian facilities are available close by.'

When property details mention 'Junction 9 of the M40' it is code for 'an hour and twenty minutes from west London'.[10] Perhaps now, in order to help afford his retirement and the odd pint in that pub, Mr Rumpling is sweeping out stables in those equestrian facilities? And maybe Windy Miller is rolling the cricket pitch at weekends? But Pugh, Pugh, Barney McGrew and the rest of the lads, however, will certainly have moved to Bicester or further afield to be able to afford their retirement.[11]

Lark Rise[12] was based on the area of Juniper Hill about three miles north-west of Fringford and the birthplace of its author, Flora Thompson. It was the slightly poorer of the two originally quite poor villages; many of its properties have now gone for good. In contrast, today, 'Fringford is a delightful, unspoilt village, with thatched houses set well back behind broad grass verges along the main street. The old post office is there . . . although it is now a private house.'[13]

A decade ago Victor Osborne retraced the fictional steps in the novel and found that almost a century earlier:

virtually all the men worked on farms for a mere ten shillings a week, which pauperised [sic] them and their families. They ate what they could grow in gardens and allotments, keeping a pig and hens for meat . . . [a century on] no one living here works the land now. Many commute to jobs in neighbouring towns and take affluence for granted.[14]

In Fringford in autumn 2010 a five-bedroom house would put you back £500,000 and six-bedroom homes were going for between £700,000 and £1,250,000. The cheapest two bed I could find on the market was for £250,000. There didn't appear to be many four-bedroom properties for sale. Who can afford property at these prices? And what effect has this change had on life in a village immortalized in fiction because of the poverty of the lives of many of its inhabitants, and the great transformation in rural life taking place there a century ago; a village of which it could so recently be written that 'poverty's no disgrace, but 'tis a great inconvenience'?[15]

Today almost all of the old families of Fringford and thousands of other similar villages can no longer live where their ancestors struggled, but survived. Just as I imagine the fate of the Camberwick Green fire crew, the fortunate ones will have moved to nearby Bicester, a slightly less salubrious market town, where a two-bedroom 'non-estate property' can be yours for around £150,000. An ex-council house, an 'estate property' in sales code, should be a little cheaper.

We are lulled into the illusion of believing inflated prices to be normal today, that you have to pay (and borrow) sometimes more than £100,000 for a home in a place such as Fringford. By taking out a large mortgage, as most people must, especially those on lower incomes, you could find that you end up paying several times your initial loan in interest over the course of the two and a half decades of regular payments, depending on interest rates and the size of your loan, of course. And goodness knows how much you'd end up paying if you ever went into arrears.

What about renting? Well, don't even dream of that in rural Fringford unless you happen to be some kind of celebrity just 'popping in' or a rich American over for the summer. In Bicester itself a one-bedroom flat rents for about £525 per month (unfurnished but with parking). And if the coalition government's October spending review recommendations become law then those who are on benefits or on a low income may not even be able to afford to rent in Bicester or other southern rural towns.

In October 2010 the statutory minimum wage in the UK increased to £5.93 per hour for those aged 21 or over. To put this in perspective, if you were earning that minimum then, after a little tax and national insurance, you would need to work at least 100 hours per month to pay the rent on that one-bedroom flat in Bicester. And after you'd paid the rent you would be left with about £12 a day to live off, for bus fares, soap, clothes, food, gas, electricity, TV licence and phone bill – or the stamp for a letter to a loved one.[16] It would become impossibly expensive yet, on 27 October 2010, during Question Time, the Prime Minister said these recommendations would be implemented.

I grew up in Oxfordshire in the late 1960s and lived there throughout the 1970s and early 1980s. What would it take to get that county, its towns and villages, and the country it sits in – as a whole – back to a broader social mix with the consequently more affordable rents and house prices we have previously enjoyed, back to the time when I was living there? Back then the M40 only just entered Oxfordshire and had not yet been extended to Birmingham; London had not yet encroached out across the south-east in general to transform local villages to commuter and weekend retreats, making life too expensive for many, even in those towns and villages that used to be cheapest.

As people mixed less, both socially and geographically, what they saw on the news and in police dramas about gritty urban estates became what they thought of as the truth.[17] But between the early 1970s and now, country and town became ever more socially, demographically and economically separated; people's visions of each other polarized, which in turn altered how we voted.

Voting turnout depends on many things – on whether a contest appears close (when voters are told that there is more chance that their vote matters), on the popularity of particular political leaders (who can influence the popularity of particular local incumbents), and on economic fortunes or misfortunes. If you can persuade voters that the economy is doing badly, hence that they personally are doing badly, because of the ineptitude of the party in power, you can help a few wavering voters make their choice against that party. Conversely, convince enough people that things can only get better if they vote for you, and you are more likely to win the vote. However, something else has been underlying all the day-to-day and year-to-year swings in voting and voter turnout: a slow and steady shift in attitudes between town and country.

Slowly, surely, year by year, our politics have become more polarized geographically, especially between the city and the countryside. To see how long this has been going on we have to go back a long way, all the way back to 1884, and we have to do a little maths. Just as it is possible to measure how the country is growing or shrinking in terms of how polarized it is becoming – for instance, where older people are choosing to live, where the married are, or those who have work, cars or own their homes, or are rich or poor – so too we can measure geographical segregation and how it rises and falls in terms of beliefs as reflected by voting. We can only do this when general elections are held, as it is only then that most people get asked to vote on issues of great importance.

There have been thirty-two general elections held since the 1884 Representation of the People's Act made the voting franchise mildly geographically consistent by its efforts to equalize the population sizes of constituencies. Back then things were different: no votes for women, rotten boroughs, and the abundance of seats in the pockets of rich vested interests; also, the eligibility to vote differed according to whether you lived in the countryside or the city.

It wasn't until 1885, as a result of the 'progressive' 1884 Act, that lodgers were allowed to vote (but only if their rent was at least £10 a year). Ten pounds was a huge amount of money then. You could rent any property in Fringford for that in 1885 – in fact you could then *buy* most dwellings there for £10! Voting, even in 1885, was only for rich men; but among the rich, lodging was far more common in cities than in the country.[18]

Between 1885 and 1910, there were only slight political differences between different areas of Britain. Town and country were not so divided, neither was the North from the South. It mattered far more if you were Catholic or Protestant; very rich or merely rich. And just moving between 4 per cent and 8 per cent of Conservative voters between constituencies, in exactly the right way, would have resulted in each constituency having the same proportion of Tory voters at all the general elections held between (and including) these twenty-six years.

In the years when Gladstone, Balfour, Asquith and Lloyd George (and also the ones who everyone forgets)[19]

160

were Prime Minster their core support was class-based, not place-based. The classes we are talking about were upper-middle and lower-upper. The table on page 165 shows the segregation index for Conservative votes at every general election held since 1884. It is just one way we can measure how these divides grow, and wane. Because the Tories were the only consistent force to be reckoned with for this entire period, political segregation is best measured over time by looking at the voting trends for that party.

In 1918 the Representation of the People Act allowed most women aged 30 or over to vote for the first time; by 1928 women could vote from the age of 21, as men could, an age that was again later reduced to 18.[20] The result of extending the franchise to women over 30 and almost all adult men, and of holding an election in wartime, was to make 1918 the most geographically polarized election result ever announced.

The Labour party secured over a fifth of the popular vote but only 57 seats – almost all in urban and mining areas. The Tories secured only a third of the vote but a huge tally of 332 seats, as they were unopposed in those by the official 'coupon' Liberals who were themselves similarly unopposed by the 'coupon' Tories. As a result the Liberals won 127 seats despite gaining only just over an eighth of the vote. David Lloyd George got to be Prime Minister again, but the Liberal party would be out of power for almost all of the rest of the century as a result of cosying up too close to the Tories.

It was in 1918 that urban-rural divides in voting first became so apparent, as a result of what has come to be seen as an unholy political alliance. Since then, political beliefs by area have become less polarized. The Liberals died out almost everywhere and Labour grew in popularity in rural areas as well as in urban strongholds. There was great poverty in rural Britain at this time, although access to a steady supply of food meant that hunger was not the central issue between Lark Rise and Candleford, but almost all those material goods we now take for granted were in short supply for the rural poor as well as for the urban masses.[21]

Rationing during the war, and then the landslide election of a radical Labour government in 1945, saw the greatest falls in poverty ever recorded[22] and, as the table on page 165 shows, political polarization reached a new low point in 1950. The interests of town and country were politically unified in reviving the nation in the aftermath of war.

However, the 1945 Labour administration was far better at policy than it was at politics, and in 1950 a few thousand extra votes for the Tories in marginal but strategically crucial places tipped the country into another election. Within a year, the 1951 result heralded thirteen years of Conservative rule under Churchill, Eden, Macmillan and Douglas-Home, during which time the geopolitical divisions rose ever so slowly and then fell again. This was the age of one-nation Toryism, the character of which was again reflected in the low levels of polarization shown in the table on page 165. The geographical measure of political polarization reached its post-war minimum in 1959.

Political polarization began to rise again following the election of Labour under Harold Wilson in 1964.[23] Far more votes swung towards Wilson in the cities than turned towards him in the countryside. By the 1960s urban dwellers had had enough of patrician Conservative aristocrats ruling over them. But, apparently, people who acted like country gentry went down better in the country. The geographical polarization increased again in 1966, and again in 1970 with the election of the Conservative Ted Heath, but then it fell slightly with the first of the two elections of 1974. The country was again becoming slightly more divided by issues *other* than those which could be neatly reflected through where we lived. Town and country became less important a division again. In both areas there was enough renewed dislike of economic turmoil and uncertainty, but also enough residual rural suspicion of the Conservatives to ensure no great swing in country areas to that party. Instead the countryside swung more towards Jeremy Thorpe's Liberals, a party whose vote continued from then on to hold south-west England and other rural areas further from London. However, in 1974 the Liberal's six million voters won the party only fourteen seats, and only thirteen by the autumn in the second general election of that year, the election that Labour won, when the Conservatives became less popular overall, but not less popular everywhere.

The moment of change was October 1974, when there was a great swell of support for the Tory party in the south-east of England, again particularly in more rural areas. These were the places where people lived who were most likely to lose out from high inflation denting their wealth, and from greater rights given to poorer people in their midst (including the right to have inside toilets and hot running water). In the 1970s rural areas were still places where the poor remained convinced that if the lord of the manor did well, the good would trickle down. The rural-south voting swing did win some Conservative seats, but the opposite larger swing towards Labour, in cities and the north of the country, was enough to bring Harold Wilson back into power, soon to be replaced by James Callaghan (but the latter with only a very small majority of seats).

Given the figures from the table on page 165 I would argue that it was that jump in the series, from 8.01 per

163

cent to 10.72 per cent in just eight months, that indicated a new geographical division opening up in Britain. This was the fastest rise in voter segregation ever to take place without a change to the voting system. British politics was seen from then on as a political battlefield that would pit the largely rural or *faux*-rural south of England against the mostly urban and pit-village populated north.

In 1975, Margaret Thatcher was elected leader of the Tory party. A grocer's daughter from Grantham, a Lincolnshire town located just south of the North-South divide, she was an industrial chemist whose one business achievement was to help invent a new and particularly nasty kind of sloppy artificial ice cream.[24] That she won her party's leadership race should not have been as much of a shock as it was. The one-nation Tory era had come to an ideological end between the months of February and October 1974, with her election as party leader in February 1975. The whole one-nation project halted when Maggie became Prime Minister in May 1979.

Initially, voting between town and country, North and South, became a fraction less polarized when Thatcher won her landslide victory, which saw her pick up many marginal seats and her vote rise most where it was weakest to begin with. She achieved this by looking a little less posh and certainly less male than the usual Tory of her day.[25] However, she quickly built on those geographical divisions and reinforced them.

Increasingly popular to rural southern voters yet rising to pariah status in northern cities, Thatcher split town and country apart in 1979. Political polarization rose in 1983, and in 1987 it reached a new post-1918 high (see table opposite). Then polarization rose again as John Major was narrowly elected to victory, in 1992, and it rose again as

Election	Concentration	Election	Concentration
1885	7.11%	1951	6.77%
1886	5.53%	1955	6.93%
1892	5.81%	1959	6.24%
1895	4.70%	1964	6.51%
1900	4.39%	1966	7.69%
1906	6.67%	1970	8.04%
1910 (January)	7.91%	1974 (February)	8.01%
1910 (December)	6.24%	1974 (October)	10.72%
1918	19.30%	1979	9.17%
1922	14.44%	1983	10.59%
1923	11.57%	1987	11.84%
1924	10.62%	1992	11.88%
1929	9.24%	1997	13.94%
1931	9.23%	2001	15.05%
1935	9.65%	2005	15.69%
1945	7.21%	2010	16.40%
1950	6.74%		

FIGURE 12: Segregation Index of
Conservative Voters, 1885–2010

Note: the percentage is the minimum proportion of Conservative voters who would have to move between constituencies if each constituency were to have an equal share, the same share as the national proportion. Source: Originally included in the book Injustice *published in April 2010, and updated to include May 2010 for the* New Statesman Magazine.[26] *Dates are of each general election held in the period.*

Tony Blair achieved a very different kind of landslide to Maggie's, first in 1997, again in 2001 and once more in 2005!

In May 2010, remarkably, political polarization increased to its highest ever level recorded outside of wartime. David

Cameron received the greatest additional support from rural southern constituencies, where he already held great majorities; whilst in Scotland, in much of Wales, in the urban North of England, in inner London and even in Oxford East, the vote swung towards Labour, denying the Conservatives a working majority, despite the fact that they had been able to secure many additional votes. The reason? These additional votes were secured in the wrong places.

The division between Conservative and Labour has increased due to a growing perception of distrust between town and country. Labour politicians used to say that in mixed post-war communities the elderly would be able to look out through their windows to see youngsters pushing 'lines of perambulators' along the street. Now the elderly look at their TVs to watch documentaries about young adults pushing drugs on unsuspecting urban children in a country they are repeatedly told has gone delinquently antisocial.

How many people would have to be moved around to allow us to get back to the social mix we had in the early 1970s? What would the consequences be? It is not that I actually want us to return to the social structures and human geography of my childhood – a lot of it was not much to write home about: endemic racism around the automobile plant, not quite enough housing for all, and near feudal hierarchies were maintained a few stones' throw from where I grew up.[27] But, still, we were much more mixed then than we are now, both within town and country and between the two. How far have we come and in what direction are we now moving?

Just after I was first appointed as a professor at the University of Leeds, a colleague[28] and I had a go at trying to answer the question of how divided we were becoming, and in which aspects of our lives we were now separating out the most, geographically. We did the work shortly after the results of the 2001 census were released. It was clear to many people that social divides had grown; that town and country had become more divided; and that things were not at all like they used to be; but to know precisely how they had changed we had to have something we could use as a concrete comparison: the census. What we found was quite shocking.[29]

To explain the gravity of the situation we began our stuffy academic report by telling a fictional tale of what would be required to unwind the mess we had got into, were that mess to be unwound in a single month. The mess we were referring to was the social polarization that had taken place, often gradually, over the course of around forty years.

Some years had witnessed turmoil: strikes by the miners in 1973 and 1984, the poll-tax riots of the early 1990s; in other years things were calmer and change less apparent. However, the country had been changing, with areas gradually becoming much less like each other over time. Just as the novel *Lark Rise to Candleford* depicted a time when rural Britain was changing quickly and for ever, so too have the last four decades seen astonishing social upheaval. And the greatest new divide to emerge has been between town and country.

Our story began[30] with the tale of how a future government, committed to increasing social justice and reducing geographical polarization, decides that indirect social engineering and pleading for a better, bigger, society are not enough. The government therefore draws up a list of those who will have to move home to ensure that we very quickly become as well mixed within each area as we last were in the early 1970s. The day after winning

167

this fictional general election the fictional new government releases the list of all who have to move, where they should go and who they must swap homes with. This is done with instructions to move within weeks, on pain of severe financial penalty, perhaps forgoing rights to any property or home whatsoever. This fictionalized government's forced home-exchanges would ensure that lone adults moved into smaller properties, larger families would be better housed in bigger properties and that the social, democratic and economic mix would be more balanced overall; however, all this change would have to be coerced.

So much for fiction. Years later, on 20 October 2010, the coalition government, in effect, ordered hundreds of thousands of people to move home within a year or so, when the Comprehensive Spending Review announced that rents would rise and that full housing benefits would cease for many erstwhile recipients.[31] The main difference between the fiction of our tale and the truth of this one was the speed of implementation and the opposite nature of the effect: rather than helping to improve our social mix, this coalition government's forced home-moves will increase social polarization, as poor people will have to move to poor areas.

I repeat our fiction of an equalizing government's coercion verbatim because, otherwise, I doubt you would believe our prescience:

The roads have been gridlocked for seven nights and seven days now. Every van, car, and lorry in Britain is piled high with the belongings of millions of households. Petrol is running short. On a trivial level, the Royal Mail, even if they could get through the traffic, cannot cope with the millions of post redirection requests. Neither can the utility companies, the tax authorities, or the dozens of other public and private bodies deal with the changing of more addresses in a week than normally occurs in a year. More fundamentally, much of the existing fabric of society is at risk.

Private schools, hospitals, golf clubs, gyms, even working men's clubs that relied on their local clientele for business are facing ruin. So too are much of the trappings of the state, from job centres to primary schools, from post offices to needle-exchange centres. The professionals who ran many of these amenities [now must] look for new employment. But that is the least of their worries, as they too are on the move, swapping their comfortable suburban homes for inner-city flats, moving into areas they would never normally consider living in, sharing streets with people whose skin is a darker shade than white.

A million university students have been sent home or, more likely, to other people's homes and will have to conduct their studies as "online distance learners". It is as if the nation's children were being evacuated again, as they were in 1939, only now the evacuation is happening to people from all groups in society and in all directions. Large numbers of the elderly are swapping their seaside bungalows for city flats. The unemployed are being scattered across the countryside. Affluent households are trying to park their multiple cars in streets never designed for more than one car per household (if that). Married couples are returning to the city centres where they spent their single years and swapping their homes with some of the groups of single students displaced from those same city centres.

> There is political mayhem. Nobody can predict . . .
> which constituency will be safe for which political
> party. The only sure bet is that most will be marginal.
> Everybody is unsettled and only the estate agents are
> happy.[32]

What we were describing was the forced movement of
some 2,452,021 people (around 4 per cent) in the UK, in
about 1.2 million home swaps,[33] the minimum number
that would have to swap homes were we to return to the
degree of social mixing we last enjoyed in the early 1970s.
A small percentage maybe, but in all cases exactly the kind
of people who were most likely to live in one particular
area forced to move to the kind of place such people had
left in great numbers since 1971. The number of swaps
was calculated on the basis that at this level we would
incur the least inconvenience. Only three aspects of the
social mix were included to calculate this measure: first,
how different was the age profile in each area; second, the
marital-status profile; and, third, the work-status profile.

If we looked at the first set of measures, age mixing, we
would see that over time rural areas in southern Britain
have attracted, or become affordable to, much older populations than they were home to in the 1970s. Over the
four decades we were initially considering, the bulk of this
age polarization had occurred in the 1990s, with earlier
retirement of the affluent to the countryside, and increasing numbers of youngsters and less affluent older people
relocating to small towns, or other places such as cities,
where they could find work, or study.

Traditionally, the population of rural Britain was far
younger than it is today: age segregation between town
and country fell in the 1970s, even though this was the

time when retirement migration to the coast became hugely popular. In the 1970s low unemployment meant that young people could stay near their families and did not need to get on their bikes or try to take long bus journeys to find work.[34] But this is also the era that is often caricatured as a time of economic distress, despite the fact that unemployment has not been as low since then.

If we look at the second set of measures, marital-status profile, we see that the countryside has become the last refuge where, among those of working age, it is still common to find a large majority of people formally married. The city is more commonly where you'll find those who are cohabiting, or those who are single, separated or divorced (and London, in 1991, was the only city where you could find a majority of working-age adults who were not married.) By 2001, in many towns and cities, married adults were in a minority of all those aged over 16 and under 65. It was during the 1980s that this particular town-country marital-status fault line grew widest and fastest.

I remember drawing the map of the proportion of working-age adults who were married, for every ward and district in the country, and finding that as recently as 1991 every single town or village outside of London had a majority of people aged 25 to 65 who were married. There was hardly any other place where it was normal to be unmarried at these ages, apart from a few suburbs of Brighton, a scattering of small areas where older singletons live among a young and single university-student population, and most inner-London boroughs.

But things changed. Within a decade it became the statistics from the rural countryside that stood out against those from inner London, which kept to its same trend. Only in the countryside were you generally guaranteed a majority who had sworn marital oaths and were apparently still sticking to them. Only in rural Scotland and, in England, in the Chilterns, a few parts of rural Dorset, the South Downs, Staffordshire and Northumberland were 51 per cent or more of the adult population married and still in that first marriage.[35] In contrast, by 2001 in Islington (north London) this applied to only 25 per cent of adults, in Norwich just 33 per cent, in Torbay 40 per cent, in Derby about 43 per cent, and in Newport about 44 per cent. What had been the majority almost everywhere was a majority now only in a few quite remote rural shires

However, the fastest increase in polarization between town and country did not concern age or marriage, it concerned work, which leads us to our third set of measures. As unemployment rose from the late 1970s it was not the rural countryside but the towns that suffered foremost and then fastest from loss of work. Subsequently many people who kept their jobs in the towns moved to the countryside and commuted, choosing in great numbers not to live near other (lower-paid or out of work) people. Polarization between UK districts by employment/unemployment rose 12 per cent in the 1970s, 35 per cent in the 1980s and by a further 9 per cent in the 1990s. By the end of this thirty-year period there were far fewer working-aged adults out of work or otherwise 'economically disengaged' in the countryside than at the start, whilst unemployment rates had grown very high in particular areas within many cities.

Unemployment continued to rise and, from the late 1970s, the numbers of young people out of work were unprecedented, even higher than in the 1930s or 1880s. Over a million aged under 25 were claiming the dole in 1984, and over a million were still 'not in employment, education or training' twenty-five years later. In between these two generations A further three distinct sets of 18- to 25-year-olds had endured similar rejection. Almost all of these out-of-work youngsters lived in towns and large cities, in contrast to the situation at the start of this cycle of unemployment, which initially had been highest in fishing villages![36]

Not everything became more polarized between the 1970s and now. When we compare censuses we find that there is now a greater housing ownership/renting mix in many areas. Also, there are fewer monolithic council estates. However, the increased mixing has occurred principally because more affluent people are facilitating the rental market with buy-to-let property ownership, now that the government's right-to-buy programme has reduced the availability of social housing.

The decline in housing available to rent from the council and other social landlords, and the reduction in people able to afford a mortgage, also fuelled this apparent reduction in the polarization between home ownership and renting. However, for council tenants, polarization did increase as the highest numbers of right-to-buy sales were in areas with the fewest council houses.[37]

Similarly, from 1971 through to 2001 the distribution of car ownership became slightly less polarized as more households acquired one for the first time, and affluent households acquired two or more. The numbers of households in early censuses owning three or more cars were not measured, nor how much the cars were worth. We could not use the censuses to show us what we later discovered using other sources: that polarization was increasing when it came to owning expensive cars and borrowing to afford second-hand or cheaper cars.

In 1971, when wages and wealth were much more equitably distributed, it was hard to tell from the cars parked along a street just what kind of people lived there. That there were cars at all told you that you were not standing in one of the poorest parts of Britain, where few households owned cars and significant numbers still lacked hot running water or inside toilets.

In the forty years that followed, most of these poorer households became able to afford the running costs of a third- or fourth-hand car, the costs of a water boiler and often the costs of building small extensions for inside toilets. The repayment of these expenses would have been spread out over a number of years but, in contrast to these modest sums, between 1981 and 2001 affluent households spent far more than did these poorer households, and on items such as new or additional cars every few years, substantial property extensions, and the installation of second, third or fourth toilets. The bulk of the spending occurred in the countryside near to towns, especially around London. And because the census is not good at measuring wealth, or distinguishing between mild affluence and great riches, a cursory study of census data alone might suggest that our standards of living have improved substantially, simply because a great deal of poverty was eradicated in the 1970s, in both town and country.[38]

The census alone cannot be used to gauge the relative extent to which some areas are becoming poorer and/or richer. To work that out we have to combine censuses with the results of surveys that tell us how the markers of poverty have changed over time. These are markers such as the inability, in 1899, to afford a stamp to send a letter to a loved one.

To understand whether poverty was becoming concentrated in certain areas we need to identify what it is, above self-sufficiency, that is seen to be the marker of social inclusiveness. In 1968 a poverty survey was conducted to determine such things as whether a family could afford a joint of meat once a week. Failure to afford this would become one marker which (if combined with several others) suggested that the household was living in poverty and was excluded from what were then thought to be the norms of society. From the 1960s onwards, times have been a-changing, very quickly, and, as the saying goes, these have been 'interesting times', times you might not necessarily have chosen to grow up in had you a choice, especially if you knew you were to be born on the wrong side of the tracks. But just how interesting have they been?[39]

In 2007, I and a group of my colleagues from Bristol and London took the results from the 1968–9 poverty survey and combined those results with the 1971 census to work out where most people lived who could not, in 1968–9, afford things such as a Sunday roast. We wanted to look back again at that time and measure, using contemporary methods, just how unequal were town and country, inner and outer city, remote rural villages and suburbia.

In many cases we found as much rural as urban poverty – from tied cottages to flats in city slums. We then compared the 1983 poverty survey with the 1981 census, the 1990 survey with the 1991 census, and the 1999 and 2005 surveys with the 2001 census. The markers of poverty changed over time: recent years indicate that one such new marker is the inability to afford a week's holiday away from home, other than by staying with friends or relatives. Had that marker been used in 1968 *most* people would have been deemed poor; most could not afford a week's holiday away.

Four decades on from 1968 the balance of impoverished areas has changed: there is now far less rural poverty and far more rural wealth; the poorest have increasingly been squeezed into concentrated areas of poverty in the major cities. These are the areas where you find most children living with parents too poor to take them on holiday, where young children have the most dental problems compared to those richer children living in rural areas, and where siblings of the opposite sex share bedrooms in their teenage years.

In 2007 my colleagues and I reported that more households were living below nationally accepted normal-living standards, below what was called the breadline. This was more families living in poverty than at any point we could calculate from the previous surveys and censuses, starting in 1968. The data for 2005 confirmed that the situation had been worsening since 2001. Some 27 per cent of all households were now poor, and a higher proportion of households with children were poor, thus, an even higher proportion of children themselves were poor – meaning excluded from the norms of society. In 2007 we said it was clear to us that:

> already wealthy areas have tended to become disproportionately wealthier. There is evidence of increasing polarization, where rich and poor now live further apart. In areas of some cities over half of all households are now breadline poor.[40]

We drew maps to show how poorer households were concentrated in the cities, appearing almost to have been sucked out of villages and into the towns. And since 2007 poverty in cities has increased further, while the effects of the most recent recession have been felt least in the countryside.

176

In practice, geographic polarization in Britain occurred partly due to the fact that past sociological trends were changing. For example, if an elderly couple moved from their house, it was no longer a given that younger people of a similar social background would take their place. Sometimes, the value of these homes had gone up so much that the kind of family the former resident belonged to usually could not afford to buy it at the new price. If the elderly person was a council tenant who did not own their own home, but the village was becoming prosperous, then the new people housed there in, say, the early 1980s, were very likely to exercise their right to buy after having secured enough years' discount, and when they sold up and moved on they would not in turn be replaced by tenants but by new owner-occupiers.

In poorer parts of cities, especially northern cities, almost the opposite occurred. As areas became more run-down, as the relative value of homes fell, as hard-to-let properties were allocated to those most desperately in need of housing, poor inner- and outer-city estates became poorer – and then places increasingly best avoided. Council estates were said to have 'residualized' in these areas (become places for a 'social residual' who cannot get out). Given the subsidies that were available to encourage people to buy the homes they were renting from the council, an area had to be pretty rough for it not to be worth buying. And when such areas became rougher, the schools' reputations fell and then worsened when aggregate exam results were published annually throughout the 1990s. Places became stigmatized, often as they last had been in the 1920s and 1930s – 'poor' became synonymous with 'disreputable'.[41]

This geographical polarization between town and country, between poorer areas and more affluent places, has become a perpetual-motion machine. The higher the price of property in villages, the more attractive they seemed and more people were tempted to live there, to purchase an apparently safe housing investment, taking on a longer commute for the money they knew their home would be 'making' for them. As cars became more comfortable and road systems improved it also became more economically viable to buy a second home in the countryside, if you could afford to. At the same time it became economically sensible to abandon living in poorer parts of northern cities, if you could afford to. So, as some areas spiralled down into a vortex of worsening poverty, others leapt up into great wealth-generators where the only thing that was really 'creating' wealth was location, location, location.

Unsurprisingly, as town and country became more economically divided, beliefs began to polarize, too. Mistrust of others spiralled as ever-decreasing contact with the lives of others fuelled mutual suspicion. People in towns began to suspect those living in the countryside of harbouring barbaric animosity to foxes and badgers – of wanting to maintain medieval rights to hunt with hounds; of seeking to gas out the nice cuddly one (old Badger) from *Wind in the Willows* or Miss Potter's rabbits[42] – while the people living in the countryside felt threatened by the impact the townies' contrary beliefs would have on their livelihoods.

Just as those in the town mix less with those in the country, so too do the young mix less with the old, the rich less with the poor, the employed with the unemployed, people who think you need to get married to have kids and those who don't. And people who vote Tory or Liberal are increasingly spatially and socially separated from those who vote Labour or do not vote at all. In May 2010 the question in the village hall was: did you vote for Clegg or

Cameron? In the city pubs it was: did you vote for Brown, or not bother?

While voting patterns tell us a lot about how Britain has been changing in its human geography, they also tend to exaggerate our difference. Within the stereotypical idyllic country cottage and decayed inner-city tenement, we are more alike than many portray us to be, despite the growing divisions in wealth, health and party affiliations. Now, we often cover up our similarities and are expected to emphasize our differences. To illustrate this, let me ask you a question concerning town and country: what do stepchildren and gun crime have in common?

Well, firstly, we discovered by looking at one of our maps that, much to our surprise, the greatest numbers of stepchildren lived in the countryside. My preconceptions were proved wrong, but still I could not believe the figures.[43] I asked my colleague, Bethan Thomas, to check the figures and draw the map again. She did, it looked the same. I checked the figures myself; she had been correct. We had drawn the map only taking into account older stepchildren, to check that this was not some artefact of children becoming stepchildren when they get older and of older children being more likely to live in the country (they are more likely but it wasn't an artefact). By 2001, the children living in the wealthier, more Tory, more God-fearing countryside were, in comparison to their urban cousins, more likely to be stepchildren rather than the natural offspring of both their parents.

What was going on was that, as our net-average summary for migratory movements indicated, in general and as people age, they move away from cities, towards the suburbs, then towards the countryside, then to the coasts.[44] The rate at which we tend to make big migratory jumps later in life is accelerated by adverse life events. Those who suffer a broken heart are much more likely to end up living along the coast in middle age than are those for whom everything (often just through good luck) tends to work out far easier. This is the kind of thing we find when we look at the statistics – by age, sex and area – for who is widowed, separated, divorced and remarried. We find we are more similar than we would otherwise believe when we filter these millions of stories of people coming together and moving apart, and when we see the traces of their movements left on the map.

When a reasonably affluent couple separates, it is usually only one parent who tends to get more access to, or custody of, their children. That parent will often be working, often out of necessity and (although they may think it unlikely at the time they split up) most meet someone else soon afterwards and then resettle with this other person, who may have their own children from a previous relationship. When the new couple combine their families, they create what is now called a 'reconstituted family'.

Creating a reconstituted family is far from easy. Both adults involved often want to get away from where they were before, both emotionally and geographically. They can often achieve this with their combined incomes. They can buy the country cottage, maybe in Fringford, given the combined capital they have accumulated (given that they're now a little older than when they first started out). But they'll usually be mortgaged until their mid-sixties if they do,[45] and when they fill in the second page of the census form both will tick the box marked step-parent.

The city of Oxford is not far from Fringford and it is in Labour-majority, urban Oxford East where children are most likely to be growing up with both their original parents; within that constituency it is the Muslim families that report the lowest divorce rates. These statistics reveal the false perception that urban areas are sites of social delinquency. In addition, the countryside is not the refuge only of step-families but also of far more tax dodgers than are found in the city. If you want to know who is costing taxpayers the most, look not to the benefit cheats but to the folk living in huge country piles who avoid paying their due. If you want to know who is living the most ecologically unsustainable lives, driving the furthest most frequently and consuming the most in general, it is not to cities that you need to turn. If you want to know where schools cost the most to run (because class sizes tend to be small), where spending per head to deliver water, electricity, and broadband is highest, where the costs of taking away sewage and supplying gas or oil are greatest, then, again: look to the countryside.

And to get back to gun crime, guess where you would be most likely to be shot dead? As you may have guessed by now, it is not the inner-city. And who is most at risk of murder? Farmers' wives and their children and, above all others, the farmers themselves. No one is safe when there is a gun in the house.[46] The figure overleaf combines twenty years' worth of murder statistics to show how, in the poorest 30 per cent of areas, most murders result from people using knives rather than guns. In the richest 30 per cent of areas, murders are less common by comparison, but murder by firearms is not, especially in 'decile-three areas' (the third richest tenth of wards in the country, which are especially rural). When comparing the same-sized underlying populations, in the areas where the best-off 30 per cent live, more murders in absolute number have taken place using guns than there are gun-crime murders in the poorest 30 per cent of the country.

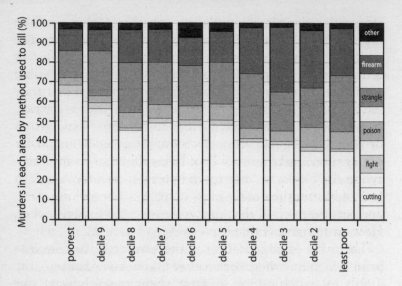

FIGURE 13: Method of Murder Used in Britain,
by Ward by Decile of Poverty, 1981–2000

Source: Mortality records by cause of death scaled to Home Office murder counts.[47]

Because I've seen the numbers I don't worry about being shot anywhere in the city, but I do worry about accidents with a gun in the country. I worry much more about what I see as I travel around Britain. We are slowly Balkanizing, driven by our misconceptions about people and places: most people in rural areas are not rich farmers, and most people in inner-cities are not on benefits. Almost everyone living in Britain, in town or country, has far more in common with each other than they realize but, regardless, our urban-rural divide is not due to change much anytime soon.

At some point political, demographic, social, economic and medical life-chances across Britain will have to stop polarizing. It is simply not possible for us to carry on becoming more and more divided. It is not medically possible for life expectancy to continue to rise so fast in affluent rural areas.[48] It is surely not financially possible for the rich to carry on getting richer at the rate that they have been in a country that is becoming poorer overall. It cannot be politically possible for a very small group of people to benefit from decisions that result in further segregation, and the wool kept held tightly down over everyone else's eyes, to keep town in fear of country, South in fear of North, the middle class in fear of the working class, and an upper class that grows disproportionately richer. How sustainable is that?

The table of polarization in the Conservative vote (see page 165), was long because we have to go back to the 1920s and 1940s to find a time when we reduced our social, spatial and ideological divisions. But we did do it. What's more, those divisions had been far greater at the outset than they are now, but we achieved things that had never been achieved before in order to cut them down: votes for people who had previously been disenfranchised; redistribution of wealth; an increase in the school-leaving age; an increase in university places available and taken up; the introduction of decent pensions. We achieved these aims partly by reducing the privileges of the very richest. In the decades following Lloyd George's imposition of 40 per cent death duties, most of the great aristocratic estates were broken up, sold, or 'bequeathed' to the National Trust, or they opened up their grounds, and houses, to paying visitors in order, in part, to afford the upkeep. This is what happened at Chatsworth in Derbyshire.

Today we are again as unequal in wealth[49] as we were when the gates to country houses were sealed to commoners, and when the wealthy maintained huge armies of servants to see to their every need. Those armies of servants are now employed elsewhere, and in other ways: they valet your car for less than the minimum wage on that disused petrol-station forecourt; they build and maintain the hotel abroad that you stay in if you are wealthy enough to have such foreign holidays; they clean your office and maybe your home. You just don't call them servants anymore.

We know we have returned to inequalities as great as those last seen around 1918 because we can compare the gaps in life expectancies between areas then and now, because we can measure the gaps in income and wealth and see that both before and after they have paid tax, the rich are again so very rich that in terms of social inequality we are all back almost to the Edwardian era of great socio-economic injustice. We know we have returned because our voting patterns reveal how geographically and polit-ically segregated we now are. We know that polarization is still on the rise because we can measure it.

And we can also feel it.

CHAPTER 7

TIME TO PUT THEM OUT TO GRASS? –
WHAT TO DO WITH THE ELDERLY

'UK's aging population is a bigger economic threat
than the financial crisis'[1]

Daily Telegraph, 12 February 2010

On a very cold February morning, the *Daily Telegraph*
attempted, ever so slightly tongue-in-cheek, to shock its
readers with the headline 'biggest threat', and the opening
gambit:

Just when you thought it was safe to come out into
the open. As if it weren't enough that the euro is
crumbling, that the banking sector is still vulnerable;
that Britain is steeling itself for its biggest spending squeeze in living memory, along comes Barclays
Capital with some really bad news.

The article claimed that the grey time bomb was finally
exploding in pension-fund balance sheets. The cost of
housing, care and the retirement of a growing number

of elderly would cause long-dated gilts to rise rapidly in price, which would then raise interest rates.

But should we really dread aging? Previous generations have looked at aging in a positive light, as we should do now. An aging population can be a happy, friendly, productive and, above all, a cooperative population. And if you don't have an aging population you have one that suffers from premature mortality, which is certainly not cause for celebration. So why have our attitudes changed?

The Barclays Capital-sourced story, as reported in the *Telegraph* that cold and snowy day, concerned the suggestion that neither company pensions nor state pensions or government workers' pensions would continue to support us as the numbers of pensioners increased. The crux of the story was that a Barclays economist was suggesting that the government would soon have to pay 10 per cent, rather than its current 4 per cent, interest per annum on its long-dated gilts to borrow money; thus, soon, it would no longer be able to run a deficit that included funding state and state-sector pensions at their current levels.

Long-dated gilts are one of the main mechanisms used by the British government to raise money. They are IOU's that are not paid back for a long time, but which pay a certain level of interest to the lender each year. The credit crunch has made it harder and more expensive for governments to borrow and, if government has to pay more to borrow money (ie, in interest), it will in turn charge banks more to lend them money, through the Bank of England. The gilts partly rise in price as money markets factor in what they see as the increased risk of lending to a country with increased obligations. So far the interest rates had not risen much by the time the *Telegraph* article came out, despite the predictions of Barclays Capital.

What the article failed to mention though was who exactly the government was borrowing money from and why these private lenders would soon, and suddenly, get 'well over' 10 per cent per year in interest for lending a little of their wealth to the nation, rather than the 4 per cent or so they currently enjoyed. Instead, the paper suggested that 'Britons have lived beyond their means, financing it by, in effect, borrowing off future generations'. It also mentioned that the privatized British Telecom had a pension deficit of £9 billion, just so that those outside the state sector should also quake a little. Again, the article failed to mention how the company had chosen to reward shareholders rather than look after its dwindling pension pot. The story left you thinking that no one's retirement fund would be safe.

All this raises questions. The rich are the usual lenders, as they have the money. The super-rich who buy gilts will do very well in retirement if they are paid 10 per cent per year in interest, and even the mildly affluent who purchase in aggregate (through small private pension funds) won't be doing badly. However, we need not borrow so much from the rich; instead we could, for example, *take* a little more from them – and a lot more from the super-rich – via taxation.

Let's start by looking at Barclays Capital, the bank that sowed the seed of that *Telegraph* article. How does the bank – especially the part of it that takes so many risks for the promise of potentially high return – make all its cash and where does the loot go? Let's do some research. The head of the bank, Bob Diamond, joined the board in 2005, which means that by law we are privy to the fact that his pay packet was £23 million a year.[2] Partly as a result of this generous reward, Diamond became both a household name and a man pilloried by the press as representative of the unacceptable face of banking. Despite all this he also became Barclays' Chief Executive Officer in 2010, in what was widely reported as a two-fingered salute from the City to the coalition government. In 2010, Diamond's income was reported to be a 'mere' £42 million – high, but not quite near the highest City salary.[3]

The coalition's Business Secretary, Vince Cable, replied to Diamond's salute with his 'spivs and gamblers' speech on 22 September 2010, which outlined that the money which high-risk, casino-style bankers make comes disproportionately from hiking short-term profits while damaging the long-term interests of business, from speculation rather than proper investment, from being paid according to how much money their banks could extract from others in the short term, not by how much they improved people's lives.

Bob Diamond had 'performance plans' that allowed him in 2008 alone to receive a £14.8 million bonus, even though the bank had to write off £1.3 billion worth of loans. For every £88 of net bad decisions made by the bank, decisions that resulted in losses, it looked as if Diamond was being rewarded an extra £1 above his standard salary. If he had 'invested' his 2008 bonus in government-backed gilts, he would have received £592,000 based on an interest rate of 4 per cent per year.

Not bad, you might think. But you are almost certainly not a top-earning City banker, so who are you to know? A 10 per cent annual return on gilts would have given him another £888,000 a year to play with, £1.48 million in total per year. That is like wining a million on the lottery every eight months, for ever. And, if the money were coming from the gilts you purchased with your bonus, then the interest would all be paid by taxpayers. A married pensioner on the basic state pension gets £11 a day to live on, some 364 times less than what a 10 per cent return on a £14.8 million bonus could secure.[4]

I was starting to get a little annoyed about the *Telegraph*'s revelation that we may soon be paying the rich even more to borrow their money, but then my eye was distracted. On the online edition of the paper I spotted an information box, where – in bold and blue text, highlighted for you to 'click' – it stated: 'Retiring Soon? Visit the *Telegraph* Retirement Service (UK only) to help you maximise your retirement income'.

I clicked the 'enquire now' box, adorned with a T in the *Telegraph*'s font. Was this a further news story, or an advertisement? It didn't look like an advertisement. I had forgotten all about what I know about Bob Diamond and my concerns over why Barclays Capital should be planting stories like this. All of a sudden what I wanted to know was how would I be affected and what I could do about it and so I quickly forgot everyone else – rich, poor, claimant or moneylender. Soon there was no such thing as society in my mind – instead it was just me and my family.

The 'enquire now' box led me to '*Telegraph* Retirement Services', which, a few further clicks revealed, were provided by a company called Aegon. I clicked on Aegon's 'about us' box and learnt that they employed 28,000 people and had their own personal finance-news service with headlines such as:

- Do children need pensions?
- Parents won't have wealth to pass on, report says
- One in four women rely on their husband's pension in retirement
- If anyone should be protesting, it's the put-upon private sector

I was intrigued. I have children, and my wife will rely on half my pension if I die before her. I clicked on each of the stories. It turned out that, headline after headline, the stories jumped from Aegon's website to the *Telegraph*'s website where, from two stories published on 15 September 2010, we learn that pensions are 'increasingly the responsibility of individuals'[5] and that women should 'start making retirement-savings plans'.[6] On 18 September, the stories continued in the same vein: 'future generations should not expect to inherit wealth from their parents'.[7] On 20 September: 'grandparents are setting up pensions for their children to combat fears they could end up in poverty in old age'.[8]

Worrying thoughts raced through my head. Do I need a private pension above the one that comes with my job and my state pension? When I die will my wife need an additional, private pension? Should I take out a private pension for my children? Just how much money should I be sending to Aegon for one of their 28,000 employees to turn into an annuity for me, and for them then to send a little the *Telegraph*'s way, too, to pay for the links from their infomercials, and a little more maybe to a company such as Barclays Capital so they may invest to create that annuity, or create press releases for these so-called news stories in the first place. Oh, and a little of that to go towards Diamond's bonus fund. After all, money does not come from thin air, profits have to be made *from* someone.

Under the online version of the 'Do children need pensions?' story two comments from *Telegraph* readers were published. The first said, 'Give them individually purchased shares, a deposit on a house, and some gold pieces. That's a far better option than a pension in the UK.' The second just said, 'Roll up suckers one and all'.[9] I wondered how long that comment would remain there!

But I was very grateful for it. I ticked the 'recommended reading' box – on the comment, not the story. Sadly I was only the second person to do so.

A great problem with the overpowering strength of the finance and advertising industries in Britain and with how they have got their tentacles into so much of the fabric of our lives – including our newspapers, the advertising boxes next to our emails, and our politicians, who they sponsor – is that they can make you begin to doubt your own sanity. I realize that I have to be wary if I buy something, and that sometimes I would be a 'sucker' if I did. I know I have an adequate pension that goes with my job, and a state pension too, and that if it all goes belly-up it would be because the financial system as a whole has gone belly-up. I know that the private-finance industry does not have my interests at heart, but is solely focused on securing its own interests – to secure as much money from me as it can while returning as little as it can get away with. I know I'll need people of good heart around me to help me make it to retirement, much more than I'll need money to get there, but that knowledge does not protect me from worry.[10]

Humans are made to worry. Our eyes are set so that our peripheral vision can detect other creatures creeping up to eat us. (Perhaps this peripheral vision might save us still from the finance industry!) We were not made to be lone predators, focusing ahead, looking for the kill; we have thumbs instead of claws. We are cooperative, tool-making creatures, but there are some of us who are a little more predatory than others. There is money to be made out of population-aging scare stories and anything else that gets people not to act collectively (in each others' interests). There is money to be made and performance bonuses to be secured if we let these stories scare us, confuse us and then fleece us. Don't click the button. Read on instead.

We can *all* afford to retire; we can also *all* afford to study. We can all afford to do a lot of things in our adult lives that are not simply about making money and giving much of it to others to supposedly make more out of it. We don't need so many people in paid work, unless we allow a few to grow fabulously wealthy at the expense of the rest of us. To perpetuate such an imbalance, retirement age would need to rise and those who couldn't work, or couldn't find work, would need to be on punitively low benefits. I think this would be wicked. Low benefits also perpetuate the imbalance: fewer students would be able to attend university (so the rich need not be taxed for that); more people would be forced into low-paid jobs. A few people cannot become hugely wealthy without millions of others becoming poorer. The profits that generate the wealth have to come from somewhere.

Top bankers are, of course, not retiring on as *little* as a million and a half pounds a year. Their pensions and benefits are set to be hugely greater than that. A million and a half pounds per year is what a single year's bonus might grant them through investment in gilts; it is what they might spend or re-invest in tax-avoiding trust funds. If they were prudent, the offspring of the super-rich need never undertake paid work. Alternatively, Bob Diamond could forget about his family's future and buy himself an annuity that pays out only until he died. Either way, he would be fabulously wealthy. But in this he would not be alone.

Britain's pensioners are collectively, fabulously wealthy. Their mean-average wealth is nothing compared to a top banker's, but it would still equate to hundreds of thousands of pounds each – enough for all their possible material wants to be satisfied until they died. But that is collectively, on average. In reality the money is so unequally distributed that millions live in poverty while others – those few who are very rich – don't have enough days in the year to spend their money on holidays. What does a top banker do with all his money? Well, like all of us, he'll want to spend some of it on himself. And, no matter how much he has, he is going to age. Even masters of the universe can't cheat time.

To find out if we can afford to support the elderly, we need to know something about how much wealth we have and where it is, as well as something about how we age and how elderly we really are.

As we age our bodies begin to malfunction. They do not do this linearly, with time, but exponentially in the same way that wealth rises exponentially as interest amasses. Rather like washing machines, for which you can purchase a (usually maximum) five-year guarantee, the early physical operation of our bodies tends to be more reliable. And, just as the washing machine starts to break down when the guarantee expires, so do our physical parts start to wear out as we age.

Washing machines did not last that long in the past. Old twin tubs rattled to a mechanical failure far more quickly than do modern-day machines, which, like today's human generations, last longer. In the developed world, increased longevity is due to various factors, including better conditions during gestation, better nutrients during childhood and a far easier life overall (no more outside toilets!). But while we humans can improve the conditions into which we are born, we cannot cheat our biology. Like washing machines, we have initial periods of our life when a fault in manufacture might cause problems. In humans these kinks in our manufacture are called 'congenital' – we are born with them, and they affect our 'mortality curve'. People in finance use this curve to figure out the probable costs and profits of annuities. The curve can also tell us if we can afford to look after the elderly.

Today in the UK about 5 babies die for every one 1,000 born and so with almost 2,000 children born each day, 10 will not live for a year. The lowest infant mortality rates the world has ever known are in Japan, Sweden and Norway, where it is nearer 3 who die per 1,000 born. In the US more than 6 babies die for every 1,000 born. Twice as many infants die in countries with the greatest disparity between rich and poor than do infants born in countries with a more equitable distribution of wealth.[11] But in all countries in the world, rich and poor, our mortality rates – our chances of dying each year – fall rapidly as we grow older, up to a certain point in our lives.

Usually, by the time children celebrate their first birthdays they are more robust, and their chances of dying diminish until the age of about 10, when these chances are at their lowest.

In poorer countries disease is what most often kills children; in rich countries it is other humans driving cars that most often kill them (and most often kill young adults). Accidents become more common after the age of 10 and, until around age 20, we become each year a little more likely to die than we were the year before. (Remember *The Drop Dead Game* from Chapter 1?) We are given more freedoms and, as a consequence, take more risks (even though, until we reach 40, the risks of dying are small compared to risks of dying between birth and age 1). Our likelihood of dying tends to plateau until we reach our mid-thirties, after which point something changes.

For teenage boys and young men the risk of death is around 1 in 1,000 a year. For girls and young women it is up to three times lower. Girls are brought up to be more careful, and go through puberty earlier than boys, which makes them more responsible adults at a time when it helps to have a more mature head on your shoulders. Girls may also be more risk averse, again for reasons that have origins in our biology and our evolutionary instinct for survival; however, until recently, childbirth had a massively adverse impact on mortality rates for young women in Britain; in fact it had the greatest impact. Until recently, women on average had much the same life expectancy as men did (such as in my great grandmother's day in the early 1900s).[12] Today, advances in midwifery and paediatrics have been one factor that has helped to increase women's lifespan to, on average, about five years longer than men's.

Back to the elderly – we really begin to suffer from the effects of aging from about 35 years old, which is the point at which there is an abrupt change in mortality rates. Sixteen years ago I drew a graph for my first atlas of Britain.[13] The graph took in all the individual digitized mortality records of Britain and showed me that from age 35 onwards, with every year that passes, our chances of dying increase, always a little higher than the year before and almost always by nearly exactly the same multiple higher.

Drawn on a logarithmic, or log, scale, as it is in the figure overleaf, the mortality curve, over age 35, is shown to be more an angled line than a curve. On a log scale, tenfold rises (and other multiplicative rises) are shown with equal distance between each rise; therefore, with the graph below, the difference between a chance of 1 in 1,000 and 1 in 100 would be the same magnitude as the change between 1 in 100 and 1 in 10 – between each of these increments the chance has risen tenfold. You can see from the graph that mortality chances increase tenfold between your thirties and your fifties, and between your fifties and seventies, but between the ages of 20 and 35 you would be just as likely to die one year as the next (the line rises vertically). When I drew my atlas, I was then a long way from 35, or so it seemed. *Great*, I thought, 35 – *that's a lifetime away.*

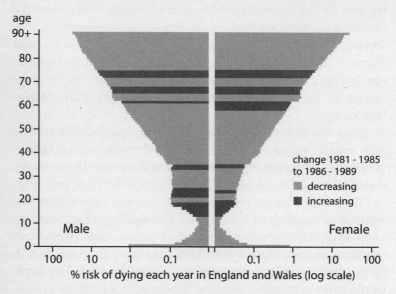

FIGURE 14: The Human Mortality Curve,
England and Wales, 1980s

Source: New Social Atlas of Britain, Figure 5.16[14]

Now I'm 43, seven years up the curve. The aches and pains have begun. Nothing worth complaining about, but I'm aging in a way I wasn't when I was 27; however, the good news is that I won't be aging in the same way someone aged 43 would have aged in the 1980s. The graph was made using data on everyone who died during the

1980s in England and Wales and distinguished between two types of ages: those with rising mortality rates and those with falling mortality rates. For most ages the rate has fallen as people have become physically fitter and so 43 in 2011 is rather like being 38 in 1985. If I make it into my eighties (or even to the 2050s), odds are it'll be a much fitter me than my grandparents were in their eighties. Health is generally improving for most people in most parts of Britain and so we do not necessarily get as old, biologically, as our ancestors did at similar ages. There is, of course, no guarantee that we will continue to see our health improve overall; this cessation has already begun in those parts of the country where life expectancy has stopped rising (and that expectancy may be on the cusp of falling in some of the poorest places). There are also social groups for whom the improvements in living standards and consequently health standards have been the slowest.

I discovered when I first drew the graph that in the 1980s some groups of the elderly, particularly around retirement ages, and some groups of young people, experienced an increase in mortality rates. These increases are indicated by the bars shaded darker in the figure above. They are part of the evidence that now shows us that Neil Kinnock was largely correct in 1983 when he forecast: 'I warn you not to be young. I warn you not to fall ill. I warn you not to get old.' That warning was repeated on 5 May 2010 by a journalist who, on the eve of the general election of that year added, 'I warn you that a chance some have waited for all their adult lives will slip away, perhaps taking another generation to come around again'.[15] In the event, hundreds of thousands of people's chances to see their children go to university were taken away within months, and their chances to retire at the usual time dashed. We were told we

197

could no longer afford such 'luxuries' due to aging and all the other supposed 'costs' of our modern economy.

Recently I saw a graph of the (legal) drugs we take, by age. It is shown overleaf for women. The one for men looks similar, although men tend to use slightly fewer lotions and potions (probably for the same reasons they go to the doctor less than women, which again fits in with their higher risk-taking profile and that might well be part of the reason men die a lot earlier than women). The curve on this graph was identical to the old mortality curve – we take medicines, on aggregate, in direct proportion to the log of our chances of dying each year, an average of fifteen more prescriptions, on average, as our mortality chances increase tenfold. That should give us hope – you see, taking the log of something makes it much smaller. If you are old enough to know about slide-rules you'll know about this. If not, you are young enough to know about graphs: compare the X axis on the previous graph to the Y axis on the figure below. Previously, it is a log scale, and based on multiplicative ratios; below, it is arithmetical, and additive. What we discover by comparison is that the costs of aging rise slightly as the risks associated with aging rise greatly.

In Britain, the people who take the least number of medicines, relative to the state of their health, are the elderly. People aged 75 to 84 take only twice as many medicines as those aged 55 to 64 even though they are about ten times more likely to die.

Given the state of their bodies, older people consume far fewer drugs per malady than do younger folk. Those over 85 might consume, on average, almost a prescription a week, but that would appear far more warranted than the average of almost a prescription a month being acquired by those half their age. Given how much healthier they

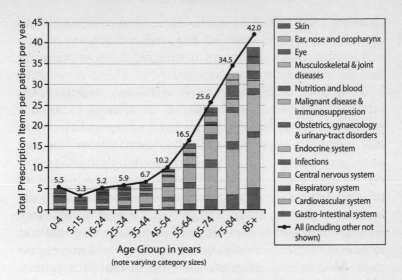

FIGURE 15: Annual Prescribing of
Medical Items to Women in Britain by Age

Source: Ruth Willis, 2010, in turn from: ONS, Key Health Statistics, 2000.[16]

should be, the middle aged appear far more costly per illness to the NHS than do the old. (Here I am using mortality rates as a proxy for physical ailments. It is not a bad proxy when it comes to considering serious physical illness.) Thus, we can determine that the elderly are not a great drain on our health services, nor are a majority of them a drain on care services. The very affluent elderly tend to privately employ people to look after them, for example, and stereotypes of bedridden, impoverished old folk inevitably requiring expensive nursing-home care can be misleading. Statistics that are properly interpreted, understood and accepted can go a long way towards changing the belief in such stereotypes. Almost three quarters of people aged 90 and over still live in private households, many alone, and with a majority of them still looking after themselves, unaided.[17]

We need to recognize this self-sufficiency, alongside the fact that one of the main sources of voluntary care for people aged over 90 comes from the young elderly, those just into their seventies. Of those elderly who do need help, only a small minority of them, some 150,000 people out of 20.5 million aged over 50 (0.7 per cent), are able to fund private care for themselves in their homes.[18] And a tiny fraction of those 150,000 will spend more again on their care and household staff in old age than will the remainder of the 0.7 per cent. But we should not expect to be able to pay privately for care in our own homes. The good news from the statistics of aging, from prescription-medicine consumption and from the surveys that show how we are already living, is that most of us can grow old without being a great burden. We do not need huge sums of money to pay for our retirements. This, I think, is great news, because we cannot all be as rich as Bob Diamond.[19]

Much of the private care purchased by that 0.7 per cent could be given to elderly people who most need it, rather than those who can most afford it. Furthermore, in a more caring society fewer of our social arrangements would be mediated through the market. Do you want the person aiding you in your dotage to be doing it because you pay their bills or doing it because they care, because they see their job as worthwhile and valued, not as dead-end? Which person do you think would do the better job,[20] especially when we are likely to need care in the years that approach our death?[21] Indeed, two-thirds of hospital beds in Britain are taken by people aged over 64[22] – a healthy (if you will) proportion of the population – for who wants to be in hospital when they're younger? Rather this way around than the other.

And contrary to what many believe, it is far better to have a person live in good health to 100 after retiring at 65 than have two people die at age 50 while still working. The idea that an aging population somehow presents us with an extra cost is a very strange idea. It is similar to the kind of thinking that results in people estimating how much having a child might cost you in terms of cots and clothes, school-kit and Christmas presents. By such logic the cheapest future for humanity would be if the planet were hit by an asteroid that wiped out all human life. Suddenly the 'costs' would disappear. There would be nothing left to worry about.

For classical economists, a society with large numbers of people who die on their sixty-fifth birthday, or thereabouts, might look on paper as if it is efficient; however, in reality, such a society looks more like the neighbourhoods around Calton in Glasgow, where male life expectancy is about 54 years old.[23] This does not ignore the fact, though, that an aging population does present us with different challenges to those we have faced before. And I'd say these aging-related challenges are far more welcome than such things as tuberculosis, measles and polio, the fight to overcome opposition to a welfare state or free secondary education, or the fight to secure women's rights. On the contrary, the challenges of aging are to be celebrated.

A recent report from the Royal College of Physicians stated:

A typical district general hospital with 500 beds will admit 5,000 older people each year and 3,000 will suffer a mental disorder. On average, older people will occupy 330 of these beds at any time and 220 of these will have a mental disorder. This means that the acute hospital will have at least four times as many older people with mental disorder on its wards as the older people's mental health service has on theirs. Three disorders – depression, dementia and delirium – will account for 80 per cent of this mental disorder co-morbidity, such that, 96 patients will have depression, 102 dementia and 66 delirium.[24]

Medical and socio-economic advances now allow those of us in developed, richer countries, to benefit from good physical health for longer; however, the one part of our bodies that wears out faster than the rest is our brains,[25] sometimes depending on how long we live. It was always thus, it was just that in our industrial and farming past, few of us lived long enough to experience this discrepancy between our physical and mental longevity.

In contrast to Alzheimer's, which is found wherever longevity is possible[26] (and sometimes where it is not), depression and anxiety are far more common to affluent countries with an unequal distribution of wealth than they are to countries with a more equitable distribution. (World Health Organization psychiatric assessments show this to be true for young and old alike. One in three families in Britain contain a member suffering from poor mental health, most often because high rates of financial inequalities in British society make the population more anxious and prone to depression than in the bulk of more equitably affluent nations.)[27]

Delirium is usually an outcome of another disease of the central nervous system and, along with Alzheimer's, depression and anxiety, could be spotted, and treated, earlier than it is currently if our health system were able to treat the poor in all areas as well as they treat the rich in others. The most pressing case for an equitable society comes from the growing numbers of us expected to reach great old age: it is much easier to have a good death in a good society. Suppose that thirty-nine years from now we could halve the instances and prevalence of dementia, depression and delirium among those who will be very elderly. If so, it would mean that those 500 hospital beds would be occupied by only 110 of us with mental disorders, most probably coupled with at least one physical ailment. But, one might note, the elderly population is rising, so those 220 beds might well still be needed even if we were to become a more equitable and caring society. In the next 19 years, by 2030, the numbers of those aged over 85 are set to double, and the numbers aged over 100 to quadruple.[28] So, yes, the numbers will be affected, and we'll have to deal with diseases of old age far more effectively than we do currently, just to stand still. There will be a growing army of young, fit older people able to care for those even older, but will they be willing or in a good enough financial position to do so?[29]

In a time of rising austerity, in a nation slipping down the world rankings of wealth but with an increasingly older population, how can we be optimistic that all will be fine? Perhaps we should look back to the past. Maybe we need more stiff-upper-lips and to be more willingly prudent. Maybe we need to reverse the effects of our selfish 'me generation'. Perhaps we should look to the nation's favourite granny for clues; amazingly, she also doubles as an agony aunt. All we need to do is log on to the 'Official Website of the British Monarch'[30] to find out how to contact her:

You can write to Her Majesty at the following address:
Her Majesty The Queen
Buckingham Palace
London SW1A 1AA

If you wish to write a formal letter, you can open with "Madam" and close the letter with the form "I have the honour to be, Madam, Your Majesty's humble and obedient servant".

This traditional approach is by no means obligatory. You should feel free to write in whatever style you feel comfortable.[31]

I resisted the immediate urge to put pen to paper (opting for what made me comfortable) to ask Elizabeth for her thoughts on how those not inheriting a household of servants should plan for their care in old age. Instead I had a little delve into the royal website and learnt, among much else, that in 1917 only seven men and seventeen women received greetings from King George V on their hundredth birthdays; that in her first year in the job, in 1952, just 255 centenarians received a congratulatory message from Elizabeth II; and that by 2007, she was sending out 8,439 such birthday cards and a further 770 to people congratulating them on reaching their 105th birthdays, and above. It is worth hanging on – you get more cards, sometimes with slightly different wording:

The oldest ever recipient of a message from The Queen was a Canadian gentleman, who reached the age of 116 in December 1984, whilst the oldest British recipient was 115, the oldest woman in Britain at the time. Occasionally, twins reach their milestone together. In 2006, three sets of twin sisters and in

2007, twin brothers reaching 100 were recorded by Buckingham Palace. The Anniversaries Office, which is responsible for sending out messages, ensures that each twin receives a slightly different greeting, aware that they will generally be together on their big day and will open their cards at the same time . . . During her reign the Queen has sent approximately 110,000 telegrams and messages to centenarians in the UK and the Commonwealth.[32]

Is such consideration worth every penny of the royal allowance? It is nice to have someone paid to write birthday cards, rather like those folk who are employed to reply from Santa if you post one yourself to the North Pole.[33] I'm just not sure that we should carry on having one very well paid person writing all these cards, especially given how many more she, or more likely her successors, will soon have to sign.

Only around 10,000 people are aged 100 as I write, by 2050 this will have increased by 2,400 per cent. Assuming all goes to plan, by 2050 King William will have sent out 250,000 cards to people simply because they were still alive.[34] If we have not become a republic by then (to save on the postage), he'll have sent out millions of other cards to those 105-, 106-, 107-year-olds, and on and on. This will possibly be more than twice the number his granny will have sent, annually, in her (projected) very long lifetime.

By 2050 advances in medicine, a better-ordered society, even huge amounts of care being provided by the young elderly will not be enough to help us care for our rising population of the very old. We'll need an increase in the numbers of younger people, if only to help the 68-year-old king with his mail bags. As far as I can see, we'll need to better distribute what we have if we are all to enjoy our retirements, the future king included. We can still have a service that sends you birthday cards on your hundredth birthday (even one that signs them as if they come from a king), but it could be done a little cheaper.[35]

More important than royalty, and despite all the concerns over immigration, there is great uncertainty over how many young people there will be in the future in Britain compared to how many we need. When the present Queen was just a couple of years on the throne, and then again a dozen years later, she was told wildly different stories about how many future subjects she should expect to reign over. Her advisors were uncertain, but such uncertainty matters when we try to prepare for our dotage. Why? Because we are no more certain now than we were then.

In 1955 and 1965 projections, published by the precursors of the Office of National Statistics for the UK, population around the time of the millennium differed by some 22 million people! The 1955 projection of 53 million by 1995 was far closer to the final outcome than was the 1965-based estimate of 75 million by 2001.[36] We tend to overestimate future populations rather than underestimate them. We are especially prone to overestimate during economic, fertility and immigration booms, such as that which occurred in the mid-1960s, and again more recently up until 2007. The 1965-based projections, published around the Queen's forty-second birthday, projected that there would be more than 1.5 million babies born in the year 2000, a projection that turned out to be over twice the actual number.[37] (It is easy to get population projections very wrong. The errors accumulate and multiply. If people don't immigrate who you thought were going to immigrate then they can't have the children you thought they would have, and so on and on.)

No matter how well we organize ourselves in future, we do have a problem with how few youngsters there are projected to be in future in Britain. Even if (like almost every other nation-state in Europe) we disband the households of servants that royalty and the super-rich have established to care for them, so that the cost of these servants can be redistributed to allow the rest of us can be cared for more efficiently, there may well not be enough younger people to go around in Britain. It is when people find that this is the case that the fear of an each-for-their-own attitude prevails most strongly.

Most of the world's population who are *projected* to be very elderly in 2050 are not living in those places where the vast majority of people *currently* born are projected to live. Those born today are people who will, by 2050, be in the prime of their lives. But almost all of them won't be living in Britain, unless we change our attitude to immigration (in this country and across all of Europe) – the greatest fall in fertility in the world recently has been in Eastern Europe, so we shouldn't expect help from Polish carers in future.

If our current population and household projections are allowed to run their course then, just as there was a 73 per cent rise in single (mainly elderly) households between 1981 and 2008, with just a 12 per cent rise in households containing more than one person, so too we should expect a similar rise over the course of the next twenty-seven years.[38]

As we can see, though, from the contradictory advice given to the Queen, there is nothing inevitable about projections. They have been out by millions before, mainly because what actually occurs is very much out of our hands. A higher proportion of single-occupancy households is what you get when you combine an aging population with a curtailment of immigration.

What is the alternative to easing immigration restrictions? Well, look to Japan. My favourite headline of summer 2010 was 'Robot Suits to Aid Elderly Japanese Farmers with Toiling in the Fields',[39] which led to the story of Professor Shigeki Toyama of Tokyo University's Agriculture and Technology Graduate School of Engineering, where he was:

> close to perfecting a robot suit that could considerably reduce the physical burden of farm work on elderly farmers. People aged 65 and older are a key pillar of the agricultural workforce, accounting for about 60 per cent of the agricultural population in Japan. Development of the robot suit may come as welcome news to such elderly farmers.

The last time I was in Japan the father-in-law of a friend of mine took me to see an area near the small city of Tōno, where people were sent when they reached their sixties. They were sent to the area to die. Here, whether they lived longer or not, they would not be a burden on younger folk.[40] There is an irony that these parts of Japan have changed in such a tiny number of generations from a pre-feudal existence when resources were in such short supply that the elderly were viewed as a burden, to a time when, post-industrially, the elderly now make up most of the remaining farm workforce. However, simultaneously in Japan, most people retire aged 60 or younger.[41] How can they afford to? How can the country afford to let them, unlike in France and the UK where the governments are trying to raise the retirement ages? The reason is that, in Japan, household incomes are among the most equitably distributed in the world. Historically it has been a patriarchal, sexist society, with few dual-earner households, but it has also been a society with fewer poorer people relative to other societies throughout the world; fewer people must continue with paid employment to sustain themselves, and their society as a whole. Fewer people in Japan than in Britain work into very old age. The Japanese also tend to be fitter in old age,[42] for a variety of reasons; thus, they are able to work for longer lengths of time in volunteer positions, post-retirement. And because they are fitter for longer they are also able to care for each other as they age. Life expectancy in Japan is 82.7 years. (But even in Japan they have a dearth of skilled nurses for the elderly.)

Such patterns, similar to those in Japan, can be found across the more affluent countries of Europe (excluding Britain). A recent report published by the United Nations lists those European countries with a life expectancy higher than ours in the UK: Iceland (almost 82 years), Switzerland, Italy, France (81 years), Sweden, Spain, Norway, Austria (almost 80 years), the Netherlands, Germany, Ireland, Malta, Cyprus, Finland, Belgium and Luxembourg (around 80 years). Australia, Canada and New Zealand also boast higher life expectancy than us, but not the United States, which falls below us with a life expectancy of only 79.1 years.[43]

In most of the rest of Europe average retirement age tends to be between the ages of 60 and 65 years (a few years earlier than ours and despite the fact that their population lives longer and only a third of people who work are aged 25 or younger). In most of the rest of Europe, working lives start later and end earlier. Far more Europeans than Britons can attend university. Most of the rest of Europe has working hours that are fewer each week than ours. Most Europeans know the joke about few people upon their deathbed expressing regret at not having stayed longer in the office: the joke's on us.[44]

In contrast to Europe, the US is the most extreme of all the affluent westernized countries that embrace workaholic lifestyles, whose citizens have longer working lives but shorter life expectancy, later retirement (or none at all) and huge inequalities between rich and poor. In the States, until the recent economic collapse and its accompanying massive rise in job losses, almost half of young adults aged 15 to 24 were in paid employment, a far higher proportion of population than in Western Europe, which by comparison has a higher proportion of young adults in employment (rather than in education) than in Japan.[45]

Millions of elderly in the States have to work until they die due to an inadequate welfare system. But the US does benefit from an influx of younger people – despite all attempts to police the Mexican border. It is partly that influx that contributes to the perpetuation of inequality. However, such high levels of immigration will not carry on for ever.

The world as a whole is aging. What is happening in Japan is a precursor to what will happen everywhere else. The *Economist* recently reported that soon, at a point now thought to lie somewhere between 2020 and 2050, the worldwide fertility rate will fall below global replacement rate and the magazine's anonymous writers concluded that 'population growth is already slowing almost as fast as it naturally could'.[46] If this prediction were true, the affluent elderly in the US should not expect a steady stream of immigrants to care for them in their old age; neither should we, even though increasingly we have grown accustomed to our care-home staff immigrating to the UK from outside of the EU. Their entry is now curtailed by the most recent immigration laws. We need to change how we view aging, as well as immigration, if we are all to have a better future.

For a very long time we humans have benefitted from our elderly in a way other animals have not. The menopause, for example is thought to be an evolutionary adaptation that allows older women to be more helpful than they would otherwise be able to if they were still undergoing the rigours of reproduction. As far as we know, all other species of animals differ from us in this regard. It may be a point of difference that is just as important as language development.

It is noticeable that no similar benefit has been found from having underproductive (and presumably somewhat grumpy) old men around. Similarly, just as women stop reproducing earlier than any other animal, so too have we all – men and women – evolved to start out on the main business of life later than almost any other animal.

The main business of human life had previously been to reproduce, but today we have far fewer offspring than our ancestors ever did. Sheep, swine and rabbits tend to go through puberty between their third and seventh month of life. Cattle, dogs and cats become adult within just a year of birth, and horses within a little over a year. Only chimps (at between age 6 and 8 years), bonobos (between age 8 and 10), and us (mostly between age 12 and 15) attain puberty so very late.[47] Our human biology divides into different life-stages, enabling us to do different things at different times of our lifespan. With this in mind, we should understand that there is nothing 'unproductive' about a large group of us being elderly.

We need not be so fearful of aging. It should be the cause of huge celebration that so many of us are now growing old, rather than suffering death more often in middle age in those years when infants made up the vast majority of bodies in Victorian graveyards. Recent scientific break-throughs have given us, among much else, three good reasons to be cheerful, although only people of a certain age will appreciate the magic number (three) and know the song it comes from:[48]

1) The human species only developed into its mod-ern form when the 'granny' evolved.
2) We are about to get a great many more grannies.
3) Grannies increase the survival chances of the species as a whole.

CHAPTER 8

THE FUTURE IS ANOTHER PLACE

When I look at maps of our social geography I often think that some parts of the country appear ahead of their time; elsewhere it is still *Life on Mars*, where the social statistics would not be out of place in an atlas from the 1970s. These areas tend to have been either the industrially abandoned towns or the most affluent of Home County and National Park enclaves that have fossilized themselves through planning restrictions.

In contrast, London now leads the way towards the future. That city in the 1980s exhibited the kind of trends in both marriage and multiculturalism that were not seen until two decades later in much of the rest of urban Britain, and which are still rare even in the more progressive rural fringes. Londoners tend to be more tolerant of a wide variety of living arrangements, and are drawn from a wider racial melting pot today than are people found almost anywhere else on the planet. (Though our MPs, now more socially liberal themselves – perhaps due to living in the capital – have nonetheless often become economically conservative. But MPs are unrepresentative of Londoners as a whole.)

Perhaps *London Citizens* is a group that better represents the potential of the nation? In the last decade it has become the most lauded of all social movements among people who think clearly about Britain.[1] Its achievements include gaining £40 million for poorer Londoners by securing living wages; ending the illegal detention of child refugees in Britain; and training more than 2,500 community organizers.[2] It is a loose organization based on a model of community action that first began to work in the poorer parts of the United States. Its members' ambition today is to spread its ideas out across Britain. If we were to base our predictions of how the future of the country might look, according to which parts appear to be most progressive today, then extrapolating current London politics and social ambition forwards would result in a picture of a place where people had recently learnt once again to start to care more for each other.[3]

London Citizens places rights at the top of the agenda: they do not accept the act of placing children in forced detention because their parents are suspected of being here without the proper papers – they fought and won a campaign to change the law on this; they do not accept the appalling misery of the greatest concentration of poverty found in Western Europe – in one of its richest cities, London – and, as a result, they have successfully shamed top bankers into paying their cleaners a living wage. A future along the lines of *London Citizens*' ideology would give Britain something to be proud of – apart from being masters of self-deprecating humour and the art of queuing and tea drinking, and that history of occasional tolerance and shelter of refugees.

There is no guarantee that our future will be more progressive than our present. For example, in the late 1920s, had you looked for the most progressive trends in

Germany you would have projected a favourable future within parts of Berlin. Alternatively, if you had been astute in the early 1930s you would have identified the signs of terrible things to come.[4] Were you to turn to the darkest corners of London today, to the insatiable pursuit of money by hedge-fund managers and the vitriolic violence of the British National Party, you could paint a similar dystopia; however, I am an optimist and so I see signs that allow us to be positive about our future.

I see messages of optimism elsewhere in the world today. In almost every other rich nation of the world, especially in most of those countries more affluent than the United Kingdom, people have achieved a comfortable standard of living and narrower gaps in social and income inequality than is now common in this country.[5] Other than in the United States, almost everywhere else in the world citizens now share out their resources more equally.[6] Countries as diverse as Canada, South Korea, Norway and Italy, are all home to more equitable societies than Britain and all have longer life spans, which in turn lead to more productive and fulfilling lives than can be found in Britain.

To see an optimistic image of the world as a whole, of a planet where resources are more equitably arranged, you have to be imaginative and to learn from the two dozen or so nations that have already given up arms and armies: places such as Costa Rica, Liechtenstein, Saint Lucia, Tuvalu, Iceland and Mauritius.[7] Within the affluent world it is in countries where inequalities in income are lowest, from Sweden to Japan, that consumption per person is lowest, despite most having far more to spend.

In parts of the world such as Kerala in India, Tanzania in Africa, Vietnam in Asia, or Cuba in the Caribbean, one finds examples of how people can live in ways where all have far more in common with their neighbours than we do in Britain. None of these are models of harmony for the future, but all show different aspects of what is possible elsewhere and what is possible with much less. For instance, there is great poverty in Cuba, but that country still manages to send far more doctors to help out in the poorer parts of Africa than does the much larger and very much wealthier USA. Cuba is home to just 2 per cent of the population of Latin America, but 11 per cent of its scientists. Cuba now uses 21 times less pesticides than it did in the 1980s and some 80 per cent of vegetables grown in that country are now classed as organic. Similar statistics can be found elsewhere. These are all places where overall consumption is not now so hugely higher than that which the parents or grandparents of current residents enjoyed when they were young, but where many people survive with some dignity rather than there being masses living in abject poverty.

In those unequal, affluent nations where most wealth is in the hands of the few, consumption levels are far higher right across the social scale: from richest to poorest. In the United States and United Kingdom people on average consume and waste far more: more meat, more water, more travel, more electricity, more of everything. They do it because in the unequal places, with the misrepresentative 'United' in their titles, all have to consume more to keep up with those near them. As a result, debt rises relentlessly.[8]

The future for Britain could easily be to make current conditions worse. If we take the worst-case scenario we aim to get through the recession by more than decimating the public sector. (Decimation means making cuts of *only* a tenth). Currently the housing market is stalling, but we have a plan for its recovery: if we build fewer homes, and

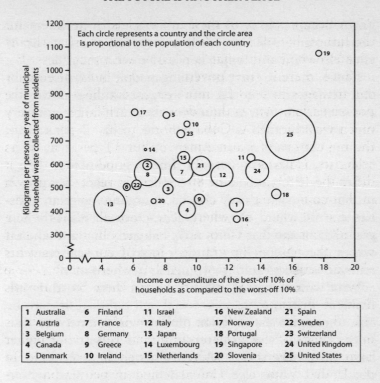

FIGURE 16: Residential Waste (kg/person/year)
Versus Income Inequality in Rich Nations[9]

*Note: how much we each throw away is one of the best measures of
how much we buy. Although among rich nations far more people are
poor in the United States than in any other affluent country, even the
poor there, through access to debt, consume a huge amount in comparison to the poor elsewhere in the world in order to maintain local
respectability and because so many more loans are offered.*

share out so unequally those we have left, demand has to
rise. Millions remain unemployed, as they have done for
the last thirty-two years, but that encourages those with

jobs to accept poor working conditions rather than demand improvement. Millions more experience short spells of unemployment and longer spells of great insecurity.

Under our current plan young people hold more debt than their parents could ever imagine holding as wealth; and older folk face destitution if they are not among the very meagre ranks of the protected rich. In this light, George Osborne's stern oratory on how there is no alternative to his parties' cuts is far from a good plan.[10]

Yet I and many others are still optimistic because it cannot go on like this,[11] and because we can see an alternative – elsewhere, in other places – today. This is the one great advantage that Geography has over History: when it comes to fortune-telling History looks back searching for certainties, Geography looks *across* at alternatives.

What alternative is there to a growing North-South divide in British economic, social and political life? To be able to imagine that division diminishing you need to consider other gulfs as apparently just as robust but which have fallen nevertheless. Across Europe the only regional divide that came close to matching that found within Britain, in terms of life-expectancy differences within a single country, had been found previously in Germany, especially just after the iron curtain fell and the country was reunited. It is worth noting that even at its height such polarization in Germany was small compared to what we now experience in Britain.[12]

In the 1990s a huge swathe of young people with get-up-and-go got up and went from East Germany and moved West. They moved to where opportunity beckoned, to where their parents had been denied entry; few people moved in the opposite direction.[13] You would have expected great polarization as a result of the fall of the Berlin Wall and, at first, there was, but then reductions in regional divisions in Germany occurred despite 1,700,000 people moving from East to West.[14]

In contrast to the United Kingdom, in Germany there was a policy of genuine economic investment in the more disadvantaged regions and both infrastructure and hope improved across the board. The East was not to be abandoned and cut off again, market forces were not allowed to replace barbed wire. All it took was the will of the people. Today people lead longer, healthier lives in the German Eastern Länder than in northern England. Forty-five years of communism was less damaging than thirty-two years of Thatcherism and neo-Thatcherism (1979–2010). Today in Germany that great geographical health divide has diminished greatly, whereas in the early 1990s it was the second greatest geographical gulf in life chances in Western Europe, overshadowed only by the British North-South divide.

Regional division has been reduced in many parts of Europe. In Spain in the 1990s regional divides were reduced by allowing greater immigration, which also contributed to an increase in birth rates; this also affected birth rates in other parts of the world. Those émigrés to Spain, who had children there, had fewer children than adults who remained in the places they had emigrated from. As a result the population of Spain rose by six million while the total population of the world fell.[15] In Italy regional divides affecting health are thought to have been reduced by a substantial redistribution of resources via their national health service.[16] (Remember us in Britain, where in certain areas we have a small ratio of general practitioners compared to those who are ill? Compare this to Italy, where doctors are assigned to the places where they are most needed. This public spending distribution is a complementary part of the reason why Italy has a greater equality in health than is seen today across Britain,[17] despite Italy also being a country that is relatively more regionally divided than we are. The same story of regional divides is true of France, Greece, Austria and Sweden.

In the past, immigration has reduced regional divides in Britain. Migration from the Indian subcontinent to former mill towns in the north-west of England and to many areas of Yorkshire meant that a great many homes were not demolished, which otherwise would have been if they had been uninhabited, and the economy has benefitted from an influx of younger workers and their offspring. Such immigration, the revitalizing of local economies that goes with it, and the birth of children to replace those dying, all make for a more cohesive society in the long run.

Where immigration has not been encouraged, and where immigrants are particularly put off by perceived prejudice and a lack of opportunity, places have become a repository of surplus men. In 2004, across all of Eastern Germany and despite the health divide being curtailed, there were only 90 women for every 100 men among adults below age 30. In some parts of the East German state of Thuringia, it was recorded recently that there were as few as 82 women for every 100 men. The town of Königstein has the fewest women of all.[18] In Britain the presence of more immigrants from abroad redresses the balance. Their presence mitigates the effects both of aging and of higher out-migration by young UK-born women, currently mostly to other parts of Britain. However, as unemployment among young adults in Britain rises to levels never experienced before we should expect net emigration.[19] If the trends of recent years are continued and internationalized then the immigration of the British into other countries should also begin to feature more highly skilled women than men leaving these islands in search of better prospects overseas.

Iceland and Ireland are both currently experiencing out-migration of their youth, but we have yet to see if there are more women than men emigrating. Women, if they form a relationship with a man abroad, have tended to return to where they grew up (usually with their new partner) to start a family. The young women of Britain may return with men from other places; however, we have yet to see this in anything more than a trickle. As I write the emigration has only just begun.[20]

I would like to think that we in Britain have learnt from our recent past, from the effects of the smaller economic slowdowns of the early 1970s, 1980s and 1990s.[21] Hopefully we will not see a ratcheting up, yet again, of young male mortality, of the kind that has occurred with each of those other post-war recessions. In Britain young men are now three times more likely to die in their youth than are young women and if the trend does not abate that will rise to four times more likely after this latest economic misfortune. To halt that trend we must offer young adults better options than economically forced emigration. We can measure our future failure, *if* we fail, in everything from the ratio of boys to girls born, to whether the murder rate among the young rises again – from its current national high of forty victims per million young men per year.[22]

People make their own history, especially in the wealthiest and most powerful nations of the world, a club of which Britain is still a prominent member. For most of my parents' lifetimes and almost all of my grandparents', the country was made a better place for all. That has not been true of almost all of my lifetime, but it still could be. The key to success is largely in the hands of older adults who are currently denying opportunities to the young, and endlessly preaching 'responsibility' to them while simultaneously irresponsibly saddling the youth with debt.

It is older adults who hold the vast bulk of the £9 trillion national-personal wealth, more of which could be going towards wages for the young. It is younger adults who hold almost all of the £1.5 trillion personal debt.[23] To a great extent the future of Britain depends upon the point at which young adults realize that this inequality exists, and then whether many leave in despondency, or whether those who stay are more active in their response. Currently only young adults with affluent parents can see, and expect to see, a secure future.

All around us are examples from other countries of how the future of Britain may look as that future is currently being played out in other places. Countries as diverse as the Netherlands and Japan show us how a greater population density can be accommodated by more efficient forms of urban living. Through such adaptation we in Britain could comfortably accommodate the numbers of people needed to balance out our aging population with younger citizens and without growing distressed about resources going to these newcomers.

There are many other countries that take far more immigrants than Britain. The United States takes the most worldwide, but in a way that maintains and even fuels inequality: continuous streams of immigrants shoring up the bottoms of steep social gradients. These create great social pyramids that (for stability) require so many more at their base than at the top that almost no one on the lower slopes realizes even a glimpse of the American Dream. And yet they keep coming because hope is eternal.

In great contrast, New Zealanders' dream of a small place of one's own is realized by a far higher proportion of those who migrate to their country, principally because a place of one's own is a more reasonable dream than the accumulation of great personal riches. A fifth of New Zealanders were born abroad, and a fifth of all people born in New Zealand now live abroad. If we were to learn from their experiences and from the experiences of the people in Australia, Canada and even Norway, we would cope with immigration so much better than we do now.[24] Alternatively we could embrace the xenophobia that has swept across much of mainland Europe in recent years with the rise of so many small, far-right parties. My gut instinct is that the ethnically and religiously diverse United Kingdom will not go down that route. Most young people in Britain know what 'bigot' means.[25] Multiculturalism might be what we could best teach those in mainland Europe, in return for everything we could learn from those on the mainland about how we could live better lives in so many ways.

If you look at the arrangement of housing in urban centres in Finland or Denmark, and especially in the Netherlands, you may see how young adults need not wait with angst until they are older before they even think of buying a property. It makes no sense to own a home until you are sure you will remain in one place for quite some time, most often when you are raising children. We are currently moving towards that situation, but only because we are being forced to, because so many of the young can no longer afford the gigantic additional debt of a mortgage.

Renting is on the rise again in Britain in earnest, and what matters most in this scenario is how well landlords behave. Not everyone can be a great landlord, but we can bring in legislation to ensure that they all are at least required to be good. One way the British could mitigate the effects of losing so much social housing in recent years would be to re-regulate the private-rented sector so that these landlords would be forced to provide a decent service or to sell to someone who could, with the sale being instigated by their tenants. This would operate in a similar way to the right-to-buy, but would be a right-to-sell, avoiding the trauma of eviction, allowing your children to stay at their school and keep their friends.

Unscrupulous private landlords are a minority, usually older and rich. Tenants are a very large majority of the young and an even larger majority of the poor. It is only the guile of the landlords and the misplaced optimism of renters (that they will soon not be renting) that inhibits housing-law reform. People in Britain will soon work out that the proportion of households able to afford a mortgage has been in decline since 1991. Not everyone will be able to own a home, many who do now will lose that ownership, but far fewer families need face eviction if we had the right-to-sell our homes to a better landlord and stay put.[26]

Similarly, the divide between town and country could be reduced if the large majorities living in cities understood the extent to which many existing planning laws have been enacted to uphold the property values of those living in nearby rural areas. If these laws were altered to protect land that was ecologically valuable, rather than to preserve the greenbelt to bolster the prestige of the affluent, then the distinction between town and village could blur. We need more parks in towns and fewer planning envelopes around cities where what is actually being protected is the urban/rural divide, not the habitats of rare species, or ancient woodland. Take this route and we shall have more small eco-towns in the future and fewer exclusive hamlets.

In France, Belgium and Luxembourg, different models of planning are already in place, making city and country less divided. So, just as we exported suburbs to the world, we should now look to see what it is we are most likely to import back from others' inventions as we begin to replace our aging semis and terraces with something that works better for the twenty-first century.

Vibrant cities are places where the large majority live in flats, rather than commute in from houses in the suburbs. Already many of our city centres contain new blocks of flats, but often these were built speculatively to house students, not to rent to more discerning adults, and hardly ever for families. We need to build our homes more for living in than to profit from.

And how should we cope with our ever growing army of elderly? To begin with we must learn to think of aging as a process that makes us more capable, careful and wise. The celebration of youth is a recent and transient illusion. Young faces sell products in television advertisements, they appeal to our instincts to care for small, large-eyed and vulnerable offspring, but in practice a world dominated by youth is a world lacking experience. Look to Greece, Italy and much of the non-European world for different models of the family and of aging if you want to see, today, one possible alternative future for Britain – one with greater contact between generations.

Just as the middle class in Britain are beginning to expect that their grown children may need to live at home for longer than in previous years, or to return after a short spell of study, so too are they expecting to pool wealth between generations. This might mean middle-class grannies returning to be nearer middle-class grandchildren (working-class families have always had to share more and live nearer to one another). In fact it was only the affluence of a single generation, accumulated during that dearth of babies from the 1930s through to 1944, who could continue, in such a majority, to buy their own homes young. They could afford not to take in their parents.

Their children in turn left home early to study and didn't return. Such a nuclear existence, with only the children and two parents at home, was a historical aberration, the final spending of the winnings of Empire.

How we age is changing, and to further institutionalize the elderly would alienate them, and us, and require a great many more badly paid young adults to provide care (for fear of being jobless and hence penniless, not because they care). Again, we may be stupid enough to allow this to happen, but I hope not, and doubt it may happen.[27] I see a different future because I look back at the statistics for the last six generations and realize that none of them predicted the progress that occurred in their lifetimes and how different their old age would be compared to that of their parents' and, most importantly, at what age they were old, or were considered to be so.

As long as maximizing profit is not our guiding motive then we may be able to live more commonly in groups in sheltered housing as we age, nearer to our relatives, and increasingly very near to them. Grandparents are already more frequently caring for grandchildren than they did in the previous generation, and this is one example of the importance of geographical proximity. With the rise in tuition fees there will be increased demand to have access to local universities, so that the large majority of students can live at home and study as they do in mainland Europe (and much of Scotland). And when people do travel, where will they turn for childcare, and other care? They head towards a more matriarchal set of arrangements, where women return to where their mothers live so that they can find the support from this network of parents; and, increasingly, the men will have to fit around this.

But, I am not always an optimist; there are many

different and dimmer futures to be envisaged. Look to Portugal if you want to see what Britain might look like if we became a bit more impoverished and an aristocracy of the rich gain greater power. If we were to become more like Portugal economically I am afraid that the weather would not alter, we would not suddenly develop wonderfully warm beaches;[28] we would remain a grey island, drab in places, but under an even more authoritarian social structure than what we already endure. We could become even more divided. You could look to Israel to see what that feels like, but note that we are already more economically divided by income and wealth inequalities than are all the people of Israel and the occupied territories.[29] You might think that Britain doesn't feel so divided, but like the frog in the kettle slowly warming up, you've acclimatized.

To see a dystopian vision of our future and, sadly, to see the country we are changing into, simply look across the Atlantic to the United States. Admittedly, we have much to learn from the US, where there are many things better than in Britain: among some, greater religious and press freedom; a more advanced civil-rights movement; and sometimes an ingrained disrespect for the arrogance of aristocracy – but there is even more to learn to *avoid* in that country.

If you want to see what the newly privatized UK higher education system will look like, look to the US. If you want to know what our health system would look like if we allowed those determined to privatize it to get their way, take another glance west.[30] If you want to know what a meaner Britain will feel like, as benefits are squeezed and rights repealed, look to the American nightmare of inadequate social security and a media dominated by a handful of rich men. We should look, learn and avoid.

There are many other, better places to look: the rapidly industrializing great states of Indonesia, Brazil, India and China. What would a race to the bottom be like if we were to try to compete more fiercely with them to retain our great wealth in comparisons to theirs, if we were unwilling to share? For that vision the best place I have found is Singapore. Stand on the beach by the airport there; it is strewn with debris from passing cargo ships, it stinks of oil; in the skies above, jets come in for landing every few minutes. Here is the world's crossroads. You can stay for a few hours or days if you are in transit, but to migrate here you must be very wealthy.

Why would you want to migrate to Singapore, to polluted beaches and a small country where it remains a criminal offence to buy non-medicinal chewing gum? Why, to enjoy the tax breaks and the sun, of course. Here is a place you could go to hide your wealth from those who would redistribute it. Singapore is the most unequal of all the world's richest twenty-five countries.[31] What would that future look like for us?

A British Singapore would be a place of repressive laws and of an immigration policy that welcomed millionaires and other high-tier migrants but gave others only guest-worker status at best, with a requirement to leave should they become pregnant. People born in Britain would also have to emigrate if they could not find work and became a so-called burden on the state, which would cease to support them. Britain would soon have some of the lowest infant-mortality rates in the world, just as Singapore has today (because poorer people have to go abroad to have their children). There would be increased ethnic division and much less inter-marriage. Instead, one set of castes would be destined to serve another. Menial jobs would be reserved for those from specific racial or religious orders.

Have a look at who does most of the menial jobs in London, who stands in doorways as 'security', who runs the Tube, who serves in hotels. We in Britain are not so far removed from Singapore; like them, we are an island, an airport hub for crossing an ocean, a stop-off point for shipping. The reason we do not easily imagine that we could be like Singapore is simple: they were one of our many colonies and should be more like us, not the reverse.[32]

We could be more than just a haven for dodgy money, more than a place of refuge for banks from the more effective financial regulation found on the European mainland. We need not slowly turn into a Singapore of the West, and we should remember that Singapore, too, could change; it is unlikely to become much more unequal.

The future is the last of the eight big issues this book promised to address. I have shown, with each of the other seven, that somewhere else in the world not too unlike Britain something is happening that could happen here, usually to improve our current situation, occasionally to make it worse. I have done this to demonstrate that an alternative future is possible, perhaps even probable, given that it already exists elsewhere and that we are currently an 'outlier' country (being one of the most unequal of rich countries). Britain is currently a place where, for your own personal future, it matters to whom and where you were born far more than it would elsewhere in the majority of the affluent world.

There is much more to say about the possible futures of Britain – and so much scope to get so much wrong. We could talk about Britain's place in the world, of Empire, colonies, Zimbabwe, Gibraltar, ex-pats, the Falklands, of shoes and ships and sealing-wax.[33] We could discuss whether or not one of our greatest problems is that the last decent invasion on to our shores took place 945 years ago. Invasions and revolutions are great equalizers. Because of recent invasions Japan and Germany no longer have an aristocracy; because of revolution France and the United States have real constitutions. However, rather than concentrate on our failings, I'd prefer to talk about the great advantage we now enjoy given that the language of the Internet is English, and just at the point when the majority of the world's population are, for the first time ever, becoming literate.[34] Our language advantage should attract more people into Britain, just as we are beginning to have so many less of our own.

To find enough space on our large island, but also to use it well, we need to build *up*, more than *out*. We need to commute less and telephone each other more, rather than meet (physically) face to face so much. It is all that long-distance commuting that causes the trains to be so full, the buses packed and the roads jammed. It is worth knowing that if you don't need to touch someone else at a meeting, then you really don't need to be there physically. Handshakes are overrated. I think they will go, just as ties are going, and the codpiece died a fashionable death long ago. (My grandfather tells me the greatest change in his lifetime has been in the clothes people wear.)

Currently the people who have least choice over where to live in Britain are the rich. We can tell this from how they have come to be the most geographically segregated of all income groups, clustered together in more tightly bound enclaves when their geographical extent is estimated between each of the last four censuses.[35] As we again become more equal, those who are very rich will become freer to live where they like and mix with whom they like. If you want to find a good man to marry, you might still, in future, be better-off heading for the countryside or to where the North begins, where the head on beer flattens and the hills rise. If society becomes more equal, you will be able to consider a greater choice of marriage partner anywhere. The hills will still rise and that head on beer will still flatten, but there might be quite a few more of us living there, but not so many moving about that we cannot move.

My surest prediction for the future is that in less than a century's time people will look back at the start of the twenty-first century and ask why those we put in power were so callous and mean-spirited, and why we did not do more to stop them from being so. For this country to be changed for the better, we all must get to know it better. The most pernicious effect of growing social divisions is that we have increasingly come to live more compartmentalized lives, commuting by differing means to different locations, shopping in differentiated places for different things, including ever more differentiated education for our children, and market-segmented retirement homes for ourselves. There are more gated communities in Britain than since we were last as unequal, and more no-go areas kept for the rich now than were last found a century ago.[36] Seventy-five years ago the middle class of England flocked to hear stories about how the other half lived and how unfair it all was, including for them.[37] We need those stories again; we need to look forward to what could be, to look more closely at many alternatives, not back at a map of what once was.

NOTES

Introduction – Geography Matters

1   We have 1 per cent of the world's adults and .5 per cent
     of the world's children. Five notes about endnotes in this
     book: 1) They are all at the end and are all superfluous 2)
     they are sequential within chapter 3) in the main they only
     refer to publicly available information – not websites hid-
     den behind pay-walls or academic journals available in a
     similar way, so I use Wikipedia where it makes public such
     private information 4) if you can easily check a fact, such
     as the one above about adults and children, then I won't
     usually put in a reference 5) my editor hates references
     so reads them last which might allow me to occasionally
     sneak in something tangential but still interesting, such as
     the fact that we are home to 5.5 per cent of the world's cen-
     tenarians. This is not an easy fact to check. You can work it
     out from the data provided here: Lopez, A. D., Salomon, J.
     et al. (2001) *Life Tables for 191 Countries: Data, Methods
     and Results, GPE Discussion Paper Series: No.9*, EIP/GPE/
     EBD, (Geneva: World Health Organization, 2001) www.
     whqlibdoc.who.int/hq/2001/a78629.pdf. It takes a long
     time. I put the spreadsheet here when I was drawing a map
     of where 100-year-olds live: www.worldmapper.org/data/
     nomap/485 worldmapper data.xls (note, that proportion
     will fall as more people in other countries age. When you
     read this it may be nearer 5 per cent.

2   By the way, this isn't the kind of book that tells you

232

where to find the shortest street in Britain, although over the years I've read it's Elgin Street in Bacup (five metres), Ebenezer Place in Wick (two metres) or Tolbooth Street in Falkirk (too short to measure!). What I will point out is that no one else in the world feels the need to make such claims for their streets as much as the British do: www.rossendaleonline.co.uk/rossendale-news/bacups-elgin-street-loses-title-shortest-street-183.html and www.undiscoveredscotland.co.uk/falkirk/falkirk/index.html

3   Give or take a million either way. See Chapter 2 and the text within pages 50–56 in that chapter for more details. We know a lot about Britain, but we don't know, to the nearest million, how many people are here. After each census it is usual to find that there were fewer than we thought.

Chapter 1: Dirty Old Town – North and South

1   Balakrishnan, A., 'North-South Divide Wider than Ever, *Guardian*, 19 June 2008, online at: www.guardian.co.uk/business/2007/jun/19/workandcareers.money which explained that 'The north-south divide in Britain is greater than ever despite the government's aim to reduce the gap'.

2   On 14 September 2010 in the Pinstone Street branch in Sheffield city centre and in Glasgow: Wallop, H., 'Police help to disperse Northern Rock queues', *Daily Telegraph*, 15 September 2007 www.telegraph.co.uk/finance/2815813/Police-help-to-disperse-Northern-Rock-queues.html

3   Martin, A., 'North-South dividing line slips southwards as recession widens economic gap', *Daily Mail*, 16 August 2010, www.dailymail.co.uk/news/article-1303291/North-South-dividing-line-slips-southwards-recession-widens-economic-gap.html

4   BBC 'Spending Review: concern across England over cuts', 20 October 2010, www.bbc.co.uk/news/uk-england-11585560

5   Office of National Statistics (ONS), 'Labour-market statistics' September 2010 release; Table 18(2) Regional labour-market summary: '70,000 more jobs in London,

2,000 in Yorkshire and falls in the North East, West Midlands but also slight falls in the South East.' www. statistics.gov.uk/pdfdir/lmsuk0910.pdf

6   Szreter, S. and Mooney, G., 'Urbanization, Mortality and the Standard of Living Debate: New Estimates of the Expectation of Life at Birth in Nineteenth-Century British Cities', *Economic History Review*, 2010, vol. 51, 1, pp. 84–112 (table 1). In Liverpool registration district itself, life expectancy in the 1880s was only 29 years, some 19 years lower than the 48 years recorded then in the affluent Clifton district of Bristol (*ibid*, table 2). Earlier, in Glasgow, rates similar to those in Liverpool were recorded (as low as age 27) in around 1840 (*ibid*, table 5). Infant mortality was a key factor in determining these low overall ages, dragging average life expectancies down as so many died before their first birthdays.

7   ONS, 'Life Expectancy at Birth and at Age 65 by Local Areas in the United Kingdom, 2006–08', (London: Office of National Statistics, 21 October 2009). www.statistics. gov.uk/pdfdir/liex1009.pdf For reconstructed records and further details see: Dorling, D., 'Death in Britain: How Local Mortality Rates Have Changed: 1950s-1990s' (York: Joseph Rowntree Foundation, 1997).

8   Thomas, B., D. Dorling and G. Davey Smith, 'Inequalities in Premature Mortality in Britain: Observational Study from 1921 to 2007', (London: British Medical Journal, 23 July 2010). www.sasi.group.shef.ac.uk/publications/2010/ ThomasDorlingDaveySmith 2010 BMJ.pdf

9   www.supanet.com/mens-room/the-northsouth-divide-over-heads-on-pints-25270p1.html

10   For an interactive version of the map see: sasi.group.shef. ac.uk/maps/nsdivide/index.html

11   The north of England wasn't being bailed out, unlike the south of England was when the banks went belly up. See reports on the divide in *The Sunday Times*, 15 August 2010; *Daily Mail*, 16 August 2010. On social divisions in general see the Guardian on 14 and 16 August 2010. At

the time of writing, *The Sunday Times* report sat behind the Murdoch empire's new pay firewall (don't bother to see *The Sunday Times* report) – it was copied by the *Daily Mail* the day after, and remains, for the time being, open-access. Just how much news you will be able to read on the web for free in future is very hard to guess.

12   Senex, Perambulators in Winter: A Plea for the Babies, *BMJ*, 2, 5 November, 1887, p. 1022 doi:10.1136/bmj.2.1401. 1022-a. Available online open access via government websites in the United States: http://www.ncbi.nlm.nih.gov/pmc/articles/PMC2535346/

13   See this volume, endnote spanning pages 243–244, for why Callaghan's 1976 and not Macmillan's 1957 is the correct year to cite for when people in Britain really never had it so good.

14   For an alternative perspective and an exposé of Victorian indolence, see: Wright, A., *Hoax! The Domesday Hide*. (Leicester: Matador, 2009).

15   Originally in German, published under the title: *Die Lage der arbeitenden Klasse in England*, see also http://en.wikipedia.org/wiki/The_Condition_of_the_Working_Class_in_England_in_1844

16   The wife of a Unitarian minister, she 'worked among the poor and knew at first hand the misery of the industrial areas', according to http://en.wikipedia.org/wiki/North and South (1855 novel)

17   The text of the book is freely available: www.gutenberg.org/cache/epub/2153/pg2153.txt

18   Chapter six concerns the outcome of the mills shortening, then cessation, of workers' hours and wages.

19   Manchester's life expectancy for 1801–50 was the lowest I have ever seen, calculated at 25.3 years, affecting a population of 235,000 people in 1841, *Ibid* (about a page up!): Szreter and Mooney (table 3).

20   See this volume, page 256, reference to Mike Davis's *Late Victorian Holocausts* below, for the most definitive account of the period.

21 Details can be found on the 'Local Local History' site: www.locallocalhistory.co.uk/open-spaces/paddington/index.htm and index here: www.locallocalhistory.co.uk/menus/main-menu-studies.htm. Well worth viewing.

22 On the book and the play see what is currently being said: http://en.wikipedia.org/wiki/Love on the Dole (quotations used here were accessed August 2010).

23 On the retrospective see: 'Rereading: *Love on the Dole* by Walter Greenwood'. An evocative portrayal of life in depression-era Britain, *Love on the Dole* sold thousands when it was first published in the 1930s. John Harris visits the Salford streets where it was set and finds some grim resonances'. Harris, John, *Guardian*, 7 August 2010 www.guardian.co.uk/books/2010/aug/07/rereading-love-dole-walter-greenwood.

24 It is 'not done' to mention on a university homepage which school you went to as it gives away the secret that universities are not meritocracies if too much of the backgrounds of academics are revealed. In the department where I now work, every member of academic staff mentions which university they attended; no one (myself included) mentions which school.

25 From 1973–86 I attended Donnington Infants, Wood Farm First school, Headington Middle and Cheney Secondary. See: Dorling, D. (2001). Anecdote is the singular of data. Environment and Planning A 33(8), pp. 1335–40. And, should you know Newcastle, at ages 18 to 21 I lived in Fawdon in 1986, Benwell in 1987, Fenham in 1988 and Heaton in 1989. http://sasi.group.shef.ac.uk/publications/2001/dorling_anecdote.pdf

26 The eponymous 1980s TV series based on *Brideshead Revisited* (1945) was filmed partly in Oxford in the colleges of Hertford, Wadham and Christ Church. Shortly after the programme was aired, the Bullingdon Club re-enacted the book's 'puking in the quad' scenes. For more details of the TV series see: http://en.wikipedia.org/wiki/Brideshead_Revisited_(TV_serial). When I was a teenager

in Oxford the Bullingdon's members included Boris, Dave and George (originally Gideon). They were what toffs in Oxford looked like. You will have seen that photograph of the Tory government as teenagers in their Bullingdon club despite all the attempts to hide it. There is a copy to be found here still: www.dailymail.co.uk/news/article-435875/Camerons-cronies-Bullingdon-class-87.html

27 Dorling, D., *A New Social Atlas of Britain*, (Chichester: Wiley, 1995). Both the PhD and that first book are available for free on the web: www.sasi.group.shef.ac.uk/thesis/index.html   http://sasi.group.shef.ac.uk/publications/new social atlas/index.html

28 Dorling, D. and D. J. Atkins, 'Population Density, Change and Concentration in Great Britain 1971, 1981 and 1991'. Studies on Medical and Population Subjects No. 58. (London: HMSO, 1995). An open access copy is here: www.statistics.gov.uk/downloads/theme population/SMPS58.pdf

29 In 1998 *The Drop Dead Show* won a Royal Television Society award. It is mainly remembered now as being among the early television debuts of the young Davina McCall. The award was for 'adult education: general'. See www.rts.org.uk/doclib/AWARDS1.pdf Although I doubt that many copies still exist of our report, in case you want to track one down it was: Shaw, M., D. Dorling, G. Davey Smith. 'Life Expectancy: A Research Report for Granada/Channel 4's *The Drop Dead Show*' (Bristol: University of Bristol, 1995). See also the booklet referenced below. We were not the only academics contributing. The show was not meant to be completely serious and featured the first live shit on TV when 'Roger the botty-doc' (I've forgotten his actual name) examined the stools of three contestants to declare which poo was healthiest. This was cutting-edge TV – all before Gillian McKeith made a TV living inspecting stools.

30 Although the introduction of good food rations for women and small children was the primary cause in the Second World War, the beneficial effect of war upon children was

also true of even earlier wars. See: Dwork, D. *War is Good for Babies and Other Young Children: A History of the Infant and Child Welfare Movement in England 1898–1918* (London and New York: Tavistock Publications, 1987).

31 These figures for life expectancy are from Table 2 'Period Life Expectancy at Age 65, 1991–3 and 2006–8' ONS news release 21 October 2009. www.statistics.gov.uk/pdfdir/liexnr1009.pdf

32 Dorling, D. and M. Shaw. 'Life Chances and Lifestyles', pp. 230, 243, 260, from V. Gardiner and H. Matthews, eds., *The Changing Geography of the UK* (London: Routledge, 2000).

33 Shaw, M., D. Dorling and G. Davey Smith. *Don't Drop Dead* (London: Channel 4 Television, 1998) (consultancy report published as book, ISBN 1 85144 209X). The questions also appear in Gardner and Matthews, eds., *The Changing Geography of the UK*. Incidentally, Mary went on to become a schoolteacher.

34 Marmot, M., *Status Syndrome, How Social Standing Affects Our Health and Longevity* (London: Bloomsbury, 2004). The social classes referred to here are the Marketing Organisation's A & B combined, C1, C2, D and E. Which are very similar to the Registrar General's I & II, IIINM, IIIM, IV and V, first defined around 1911 along with a few 'industrial classes'.

35 Komlos, J. and M. Baur, 'From the Tallest to (One of) the Fattest: the Enigmatic Fate of the American Population in the Twentieth Century' *Economics and Human Biology*, 2, 2004, pp. 57–74, see: http://ideas.repec.org/p/lmu/muenec/76.html. For older data look up the work of John Boyd Orr: www.rowett.ac.uk/institute/jbo/jbo3.html and also studies such as that held at the ESRC archive labelled 'SN 3546 -Heights and Weights of British School Children, 1908–1950' www.esds.ac.uk/findingData/snDescription.asp?sn=3546

36 Dorling, D. 'Unemployment and Health: Health Benefits Vary According to the Method of Reducing Unemployment'

BMJ, 2009, 338, b829. www.sasi.group.shef.ac.uk/publications/2009/dorling_BMJ_2009_authors_version.pdf

37 Brimblecombe, N., D. Dorling and M. Shaw, 'Mortality and Migration in Britain – First Results from the British Household Panel Survey', *Social Science and Medicine*, 1999, 40, 7, pp. 981–88. On New Zealand, see: Pearce, J. and D. Dorling. 'The Influence of Selective Migration Patterns among Smokers and Non-Smokers on Geographical Inequalities in Health' *Annals of the Association of American Geographers*, 2010, 100, 2, pp. 393–408. www.sheffield.ac.uk/geography/staff/dorling_danny/papers.html

38 Shaw, M. and D. Dorling. 'Mortality amongst Street-Sleeping Youth in the UK', *The Lancet*, 29 August 1998: 743 http://sasi.group.shef.ac.uk/publications/1998/shaw_and_dorling_street_sleeping.pdf

39 Later we used the same estimates to work out a simpler statistic: Shaw, M., R. Mitchell and D. Dorling. 'Time for a Smoke: One Cigarette Is Equivalent to 11 Minutes of Life Expectancy', *BMJ*, 2000, pp. 320–53. http://sasi.group.shef.ac.uk/publications/2000/shaw_BMJ_time_for_smoke.pdf

40 These areas listed are the old European parliamentary constituency areas where people experienced the highest mortality rates from liver disease according to deaths recorded between 1996 and 2000 inclusive. The data used to make this assertion is available here: www.sasi.group.shef.ac.uk/hguk/files/Chapter7_figs.xls

41 On Sheffield and Hull see Thomas, B. and D. Dorling. *Identity in Britain: A Cradle-to-Grave Atlas*, (Bristol: Policy Press, 2007). Page 147 (and page 185 for those aged 40–59; younger adults cycle even less than those aged 25–59).

42 Poor Davina wasn't coping very well at this point although I like to think that putting her through this proved the real-life audition that secured her the job on *Street-Mate* (we can all fantasize)!

43 It was a story from the credit-reference agency Experian that resulted in the 1 March 2004 BBC headline: 'Britain's Fattest Areas Revealed – Researchers Say the "Fattest" Cities Have Too Many Chip Shops – Hull is the Chubbiest Town in Britain – While Kingston upon Thames is the Leanest, an Obesity League Table Has Revealed, http://news.bbc.co.uk/1/hi/health/3521551.stm

44 BBC headline 6 October 2009: 'Injecting Drug Users Rise by 30% – The number of injecting drug users in Scotland is continuing to increase, according to the latest figures'. http://news.bbc.co.uk/1/hi/scotland/8292817.stm

45 Intriguingly the study is only of men, but the email of the corresponding author is given at the top of the paper should you wish to inquire further about where the estimates for women came from: Davey Smith, G., S. Frankel and J. Yarnell 'Sex and Death: Are They Related? Findings from the Caerphilly Cohort Study', *BMJ* 1997;315:1641–1644. www.bmj.com/cgi/content/abstract/315/7123/1641

46 The Tennyson quote from the poem *Memoriam: 27*, if the musings of one man's blog about his journey into what he calls 'extremely average' woodworking are to be believed (it is amazing what you find on the web), see: http://extremelyaverage.com/tag/alfred-lord-tennyson/

47 You can find a map here: www.sasi.group.shef.ac.uk/hguk/fig4 5.htm and much more. This is on the website of the research group I work with. Incidentally, very shortly after we created the Spatial and Social Inequalities website at Sheffield (SASI) the 'SaSi Intelligent Vibrator' was launched by *JeJoue* (those French again). I sometimes wondered whether we received many hits to our website from women looking for something else (and vice versa). The vibrator is called 'intelligent' because apparently it remembers what each woman prefers. Who needs men anymore?

48 'North-South Health Divide "widening"', BBC, 2 December 1999, repeated the claim that 'The north-south divide in standards of health and wealth is at its widest since records began'. http://news.bbc.co.uk/1/hi/health/545517.stm

49 'Blair: North-South Divide "a myth"', BBC, 5 December 1999 http://news.bbc.co.uk/1/hi/uk politics/550520.stm

50 Lee, C. *Home: A Personal Geography of Sheffield*, (Sheffield: Fou Fou Publishing, 2009).

Chapter 2: Where Have All the Good Men Gone?

1   From the 2001 film adaptation of the book, *Bridget Jones's Diary* by Helen Fielding, (London: Picador, 1996).

2   Michaels, S. 'Lily Allen to Score Bridget Jones musical? Singer rumoured to be writing songs for forthcoming stage adaptation of Helen Fielding's novel', *Guardian*, 2 June 2010, www.guardian.co.uk/music/2010/jun/02/lily-allen-bridget-jones-musical

3   Headline in the *Independent* newspaper, 19 January 2003: www.independent.co.uk/news/uk/home-news/speeddating-boom-hit-by-shortage-of-men-602176.html Tellingly it was written anonymously and the article celebrated travel and spending as superior to settling down: 'I probably don't look like the typical single 34-year-old. I dress sharply and expensively, because no one wants to look like a victim when people are expecting them to.' Anonymous.

4   'What I'm Really Thinking: The Single Woman – It's been four years since I had a relationship, and I've developed into a conscious and proud singleton', *Guardian*, 25 September 2010. www.guardian.co.uk/lifeandstyle/2010/sep/25/single-woman-what-really-thinking

5   The authors of the study are being quoted in 'Cancer Rate in Fallujah Worse than Hiroshima' by Tom Eley, *Teheran Times*, 25 July 2010. www.tehrantimes.com/index_View.asp?code=223580

6   Data given in chapter 2 of Dorling, D. *The Human Geography of the UK*, (London: Sage, 2005); and online at: www.sasi.group.shef.ac.uk/hguk/chapter2.htm

7   Looking at the longer record 1973 may be the year of the greatest ever surplus of baby boys over girls. Previous record years had been 1944, when it was generally known

the war would be won by the allies (6.6 more boys born for every 100 girls) and 1919 (6 more boys than girls per 100 born).

8   On notable hermits, only one woman is listed in this popular source, is that because of surplus boys?: http://en.wikipedia.org/wiki/Hermit#Notable_hermits

9   Catalnao, R. and T. Bruckner. 'Secondary Sex Ratios and Male Lifespan: Damaged or Culled Cohorts', Proceedings of the National Academy of Sciences, 2006, 103, 5, 1639–43 www.ncbi.nlm.nih.gov/pmc/articles/PMC1360590/pdf/pnas-0510567103.pdf (page 1639).

10   Thomas, B. and D. Dorling. *Identity in Britain: A Cradle-to-Grave Atlas*, (Bristol: Policy Press, 2007).

11   Data given in chapter 2 of Dorling, D. *The Human Geography of the UK*, (London: Sage, 2005); and online at: www.sasi.group.shef.ac.uk/hguk/chapter4.htm

12   In fact life expectancies are lower in Glasgow, but it is part of a country not, in effect, a separate state. Channel 4 checked the oft quoted 'fact' recently and found it to be true, but also of other poor countries too: www.channel4.com/news/articles/society/health/factcheck+glasgow+worse+than+gaza/2320267

13   Remember tape decks? Should you be under 30, or from another planet and need some details: the tape was made of cellulose acetate coated with iron oxide. Remember Chesney? His name conjures up one of the most famous anagrams of the time. You do have to substitute 'n' and 'r' for 'h' and 's', but early 1990s teenagers were happy to play such games, they didn't have access to the web then.

14   The 'Estimating with Confidence' project for making small area population estimates in Britain was funded by the ESRC from September 1993 to September 1996, under its 'Analysis of Large and Complex Datasets' programme. Co-directors: Ian Diamond (then) at the University of Southampton and Ludi Simpson (then) at the University of Manchester. For details see: www.ccsr.ac.uk/research/ewcpop.htm

15 To translate, for any future historian who has stumbled across a discarded copy of this book (or any of the MP3/4 generation reading today), a CD, a Compact Disc, was an object made of polycarbonate plastic upon which music was recorded in digital form. S Club were also manufactured. They were an object made of seven carbon-based human life-forms selected from auditioning 10,000 hopefuls.

16 Large numbers of young people even rioted in small towns like Gothenburg where the demonstrations against the World Trade Organization took place in summer 2001. These resulted in fifty years of prison sentences being awarded, see: http://en.wikipedia.org/wiki/Protests_during_the_EU_summit_in_Gothenburg 2001#Statistics. And, in proportion to the size of the town these protests were bigger even than the poll-tax riots of London, again police provoked, but in March 1990. See: http://en.wikipedia.org/wiki/Poll_Tax_Riots

17 The 2001 Census Coverage Survey was undertaken by over 4,000 field staff who interviewed people in 320,000 households: www.statistics.gov.uk/census2001/proj_ccs.asp

18 These figures and many maps of the changing characteristics of the UK's people are in: Dorling, D. and B. Thomas. *People and Places: A 2001 Census Atlas of the UK* (Bristol: Policy Press, 2004).

19 An LP was a long-playing record. It was made of vinyl and was circular in shape, although square ones worked too, apparently because the tracks on them were circular and the corners of the squares were unused. Soon audio tape, CDs and MP3s will be as archaic objects as the LP is today and perhaps as the idea of surplus men will be, too, unless we become more equal and less stressed.

20 According to the BBC, he said, 'Go around the country, go to the industrial towns, go to the farms and you will see a state of prosperity such as we have never had in my lifetime – nor indeed in the history of this country'. In this volume I rely on the report referred to by Ian Herbert two notes below on p244, to explain why July 1957 was not so great,

and hence why people had *not* really *never* had it so good then: http://news.bbc.co.uk/onthisday/hi/dates/stories/july/20/newsid_3728000/3728225.stm

21 Remember that the early 1970s Conservatives then were far to the left of 1990s New Labour.

This was the time when the majority of the population or at least the younger population, apart from those minorities who discovered Funk and similar 1970s treasures (sadly now too often forgotten). The high point, in 1976, was: http://en.wikipedia.org/wiki/Give Up the Funk (Tear the Roof off the Sucker)

22 As reported by Ian Herbert in the *Independent* 17 March 2004, 'the New Economics Foundation (NEF) think-tank, which has adjusted the official gross domestic product (GDP) to provide a more accurate sense of well-being, insists that the year represents a golden age of lower crime, lower energy consumption and less global destruction'. www.independent.co.uk/news/uk/this-britain/1976-when-national-happiness-peaked-566594.html

23 On Mary Poppinses: Dorling, D., *New Social Atlas of Britain*, (Chichester: Wiley, 1995), p. 54 (available free online).

24 In fact, in London the national proportion of all graduates in the UK who lived in that one city had risen steadily from 1971 onwards, despite it becoming harder and harder to fit all the extra graduates in as graduate numbers were rising rapidly overall. By 2001 there were over half a million graduates living in the old Euro-constituencies of central- and south-inner London alone, more in the rest of the capital. See: http://www.sasi.group.shef.ac.uk/hguk/chapter3.htm (see figures 3.9 and 3.10).

25 That post-census imputation was possible at all was largely thanks to people like Kate filling in their post-enumeration surveys, but hundreds of thousands of young men still appeared to have left Britain even after including those imputed. My friend Carl tells me that they were called 'Ibiza man', but far more were most probably in

Rotterdam, Utrecht, Hamburg or on the Costas than in Goa, Koh Phangan, Punte del Este, or wherever else the latest place to be might be.

26 Just to recap: capture-recapture works by taking a large sample, say a census. Then, a few weeks later, you take a second smaller sample of the population. You then match the records. By knowing the proportions of people caught in one survey but not the other, and the proportions caught in both, it is possible to estimate the numbers caught in neither. The method is best known as the mechanism to estimate the numbers of whales surviving in the southern oceans. Whales are harpooned and then released when tagged. If a tag is found on a newly harpooned whale then capture-recapture has worked and the estimates can be made for the whale population as a whole. The maths is wonderfully simple, if all is independent: n=mc/r where n is population to be estimated, m is first capture total, c is second capture total, and r is the number captured at both times. For further details and why it is not always as simple as that, especially with clever humans, see: http://en.wikipedia.org/wiki/Mark_and_recapture

27 Chesney Hawkes has an official website now (something else which was not possible in 1991); however, the news on that hasn't been updated since February 2009, when he entered Ant and Dec's prison. The website does report that he was playing Skegness Butlins on May 2010 and Bognor Butlins later in the year. See: www.chesneyhawkes.co.uk

28 The London graduate job count is a claim substantiated in Dorling, D. *The Human Geography of the UK*, (London: Sage, 2005). Chapter 3. The conveyor belt of graduates to London ran continuously from 1986 onwards, speeding up every year, taking more and more in, while more and more adults in their forties left London.

29 Coughlan, S., 'Majority of Young Women in University', BBC, 31 March 2010: http://news.bbc.co.uk/1/hi/education/8596504.stm

30   ONS 'Wealth in Great Britain: Main Results, 2006/08 Executive Summary', (2010), page xxiv, www.statistics.gov. uk/downloads/theme economy/wealth-assets-2006-2008/ Exec_Sum_Wealth-in_GB_2006_2008.pdf

31   Belief in God is on the rise again in Britain, particularly in some of our poorest areas so it would not appear to be a lack of religious fervour that correlates with too much debt and shopping.

32   The 2021 census would not cost a penny until the end of the Government's period of office (2015 at the latest). There is a good chance the 2021 census will be reprieved. However, it might take an army of far-sighted family and local historians to achieve this rather than ineffectual demographers.

33   Sherlock , T., 'Scrapping Long Form Will Be Hot Topic as Statisticians Meet', *Vancouver Sun*, 28 July 2010 www. vancouversun.com/technology/Scrapping+long+form+will +topic+statisticians+meet/3331194/story.html

34   United National Statistical Division, 2010, World Population and Housing Census Programme (online): 'The 2010 World Programme is primarily aimed at ensuring that each Member State conducts a population and housing census at least once in the period from 2005 to 2014 and disseminates the results': http://unstats.un.org/unsd/ demographic/sources/census/2010 PHC/more.htm

35   Barford, A. et al., 'Life Expectancy: Women Now on Top Everywhere. During 2006, even in the poorest countries, women can expect to outlive men', *BMJ*, 2006 April 8; 332(7545): 808, Public domain version: www.ncbi.nlm. nih.gov/pmc/articles/PMC1432200/

36   Table 2 of the *United Nations Demographic Year Book, 2007*. Estimates of population and its percentage distribution, by age and sex and sex ratio for all ages for the world, major areas and regions: last updated 9 October 2009: http://unstats.un.org/unsd/demographic/products/dyb/ dyb2007/Table02.pdf Just as this book was going to press the 2008 figures were released: 3,404 million men, and

3,347 million women, the gap had increased by a million on the figures reported for 2007, well within any margin of error, but no great sign of improvement during that first year of worldwide economic recession, see: http://unstats.un.org/ unsd/demographic/products/dyb/dyb2008/Table02.pdf

37 Ahmed, H. from the Asociated Press, 2 August 2010, 'Iraq: 8 Killed on Day Obama to Outline New Mission'. All this makes me wonder if there will one day be an envoy from the US attending remembrance ceremonies in Fallujah in sixty-five years' time. By October 2010 the best place to find the article was on an Israeli news site: http://www. ynetnews.com/articles/0,7340,L-3928936,00.html

38 McLendon, R. from the Associated Press, 16 July 2010, 'Speed Dating Gets Revival among 20-Somethings'. The story is at the ABC news website still, as of October 2010 when I last checked: http://abcnews.go.com/Entertainment/ wireStory?id=11182135

39 Updated figures for England and Wales since 2000 come from ONS Table 1.1: 'Live births, occurrence within/out- side marriage and sex, 1998–2008' http://www.statistics. gov.uk/downloads/theme   population/FM1-37/FM1   37 2008.pdf and from GRO(S) Tables 3 and 11 given in the eight annual publications on births available here: http:// www.gro-scotland.gov.uk/statistics/publications-and-data/ vital-events/index.html

40 'Auf Wiedersehen, Pet first touched our funny bones when it appeared on TV screens in 1983. Featuring an intrepid band of British brickies trying their luck on building sites in Germany and Spain, the show was an instant hit.' BBC, TV on Tyne, 22 October 2008: www.bbc.co.uk/tyne//content/ articles/2008/05/29/auf wiedersehen pet feature.shtml

Chapter 3: When Enough is Enough – Optimum Population

1 Wilson, Graeme, 'An Extra 196,000 People Flooded into Britain last Year, New Figures Revealed last Night', the *Sun*, 27 August 2010, www.thesun.co.uk/sol/homepage/

news/3113659/UK-is-the-2nd-most-congested-nation-in-EU-behind-Malta.html?OTC-RSS&ATTR=News

2   'Mass car driving is the simplest example of what happens when greed begins to be valued in its own right. When you next look at a congested street, with cars jostling to move a few metres forward, pedestrians dodging in between, cyclists weaving dangerously around them, children walking past at the level of exhaust pipes, no one getting anywhere fast, and all those petrol engines continuously running, this is both the symbolic but also very real collective outcome of individual greed encouraged to grow by the mantra of personal freedom.' Dorling, D., 'Ideas in Place of Fear: Reducing Inequality and Fermenting Justice', Compass Think Piece, number 57, (London: Compass, 2010), p. 6. www.equalitytrust.org.uk/docs/ctpdorlinginequality.pdf

3   One influential report to Government in 1973 explained that the 'concept of "optimum" population was originally conceived in economic terms: i.e. that population which would produce maximum income per head, or per household, from given economic resources. Other definitions of "optimum" relate to subjective assessments of "optimum" density or to criteria such as "national self sufficiency" . . . Britain has not been self sufficient . . . for centuries, so that any attempt to calculate the size of population which would be consistent with self-sufficiency is difficult, if not impossible.' Report of the Population Panel, March 1973, Cmnd 5258. Paragraph 381.

4   Connelly, M., *Fatal Misconception: The Struggle to Control World Population*, (Massachusetts, Harvard University Press, 2008), p. 70. . . . reporting the mathematically ornate musings of Henry Pratt Fairchild.

5   *Ibid.* (on pp. 90 and 411), and also referring to Sir John Megaw, later the Director General of the Indian medical service, who complained that the population 'multiply like rabbits and die like flies'.

6   Laughlin, J. M., 'The Evolution of Modern Demography and the Debate on Sustainable Development', *Antipode,* 1999,

31(3): pp. 324–33 (p. 329 quoting from Ehrlich's 1968 'Population Bomb').

7   Select Committee of the House of Commons on Science and Technology, first report of the 1970–1 session on the population of the United Kingdom, House of Commons paper 379, May 1971. Some thirty-eight years later, in March 2009 The Royal Commission on Environmental Pollution announced it would again study the implications of future demographic change. I gave evidence to that commission, due to report in early 2011. Thankfully its members knew all about this past set of errors and understanding.

8   Report of the Population Panel, March 1973, Cmnd 5258. Paragraph 333. The next paragraph continued: 'Noise, particularly from road and air traffic, is felt to be a serious and growing nuisance. It is not, however, mainly a population problem. Rising standards of living have contributed much more than rising population to the increase in noise levels.'

9   Not all demographic accounting is about imaginary beings. Real people are the net sum of births less deaths. That is us. The more that are born and the fewer that die, the more of us there are. That is the *real* part of the demographic equation. The *imaginary* part, just like the imaginary part of a complex number in mathematics, is useful for making calculations, but is not something you can see. You need to know about complex numbers in maths to know why $e^{i\pi} = -1$. The numbers e and π are real, i is the imaginary number that connects them. Births and deaths are real, net migration is the imaginary number that connects them in balancing out the equation that tells us how many people there are.

10 The deficit occurs when the tap is on but the plug is pulled out. Even with the tap kept running, if the plug is out then eventually all the water would drain out. In practise, just as in your bath, the plug tends to be put back in when the water level has gone down a little: fewer people leave after many have left.

11 There is a basic rule of reciprocity. It features in all the

world's religions and in all the most successful and sustainable social movements. For a great historic guide to the rule read Henry Tam's *Against Power Inequalities: Reflections on the Struggle for Inclusive Communities*, (2010), made available for free at www.equalitytrust.org.uk/resources/against-power-inequalities

12   The phrase was used by the *Sun* on 6 May 2010 when the headline ran: 'If Brown Wins Today Will the Last Person to Leave Britain Please Turn Out the Lights', aping their headline from eighteen years earlier naming Kinnock in place of Brown, and then placing Kinnock's head in a light bulb. The *Telegraph* gave Brown the same treatment in 2009. If Ed Miliband does well he should expect similar treatment: www.telegraph.co.uk/news/newstopics/politics/labour/5215414/Will-the-last-person-to-leave-Gordon-Browns-Britain-turn-out-the-lights.html

13   At times the story referred to 'Britain' in the text, but at other times (and in the headline) to the 'UK'. The story's headline appears in quotation marks at the head of this chapter, the reference is in the first endnote to this chapter, referring to the piece in the *Sun* written by Graeme Wilson, tellingly its Deputy Political Editor. The word 'England' did not appear once in the story, even though that is the area of higher density.

14   Migration Watch (undated), 'Economic 1.7: Inquiry into Economic Migration to the EU, from Sir Andrew Green KCMG, Chairman, Migration Watch UK', possibly first drafted in June 2005 given the footnote at the end of the document. See: www.migrationwatchuk.org/briefingPaper/document/9

15   The quotation is drawn from point 12b found in that Migration Watch document 'Economic 1.7'. It is possible that the writer of this did not consider Belgium to be a country and thought England was an EU member state (the UK is). In February 2010 the former leader of UKIP, who favours the Migration Watch approach, announced that he agreed that Belgium was not a country as far as

he was concerned: 'Farage Defiant after Calling Belgium "a non-country"', BBC, 26 February 2010, http://news. bbc.co.uk/1/hi/8538281.stm (Nigel Farage was formerly a member of the Conservative party, but left a couple of years after Margaret Thatcher was deposed).

16   Incidentally, but importantly, the story of the population density of the Netherlands recently reported as not having risen as much as it has in England almost certainly owes more to the Netherlands registering the location of its citizens so accurately than it does to any real extra increase in people there. The Netherlands' population registers include even the locations of those living abroad (who register with their local embassy). The Dutch authorities have a better idea about how many Dutch people are resident in England than do the English have of the English! The English tend to constantly overestimate how many people live in England, including how many British citizens have not left.

17   In the United States some 60 per cent of the population gave to charity in 2010, the same proportion as in Switzerland. The people of the Netherlands were the second most likely to give (77 per cent of them). See: Fischer, M.S. 'CAF America's World Giving Index Ranks US Fifth Most Charitable', *Investment Advisor* magazine, 9 September 2010, www. investmentadvisor.com/news/2010/9/Pages/CAFAmericas -World-Giving-Index-Ranks-US-Fifth-Most-Charitable. aspx The survey also suggested that 73 per cent of folk in the UK gave to charity each year, more than the Swiss and Americans who on average live at lower population densities. For more information and some ideas as to why some people give more than others, see: The World Giving Index 2010: www.cafamerica.org/dnn/Portals/0/Press%20 Releases/World%20Giving%20Index%20Final%20 Report.pdf

18   There are many sources of data on who is living in Malta, the most succinct suggests that 'there are minorities, the largest of which are British people, many of whom retired to

Malta'. This quotation is taken from: http://en.wikipedia.
org/wiki/Malta#Population (as of October 2010).

19 We get 780 square metres by not rounding everything to
the nearest metre; $780 = (1000/\sqrt{1282})^2$.

20 Mason, C., 'England "most crowded in Europe"', BBC,
16 September 2008. http://news.bbc.co.uk/nol/ukfs_news/
hi/newsid_7610000/newsid_7618900/7618994.stm.
On London: 'The region covers an area of 1,579 square
kilometres (610 sq mi). The population density is 4,542
inhabitants per square kilometre' http://en.wikipedia.org/
wiki/London#Demography. On Westminster, 'Density
10,988/km² http://en.wikipedia.org/wiki/City of West-
minster#Demography. On Catalonia, 'The Urban Region
of Barcelona includes 5,217,864 people and covers an
area of 2.268 km²' http://en.wikipedia.org/wiki/Catalonia;
and on Barcelona specifically see the website at: http://
en.wikipedia.org/wiki/Barcelona#Population_Density
where the claim is made that there are some '936,406 people living at an average density of 40,322 inhabitants per
square kilometre'.

21 The number 1572km² comes from http://en.wikipedia.org/
wiki/London. I checked it by using the formula for working out the radius of a circle when given its area ($a = \pi r^2$),
which suggests that the radius of London, the distance from
its centre to edge, is on average 22.4 km, or roughly where
the M25 lies.

22 The data I used on road length can be found at: www.
worldmapper.org/display.php?selected=35

23 In some ways Monaco is more a casino, race track and tax
exile's hangout than a city. Many of its affluent residents
have a home elsewhere and so for them it is less densely
populated, but not for their housekeepers or all the other
people needed to make life very comfortable for those with
great wealth.

24 Now there's a useless fact concerning laying the residents
of Monaco head to tail on their roads – which no one has
yet entered in Wikipedia. It's also not a very true fact.

Only 16 per cent of the population of Monaco are native Monégasques (which means born there, or whose mother was born there or whose father or father's father or father's father's father, ever backwards, was born there). The other 84 per cent are immigrant 'Monacoians', mostly French, but you can't help wondering if that is not a word that was invented within a single Wikipedia entry – and now it's published in print (here) it *exists* and the OED can list it! See: http://en.wikipedia.org/wiki/Monaco for where that new word first appeared in the ether, and on citizenship (should you wish to dodge your tax obligations), see: www.monaco-consulate.com/index.php/useful-links/monegasque-citizenship/

25   These maps are Prints XLV and XLVII from my PhD thesis, see them, along with both maps on the normal equal area projection: www.sasi.group.shef.ac.uk/thesis/prints.html

26   The population density numbers here are taken from a date around 2002, which remains the most recent date of widely available reliable information for many countries in the world. www.worldmapper.org (see maps 1 and 35 and the notes to them on further data sources).

27   What is even worse is that individual decision making occurs in such a way that if just one person thinks it is worth building a home on the edge of town, that extra home gets built; thus a free-market approach to city planning results in the most irrational of individuals taking the lead.

28   The first report recommending huge cuts was released by Richard Beeching in 1963. Over 1,000 miles of track were closed in 1964 alone. The new Labour government elected in that year reduced the speed of the cuts but did not stop them. The cuts saved very little money as most of the lines cut were making only very small losses. Half of all rail stations in Britain were closed. The overall result was to dramatically curtail rail use for both freight and passengers. Once people had to drive to a station, why not continue driving to their final destination?

29   The Optimum Population Trust (OPT) is a membership

organization, but its trustees are elected by 'guarantor members'. Its website does not explain the difference between members by status. Maybe the 'guarantor members' are some optimum number of individuals, identified by some arcane mathematical formula for the 'perfect' solution? www.optimumpopulation.org/opt.aboutus.html

30 The OPT trustee list goes on and on and does sound very grand, although it is dominated by aging, affluent semi-aristocratic white men with the exception of Lady Kulukundis whose appeal, apparently, 'has always been that of an "English rose"'. http://en.wikipedia.org/wiki/Susan_Hampshire. Her husband's entry may be a little more accurate: 'My luck, is that my parents were very wealthy' it reports him as saying here: http://en.wikipedia.org/wiki/Eddie_Kulukundis (as of October 2010).

31 The claim on overpopulation can be found here, in the Trust's news release of 8 July 2010: www.optimumpopulation.org/releases/opt.release08Jul10.htm

32 Of course, they may have other ideas not on their website. The estimate of 555 is derived by knowing that 60 times $0.9975^{555} = 15$. Multiplying by 0.9975 is to reduce by a quarter per cent.

33 See endnote 1, Chapter 1 (page 232). These percentages come from www.worldmapper.org maps 2 and 5.

34 Our congestion is caused by our behaviour, not by our numbers. But it is very unlikely that any 'Lord', 'Lady' or 'Sir' will fund or front an organization that questions the status quo. Even those without titles find this way of thinking very hard. George Orwell suggested (sixty-six years ago) that it was wrong to believe that our amassing of wealth was a result of our own labours, and it was that which resulted in the high value of our land. He commented that 'the chief danger of the situation lies in the fact that the English people have never been made to grasp that the sources of their prosperity lie outside England'. He then said that this was 'incompatible with the spirit of Socialism' and that the source of the problem was unambiguous: 'the parochial

outlook of the Labour Party itself is largely responsible for this'. Gerry Hassan, who recently made this point, suggests that Orwell concluded that, with the odd exception, he had 'never met an English Socialist who would face it'. *As I Please 1943–1945: Collected Essays, Journalism and Letters of George Orwell: Volume Three*, (London: Secker and Warburg, 1968). As quoted by Hassan, G. in 'After "New Britain": The Strange Death of "the Labour Nation"', in *Renewal: A Journal of Social Democracy*, autumn 2010. www.gerryhassan.com/?p=1374

35   I think we should behave as we would like others to treat us, but also without being sure of the outcome, and to see where it takes us. In the *British Medical Journal* recently, such an approach was questioned, the approach of 'the intuitively attractive Australian Aboriginal saying: "Traveller, there is no path, paths are made by walking." But surely we now know enough to put an occasional signpost in the sand?' Stott, R., 'How Can We Rediscover the Magic of More Equal Societies? *BMJ*, 4 August 2010, 341 c4155, doi: 10.1136/bmj.c415. I think we can put a signpost down when it comes to population – for as long as we see each as our enemy and competitor, we are doomed.

36   In how many people can be fitted in, my first research paper concerned housing. See next endnote directly below for the reference to that work.

37   It is possible that we had fewer bedrooms per person just after the terrible effects of the Black Death, but housing statistics then were even worse than today. What we know today of our housing stock is not great. We do not routinely measure floor space in surveys and censuses. We do not know who owns every property, or what can be used as a bedroom, what really is empty or not. For all these reasons I am vague on exactly how many rooms we each have, but I began my academic career looking at housing need and supply and I have a feeling I might end it that way: Dorling, D. 'The Demand for Housing in Britain 1971–2001', NE.RRL research report, (CURDS: The University

of Newcastle upon Tyne, 1991). More recently: Dorling, D., 'Daylight Robbery: There's no shortage of housing, the stock has just been shared out abysmally – and that's the fault of the market', *Roof Magazine*, 2009, 34, 3, 11. See: www.sasi.group.shef.ac.uk/publications/commentary/dorling_2009-05_roof.pdf

38   The 200,000 second home figure is from Moran, J., *On Roads: A Hidden History*, (London: Profile Books, 2010), p. 73.

39   On Dave's request to not be made out as 'a prat', see: 'Who is David Cameron?' www.timesonline.co.uk/tol/news/politics/article6267193.ece?token=null&offset=84&page=8).

40   On world population projections see page 210 of this volume, referring to the *Econonmist*

41   If all this is new to you, please read Mike Davis's *Late Victorian Holocausts: El Niño Famines and the Making of the Third World*, (London: Verso, 2002). For more on that book see the web here: http://en.wikipedia.org/wiki/Late_Victorian_Holocausts and for more on Mike and how well he writes see here: http://en.wikipedia.org/wiki/Mike_Davis_(scholar) (both as accessed in October 2010).

42   For a good introduction to how many environmental niches humans now occupy, from a (University of California) geographer who is less sanguine than I am about higher populations being possible, see Jared Diamond's *Collapse: How Societies Choose to Fail or Succeed*, (London: Allen Lane, 2005). More details can be found here: http://en.wikipedia.org/wiki/Collapse:_How_Societies_Choose_to_Fail_or_Succeed

43   For the best assumptions I have been able to find of where the estimated 230 million humans alive 2,000 years ago lived, see Worldmapper Map 7: Population in the Year 1, and my technical notes to that webpage that are to be found here: www.worldmapper.org/display.php?selected=7

Chapter 4: Overkeen, Underpaid and
Over Here – Immigration

1   Transcript: Gordon Brown's exchange with Gillian Duffy, *The Times*, 28 April 2010, www.timesonline.co.uk/tol/news/politics/article7110540.ece

2   Collins, L., A. Chapman and S. Walters, 'Gordon won't be getting my vote: Gillian Duffy reveals what REALLY upset her about that devastating exchange with PM', *Mail on Sunday*, 2 May 2010 www.dailymail.co.uk/news/article-1270337/Gordon-wont-getting-vote-Gillian-Duffy-reveals-REALLY-upset-devastating-exchange-PM.html

3   Flynn, D., R. Ford and W. Somerville, 'Immigration and the Election', *Renewal*, 2010, 18, 3/4, 102–114 (table 1). www.renewal.org.uk/articles/immigration-and-the-election. The paper reports from the British Election Study that 47 per cent of voters said the economy was the most important issue for them, 14.3 per cent that it was immigration, 5.2 per cent crime, 5.1 per cent unemployment, and 3 per cent consumer debt.

4   The commitment to lowering immigration numbers appeared in the 'Programme for Government', announced on 20 May 2010, which stated that: 'We will introduce an annual limit on the number of non-EU economic migrants admitted into the UK to live and work. We will consider jointly the mechanism for implementing the limit.'

     On 18 November 2010, the migration advisory committee recommended just reducing Tier 1 migration by one quarter of its limit to achieve this.

5   Rawstorne, T., 'Some Ordinary Northerner! How Nick Clegg is really a man of extraordinary privilege whose family own a chateau', *Daily Mail*, 24 April 2010, www.dailymail.co.uk/news/article-1268436/Some-ordinary-northerner-How-Nick-Clegg-really-man-extraordinary-privilege-family-chateau.html

6   See the blog 'Salut!' described as 'Colin Randall on France, current affairs, travel, the media – and more besides', where

a journalist staying at the same resort as Dave Cameron's parents reports on the kind of place it is and on those who stay there: www.francesalut.com/2010/09/david-camer-sons-father-and-one-of-lifes-odder-coincidences-1.html

7   But, just as with the spending cuts of that year, this regret at 'having' to introduce legislation so quickly appeared to be tinged with a sense of glee at finally getting to do what some had wanted to do for so long and would now be doing at breakneck pace. This became obvious on 20 October 2010 when measures were announced among the £81 billion cuts of the 'spending review' that would effectively clear poorer people from living in affluent cities. Two weeks earlier one minister had suggested that these would be as effective as the Highland Clearances had been in previous centuries, those acts by lairds, often based in London, which forced so many poorer Scottish people to emigrate. As changes to housing benefit and council housing rents were revealed it became obvious that clearance would again be the effect. See: Murphy, J. 'Welfare Cuts "Will be like the Highland Clearances"', *Evening Standard*, 7 October 2010: www.thisislondon.co.uk/standard/article-23885725-welfare-cuts-will-be-like-the-highland-clearances.do

8   The word 'regret' appeared in the 'Statement of changes in immigration rules' laid before Parliament on 15 July 2010 under section 3(2) of the Immigration Act 1971 ordered by The House of Commons, to be printed 15 July 2010: www.ukba.homeoffice.gov.uk/sitecontent/documents/policyand-law/statementsofchanges/2010/hc96.pdf?view=Binary

9   Migration Advisory Committee, 'Consultation by the Migration Advisory Committee on the Level of an Annual Limit on Economic Migration to the UK', June 2010, p. 3, para. 1.3: www.ukba.homeoffice.gov.uk/sitecontent/documents/aboutus/workingwithus/mac/mac-consultation-annual-limit/

10   'Why the breakneck speed' was the thought that kept crossing my mind when I was being 'consulted' by the

government-appointed Migration Advisory Committee (MAC) on Friday, 3 September, with just four days to go before the deadline. It struck me, and so I said: that all the haste appeared to reflect a concern that if they were not seen to act this fast then government would be unable to try to claim credit for when net migrant numbers inevitably fell, as the recession bit deeper.

11 I have used birth and death records to estimate that some 2,000,433 more people born between the years 1876 and 1920 inclusive left Britain and died elsewhere, than came here and died here. This means of estimating is only reliable for events in the past where most of the people affected are now dead, but it can be combined with population projections to see how plausible are future estimates of immigration. For examples of the method in use see: Dorling, D., 'Migration: A long-run perspective', (London: IPPR, 2009). www.ippr.org/publicationsandreports/publication.asp?id=660

12 The dismissal of Enoch Powell's speech as evil appeared in *The Times*, 22 April 1968, Editorial Comment. 'Enoch's speech helped strengthen the growth of fascist groups in Britain'. For details: http://en.wikipedia.org/wiki/Enoch_Powell#cite_note-62

13 All these net migration figures are calculated for England and Wales from publicly available data provided via the world's human-mortality database: www.mortality.org

14 On the effect of the poll tax on census enumeration see: Dorling, D. and S. Simpson, 'Gone and Forgotten? The census's missing one-and-a-half million', Environment and Planning A, 1994, Commentary, 26(8), pp. 1172–3. Copy available here: http://sasi.group.shef.ac.uk/publications/1994/dorling_and_simpson_1994.pdf

15 On the 'academic analysis' referred to see: Simpson, S. and D. Dorling, 'Those Missing Millions: Implications for Social Statistics of Non-Response to the 1991 Census'. *Journal of Social Policy*, 1994, 23(4), pp. 543–67.

16 On people 'going abroad undetected' see: Dorling, D.,

A New Social Atlas of Britain, (Chichester: Wiley, 1995) p. 14, table 1.13. An online version is available via www. shef.ac.uk/sasi

17   See endnote on page 245 for a reminder of what the capture-recapture technique is. A population register would have been far easier, but to get a register you have to have a government you trust, as the Dutch have, otherwise you get a 'No2ID' campaign, as we had (the anti-identity card and population-register movement).

18   The name 'McJobs' is used to describe work such as that in a McDonald's restaurant and to juxtapose such tasks with the dream 'Apple Mac' jobs of the so called 'creatives'. Hence 'McJobs' and 'MacJobs' are very different.

19   The long quotation is taken from: Dorling, D., 'How Many of Us Are There and Where Are We? A Simple Independent Validation of the 2001 Census and Its Revisions', Environment and Planning A, 2007 39, pp. 1024–44. Open access copy at:

      www.sasi.group.shef.ac.uk/publications/2007/dorling_how_many.pdf

20   Browne, A., 'UK Population Soars above 60 million', *Observer*, 26 August 2001. For a letter on the article see: www.guardian.co.uk/news/2001/sep/02/letters.theobserver1

21   Carvel, J., 'UK Population is Poised to Pass 60m', *Guardian*, 10 September 2004. www.guardian.co.uk/society/2004/sep/10/britishidentityandsociety.uknews

22   The story was originally located here: www.telegraph. co.uk/news/main.jhtml?xml=/news/2006/08/24/upopulation.xml – but can now be found on the BBC source that the *Telegraph* reporter most probably used: BBC News, 24 August 2006: http://news.bbc.co.uk/1/hi/uk/5281360.stm

23   http://news.bbc.co.uk/1/hi/8224520.stm and duly reported in the *Telegraph* as Whitehead, T., 'Baby Boom Sees UK Population Pass 61 Million', 27August 2009.

24   Wanting your child to be the 'millionth' individual is a very sad pastime, I know. By the way, the chance that the 60-millionth or 61-millionth resident of Britain entered hidden in

the back of the lorry is even lower than the chance of it being a newborn. The 62-millionth most probably came through Heathrow's newly opened Terminal 5 rather than Terminal 3.

25   Ware, J., 'Crammed Britain: And why no politician is being honest about the devastating consequences of immigration, *Daily Mail*, 21 April 2010, www.dailymail.co.uk/debate/election/article-1267128/General-Election-2010-UK-population-hit-70m--immigration.html

26   Curtis, P., 'Gordon Brown calls Labour supporter a "bigoted woman"', *Guardian*, 28 April 2010, www.guardian.co.uk/politics/2010/apr/28/gordon-brown-bigoted-woman

27   I think the BBC became desperately scared that if they did not turn to the Right then the new coalition government would privatize them: 'Can the UK Cope with a 78m Population?', BBC, 13 July 2010, http://www.bbc.co.uk/blogs/haveyoursay/2010/07/what_will_be_the_effects_of_a.html

28   32,700 American-born children living in Britain is a third more than all the children born in Pakistan living in Britain, twice as many as born in India living in Britain, five times as many as from the whole of North Africa, almost ten times as many as from China, and more than twenty times as many children born in Poland and living in Britain! Slightly more children were born in Germany and living in Britain, but usually to the British army stationed there.

29   The 'more than one in seven' figure is from Thomas, B. and D. Dorling, *Identity in Britain: A Cradle-to-Grave Atlas*, (Bristol: Policy Press, 2007). p. 44. (Note the education costs are often through private school fees that could otherwise have been taken in taxation and used to finance more equally the education of all children living in Britain). Only a few children born in the US go on to live the lives or have the riches of so many of their cousins who have emigrated to London. We know these American children are affluent because they are located disproportionately in some of the most expensive parts of London.

261

30 Bruce Springsteen certainly wasn't thinking of these American children when he wrote about what it was like to be 'born in the USA'. Tragically one of the best ever indictments of the American dream is now usually sung with few people listening to the lyrics. It is worth looking them up. Two hundred years ago William Blake wrote the poem 'Jerusalem'. Today William Blake, similarly to Bruce, might fail to understand that people could bellow proudly about 'Dark Satanic Mills' during the last night of the proms. Blake, like Bruce, was writing about the desire to make a better country.

31 Britain has always used its colonies. First Wales, colonized in 1283, then Scotland incorporated as a source of labour for England and especially for London (and later brought into full union and used to raise armies to run England's empire), and then Ireland. From the year 1171 onwards, for centuries the city of Dublin was owned by the city of Bristol, as its own personal colony. See: www.localhistories.org/bristol.html

32 As concerns the Caribbean flows, on the figure as it is reproduced in this book the bands are drawn too small to see these distinctions. I read them from looking at the figure in: Dorling, D., *New Social Atlas of Britain*, (Chichester: Wiley, 1995) p. 42. If you want to check what I am saying, please see Chapter 2 where it is freely available here: www.sasi.group.shef.ac.uk/publications/new_social_atlas/index.html

33 On the quarter of a million Germany-born folk, see Dorling, D. and B. Thomas. *People and Places: A 2001 Census Atlas of the UK*, (Bristol: Policy Press, 2004). p. 68.

34 On the perils for the Home Office of locating detention centres, see for example the campaign to close Campsfield detention centre, in Kidlington near Oxford: www.close-campsfield.org.uk It might be better if the centre were to stay there rather than be put somewhere more remote. Similarly the location proved problematic of what was Europe's largest detention centre, Yarl's Wood, which

opened in 2001. That location resulted in us now knowing stories of modern Britain such as this: 'In September 2005 Manuel Bravo, an asylum seeker from Angola, hanged himself while in detention awaiting deportation with his 13-year-old son following a dawn raid at his home in Leeds'. Just take a little time to read how we treat people; details at this website: http://en.wikipedia.org/wiki/Yarl's_Wood_Immigration_Removal_Centre

35 The phrase 'true-born Englishmen' was evoked by Daniel Defoe in 1701 to attack the idea of English racial purity. For more details: http://en.wikipedia.org/wiki/The_True-Born_Englishman.

36 In 2009 it was revealed that there were more British soldiers in British prisons than there were serving in Afghanistan: Travis, A., 'Revealed: the Hidden Army in UK Prisons. More veterans in justice system than soldiers serving in Afghanistan', Guardian, 24 September 2009: www.guardian.co.uk/uk/2009/sep/24/jailed-veteran-servicemen-outnumber-troops

37 Dorling and Thomas, People and Places, p. 78, note 12.

38 'Supermarket Supplier Demands Workers Speak Polish: A British supermarket supplier has been accused of discriminating against local workers after insisting new recruits speak fluent Polish', Telegraph, 14 March 2010. It was, of course, a non-story, which read 'We would never turn down an English person for a job on the basis that they didn't speak Polish or any other language.' What the advert meant was that they could accommodate workers who spoke Polish, but as the Telegraph had the job of scaring its readers about immigration it ran the story anyway to get what it thought was a good headline. See: www.telegraph.co.uk/news/uknews/7441467/Supermarket-supplier-demands-workers-speak-Polish.html

39 You might say it would be better to have more people on 'better than average wages', but for everyone paid over the average, someone else has to be paid under (by the definition of an 'arithmetic' or 'mean' average). What is better is

for average wages to rise overall, and for the gap between the top and bottom wages to narrow simultaneously, at such a rate that no one is seriously disadvantaged. Because a few are paid so very highly it can be cheaper in the long run to raise most people's incomes but also narrow the gap.

40 See the Runnymede Trust document 'Who cares about the White Working Class?' (Runnymede, 2009). I wrote Chapter 8: 'From Housing to Health – To Whom are the White Working Class Losing Out? Frequently Asked Question'. A free copy can be found at: www.runnymedetrust.org/ projects/community-cohesion/white-working-class.html It contains the references to statistical claims on these myths.

41 The myths being discussed here were written up for the Runnymede Trust (see above). A set of PowerPoint slides concerning the myths can be found at the bottom of the page here: http://sasi.group.shef.ac.uk/presentations/ and also on the Runnymede Trust website.

42 Conversely, introducing free schools would almost certainly increase class, racial and religious segregation of children's education; but as I write in October 2010, only a dozen or so 'free' schools have been approved to start in September 2011. Such low numbers would have negligible effect.

43 For the text that commemorates that defeat of the British at the hands of the immigrants see the medieval Welsh poem Y Gododdin: http://en.wikipedia.org/wiki/Y_Gododdin Almost all the British soldiers were slain in the battle, but of course the Briton' families from then on lived under Anglo rule. Modern-day 'Britain' is largely an imaginative Victorian creation designed to forget a large part of the history of the islands, such as the Battle of Catraeth: http://en.wikipedia.org/wiki/Battle_of_Catraeth. The Victorians even tried to rename Scotland 'Northern Britain'.

44 On what 'researchers recently showed in exacting detail' see: Finney, N. and L. Simpson, *Sleepwalking to Segregation?: Challenging Myths About Race and Migration*, (Bristol: Policy Press, 2009).

45 Soames, N., Intervention in House of Commons Debate on Population and Immigration, 3 February 2010, Column 6WH of *Hansard*. For the full transcript see: www.publications.parliament.uk/pa/cm200910/cmhansrd/cm100202/halltext/100202h0002.htm

Chapter 5: The Human Mosaic – Neighbours and Neighbourhoods

1 Brown, C. and T. Judd, 'Britain "Is Sleepwalking into New Orleans-style Segregation"', *Independent*, 19 September 2005: www.independent.co.uk/news/uk/politics/britain-is-sleepwalking-into-new-orleansstyle-segregation-507403.html

2 Alastair Leithead for the BBC, reporting from Los Angeles, 1.30 p.m. on 1 September, 2005; for details, see: http://news.bbc.co.uk/1/hi/world/americas/4203890.stm

3 Matt Frei for the BBC, reporting from New Orleans, [9.03 p.m.] on 1 September, 2005, from his video clip 'New Orleans Descends into Anarchy', where he predicts a riot (which never occurred) see: http://news.bbc.co.uk/1/hi/world/americas/4211404.stm

4 The source of this graph is: UK 'is still divided and unequal', BBC, 1 September 2005, online at: http://news.bbc.co.uk/1/hi/business/4201236.stm It was in turn reproduced from our reports. We produced ten reports on 1 September 2005 – all are available for free here: www.sheffield.ac.uk/geography/staff/dorling_danny/reports.html

5 Ross, N., D. Dorling, J. Dunn, G. Henriksson, J. Glover, J. Lynch, and G. Ringbäck Weitoftl, 'Metropolitan Income Inequality and Working-Age Mortality: A Cross-Sectional Analysis Using Comparable Data from Five Countries'. *Journal of Urban Health: Bulletin of the New York Academy of Medicine*, 2005, 82(1), pp. 101–110(10). An open access copy is available at: http://sasi.group.shef.ac.uk/publications/2005/ross_dorling_etal_fivecountries.pdf

6 I am not arguing that every household needs a car, but few

households need many cars and many households with small children or disabled adults do now need one (many corner shops have gone). People in the world would be better off if we had fewer cars overall, and especially fewer cars in more affluent and congested nations. With colleagues, as part of the worldmapper project, I have counted the number of cars and how many people die young on the roads. The US does not have the highest proportion of cars per person, but it has the highest numbers of cars overall. The 'honour' of having most cars per head is held by New Zealand, with more than 61 cars for every 100 people, but NZ is a far more rural place than is the US; more cars in NZ are needed. For further details see: www.worldmapper. org/posters/worldmapper_map31_ver5.pdf

7   In the newspaper article this chapter began with (for reference see web address given in the Brown and Judd citation on page 265

8   On those extra university places going to working-class children see: Dorling, D., 'Expert View: One of Labour's Great Successes', *Guardian*, 28 January 2010. www. guardian.co.uk/education/mortarboard/2010/jan/28/ labours-great-successes-university-access-danny-dorling

9   On why Trevor and Harriet were wrong, see: Finney, N. and L. Simpson, *Sleepwalking to Segregation?: Challenging Myths About Race and Migration*, (Bristol: Policy Press, 2009).

10   Trevor Phillips is reported to have spoken about the 'trebling' or Pakistani 'ghettoes' in his 'assessment of the UK after the July 7 terror attacks', as quoted by the *Independent* on 19 September 2005. See the first endnote for this chapter, above, for reference.

11   On Trevor being badly advised see: Dorling, D., 'Why Trevor Is Wrong about Race Ghettos', *Observer*, 25 September 2005, pp. 14–15. www.guardian.co.uk/uk/2005/sep/25/ communities.politics

12   Peach, C., 'Does Britain Have Ghettos?' Transactions of the Institute of British Geographers, 2007, pp. 216–35

(the definition is from pp. 216–17). www.humanities. manchester.ac.uk/socialchange/research/social-change/ summer-workshops/documents/doesbritainhaveghettos.pdf Summary: using results from the 2001 census to determine the direction of change, Ceri Peach's seminal paper concluded: 'Despite fears of following the African American model of inner-city segregation, the 1991 Census suggests rather more optimistic conclusions. Ghettos on the American model do not exist and, despite an unfavourable economic position and substantial evidence of continuing discrimination, the segregation trend amongst the Black Caribbean population in London is downwards.' On 28 September 2005 the *Guardian* published a letter from Ceri Peach entitled 'Britain has enclaves, not ghettos', the distinction between enclave and ghetto is far from academic, see: www.guardian.co.uk/uk/2005/sep/28/race.world

13 Books on Britain rarely use many statistical facts systematically to tell you about people. As a result, although well worth reading, often they tell you as much about the backgrounds and beliefs of those who write them as about the people of the country they try to describe. No one is immune from this bias, and I have peppered the endnotes to this book with details about where I come from and what I have done to explain why I think what I do. However, when I turn to most contemporary accounts of even a subset of the British, I often wince at what they reveal about the author's prejudices and which small social circles they revolve in, and then I worry at who winces at me! For some of the best accounts, though, see Fox, K. *Watching the English: The Hidden Rules of English Behaviour*, (London: Hodder and Stoughton, 2005); Paxman, J., *The English: A Portrait of a People*, (London: Penguin, 2007); and my favourite, partly as he used geo-demographics to decide where to begin, but mainly for his style: Baggini, J., *Welcome to Everytown: A Journey into the English Mind*, (London: Granta, 2008).

14 On the majority of children above the fourth floor not being white in England, see: Dorling, D., *Injustice: Why Social*

Inequality Persists, (London: Policy Press, 2010), p. 117. For open access to the statistics see: http://sasi.group.shef. ac.uk/publications/2010/2010_Dorling_CABE.ppt

15   The '271' times figure is from the Hill's enquiry of January 2010. The report of that enquiry in the *Guardian* suggested that the best-off tenth of people in Britain were 100 times richer than the worst-off tenth, but in London that ratio was 271 to 1. The 90 to 10 ratio was still more than 50 to 1 even when a single-age cohort was compared by the enquiry (those aged 55–64 living in the capital). See: Gentleman, A. and H. Mulholland, 'Unequal Britain: richest 10% are now 100 times better off than the poorest', *Guardian*, 27 January 2010: www.guardian.co.uk/society/2010/jan/27/unequal-britain-report (and see also the statistical appendices of the report itself. The report in October 2010 could be found at: www.equalities.gov.uk/pdf/NEP%20Report%20book-marked.pdf

16   Some 23 of the 29 ministers entitled to attend Cabinet meetings in the new coalition government were millionaires, including a majority of the Liberal Democrat members of that first Cabinet (Nick Clegg, Chris Hume and David Laws); Owen, G., 'The Cabinet Rich List', *This is Money*, 23 May 2010: www.thisismoney.co.uk/news/article.html?in_article_id=505027&in_page_id=2 The *News of the World* published a list on 27 July 2008 but that is now out of date.

17   Szegö., J, *A Census Atlas of Sweden*, (Stockholm: Swedish Council for Building Research, 1984), p. 20. An extended extract of his writing is included here: Dorling, D., 'Human Geography – When It Is Good to Map', Environment and Planning A, 1998, 30, pp. 277–88. You can find it open access at: http://sasi.group.shef.ac.uk/publications/1998/dorling_human_cartography_1998.pdf

18   Dorling, D., 'Anecdote is the Singular of Data', Environment and Planning A, 2001, 33, 8, pp. 1335–40, p. 1339. http://sasi.group.shef.ac.uk/publications/2001/dorling_anecdote.pdf

19   Not the Beatrix who wrote about hedgehogs (1866–1943), but the one (1858–1943) who co-founded the London School of Economics, the *New Statesman* magazine, and who married Sidney Webb.

20   Ansell's survey also revealed that, in the poorest of London districts, 29 per cent more babies died than in the better-off areas. The ratio is derived from knowing that, 'By London districts: infant mortality was less than 140 in the better off and over 180 in the poorest districts.' Woods, R. 'Newman's Infant Mortality as an Agenda for Research', Chapter 3 of Garrett, D., C. Galley, N. Shelton and R. Woods, *Infant Mortality: A Continuing Social Problem*, (Aldershot: Ashgate, 2006). p. 39. This is of course a much narrower percentage divide than today, although the 40 in 1,000 extra infant deaths in the poorest London districts then was a much greater absolute divide. I prefer to use overall life-expectancy estimates as a way of comparing inequalities in health over a long historical period because life expectancies are statistics that merge these two kinds of differences, and which are understandable to a much wider audience than are rates and ratios.

21   Think of Robert Tressell's *Ragged Trousered Philanthropists* (first published 1914), George Orwell's *Down and Out in Paris and London* (1933), *Cathy Come Home* (1966) directed by Ken Loach, or Nick Davies' *Dark Heart of Britain* (1998) – all so well known now that no detailed references are required.

22   It was a major study given the dozen significant funders who supported the work. See: The Young Foundation, 2009, 'Sinking and Swimming: Understanding Britain's Unmet Needs : www.youngfoundation.org/general-/-all/news/sinking-and-swimming-understanding-britains-unmet-needs. And see Chapter 6 of this volume, page 158. The Young Foundation report was just one of many similar reports produced between 2007–10.

23   The impact of Robert H. Frank's masterpiece on 'Falling Behind' was not missed by, among others, Richard

Wilkinson and Kate Pickett in their bestselling study, *The Spirit Level: Why Equality is Better for Everyone*, (London: Penguin, 2009) see: www.equalitytrust.org.uk/resource/the-spirit-level

24   Frank, R. H., *Falling Behind: How Rising Inequality Harms the Middle Class*, (Berkeley: University of California Press, 2007) www.ucpress.edu/book.php?isbn=9780520252523

25   I can recommend his younger son Haydon's cover of 'Ain't no sunshine' http://www.robert-h-frank.com/band.html His older son's band is *New Neighbors*, and very pleasant they are too: www.myspace.com/newneighbors But I'm jealous of their success (see endnote 27, below).

26   Frank, R. H. and B. Bernanke, *Principles of Economics*, (New York: McGraw-Hill, 2003).

27   Frank, R. H. and B. Bernanke, *Principles of Macroeconomics*, (New York: McGraw-Hill, 2006).

I'm not saying that Bernanke is a saint or that Frank is always right. In fact, I suspect there are some embarrassing statements made in their 2006 book concerning how equilibrium works. Incidentally, there are only five short degrees of separation between Obama and the groupie writing on Frank's son's website. I'll admit it, I'm just jealous. I was never in a band. But is this for real?: 'Pretty sure John [a member of Frank's son's band] is sitting at the table in front of me. I'm in the physical sciences library, but too shy to say hello . . . plus he looks very busy. He may have seen the IY sticker I have on my laptop and smiled bc of it . . . ? So, Hi John. You are a geniusssss! :)' Found on www.myspace.com/newneighbors on 9 December 2008 and still there as of October 2010.

28   On the orange-juice experiment, to quote Frank, who had given his young sons pseudonyms: 'I came to this view in part because of an experiment I did years ago with my two oldest sons when they were five and seven years of age. This experiment took three days. On day one, I poured each of them a full glass of orange juice. On day two, I poured each only half a glass. Then, on day three, I poured

David (then age seven) seven-eighths of a glass and Jason (then age five) only three quarters of a glass . . . (I am not sure that a human-subjects committee would approve this experiment today.) You can guess what happened. On the first two days, each drank his juice without comment. In particular, neither asked on day two why he'd gotten only half as much as the day before. But things played out differently on day three. Jason looked first at his own glass, then over at his brother's, then back at his own, his face registering growing signs of distress. It was obvious that he was struggling not to react. But finally he blurted out, "That's not fair, he always gets more than me!"' As we know now, the end result is that the older one goes on to form a band. I do wonder if the one deprived of juice became an economist? The age gap between them is too small for him to now be the second musical one. Ibid, pp. 65–6.

29   Figure 2.2 is found in: Frank, R.H., *Falling Behind*, pp. 19–20. Which in turn gives the source as the now defunct web page: www.census.gov/hhes/income/histinc/h03ar.html

30   The eleven-year 1979–90 estimates are made simply by raising each annual percentage to the power of 11. The initial quintile annual estimates can be found in: Dickens, R., P. Gregg and J. Wadsworth, *The Labour Market under New Labour: The State of Working Britain* (London: Palgrave Macmillan, 2003), p. 11, fig. 1.2.

31   The 'Family Resources Surveys' allow us to assess changes in inequality. There is a lag of between one and two years in the release of these surveys. According to the Institute of Fiscal Studies' estimates, Alistair Darling's final budget as Chancellor, under Brown's Premiership, was highly redistributive from rich to poor. When that is included in Brown's record he may appear to have reduced inequalities overall. Very preliminary health data for 2009, first released in late October 2010, suggests that the health divide may even have narrowed in Brown's last year of office, as we know the education divide did earlier. Gordon Brown was

an unfortunate politician. It is possible that his best year in office was his last year, but for all his mastery of statistics, he did not then have the most recent figures to prove this, let alone the panache to convey them. Gordon Brown may in fact appear saintly when the budgets under his leadership are seen in contrast to the incredibly regressive effects of George Osborne's first budget, the local authority allocation from April 2011 (announced in June 2010 to penalize the poor the most), and then the cruelly highly regressive October 2010 spending review. The increases in inequality budgeted now to occur between May 2010 and April 2012 may be the greatest we will have seen in our history but it won't be until one or two years after that for us to know the precise figures – the outcomes on the ground (and only then as long as the Family Resources Surveys are not themselves victims of the cuts).

32   The precise figures from the 1979–2000 changes, calculated from the graph shown above in this chapter are 28 per cent, 72 per cent, the average (100 per cent), 171 per cent, and 363 per cent of the average respectively. On a log graph they form an almost perfectly straight line. It is as if there had been a plan to increase inequality symmetrically.

33   It was thought that some of the Jews were plotting to use bombs. In many ways the situation was similar a century later, with the many poor and recent immigrant-origin Muslims now the scapegoats for the acts of a few Muslim extremists who in turn were reacting to our wars and complicity with the US.

34   On the greater momentum after October 2010 see this chapter, endnote 31, just above, on the key events of 2010 and on when we will know for certain why, and the degree to which, increases in inequalities have accelerated.

35   As I write infants are still buried in £300 half-plots in Undercliffe Cemetery. There are no new full-sized plots for adults. www.undercliffecemetery.co.uk/undercliffeburials.html

36 Most southern England cemeteries are now full, as they were never built for a century of southwards population drift. One borough in the heart of London reports that 'St Pancras Cemetery is running out of new burial land. This means that we are looking at all the available spaces that were not used in the past. Sometimes, we can find a grave space in an older area of the cemetery near other members of the family. But we will also have to use land which current grave owners assumed we would never use.' www.camden.gov.uk/ccm/content/community-and-living/ lifetime-events/cemeteries---opening-times-and-location- maps.en

37 HMSO, 1875 (xli) *Annual Report of The Registrar General*, (London: His Majesty's Stationary Office), William Farr, quoted in Garrett, D., C. Galley, N. Shelton and R. Woods, *Infant Mortality: A Continuing Social Problem*, (Aldershot: Ashgate, 2006), p. 25. No open-access version – you'll have to use the library. I hope it hasn't been closed in the cuts, but many will be, especially those built by the Victorians.

38 On the cotton famines, see this volume, Chapter 1, pages 14 and 15.

39 The evidence being used here as a source continues: 'White and black pupils from social class I were around 100 times more likely to gain a place at medical school than those from classes IV or V. Asian pupils seemed to compensate better for poor origins, but those from social class I were still 6–10 times more likely to gain a place than those from classes IV or V'. See: Seyan, K., T. Greenhalgh and D. Dorling, 'The Standardised Admission Ratio for Measuring Widening Participation in Medical Schools: Analysis of UK Medical School Admissions by Ethnicity, Socioeconomic Status, and Sex', *BMJ*, 2004, 328, 1545–1546: http://sasi. group.shef.ac.uk/publications/2004/seyan_greenhalgh_ and_dorling.pdf

40 On current polarization in the UK, it should be noted that a more extreme version of current UK trends is found in the US. See: Dorling, D., 'The Fading of the Dream: Widening

Inequalities in Life Expectancy in America'. *International Journal of Epidemiology*, 2006, 35 (4): 979–980. http://ije. oxfordjournals.org/content/35/4/979.full.pdf?keytype=ref &ijkey=nb4fbku3KDK9m9C

41   The figure of 82,000 poor families to be cleared out of London is from: Helm, T., and A. Asthana, 'Councils Plan for Exodus of Poor Families from London . . . More than 200,000 may leave capital in "social cleansing"', *Observer,* 24 October 2010: www.guardian.co.uk/politics/2010/oct /24/exodus-poor-families-from-london On the Coalition plans to do this prior to the review, and for one of their ministers saying that they aimed to emulate the Highland Clearances, but now within London, see endnote on page 258.

42   In the census in New Zealand they ask about smoking habits as well as last usual address, and so we are able to measure these movements directly. See: Pearce, J.R. and D. Dorling, 'The Influence of Selective Migration Patterns among Smokers and Non-smokers on Geographical Inequalities in Health', *Annals of the Association of American Geographers*, 18 March 2010. www.sasi.group.shef.ac.uk/ publications/2010/PearceDorling_2010_AnnalsAAG.pdf

43   The correlation coefficient is a statistic of how well two sets of numbers are related. If both rise together it is positive, if one goes up and the other down, it is negative. When the two sets are unrelated it is 0. The highest and lowest that a correlation could be, when both series are exactly in step, is +/- 1.

44   Shaw, M. and D. Dorling, 'Who Cares in England & Wales? The Converse Care Law', *British Journal of General Practice*, 2004, 54, 899–903. http://sasi.group.shef.ac.uk/ publications/2004/positive_care_law.pdf. Thankfully doctors in poorer areas no longer work much longer hours.

45   The figure is redrawn from: Shaw and Dorling, 'Who Cares in England & Wales'. Each circle is a county, unitary, or former metropolitan authority drawn in proportion to its population in 2001. Circles are shaded light if they lie west

or north of the counties of Gloucestershire, Warwickshire, Leicestershire or Lincolnshire (the Severn-Humber divide). Circles are drawn with area in proportion to total population (with the largest circle representing London). Each circle is positioned on the X-axis according to the proportion of the population who live there who have both poor health and limiting long-term illness, and on the Y-axis according to the proportion of the population who live there who provide fifty hours or more per week unpaid care, which includes: looking after, giving help or support to, family members, friends, neighbours or others, because of long-term physical or mental ill-health or disability or problems relating to old age.

46   Only about 1 in 1,000 people in Britain report having no family or friends, but the reports you can access on deaths at home alone, often of young men in London, suggest the numbers are higher and are growing. The statistics are too patchy to be sure of how fast (but coroners' courts have to report them). On loneliness, see: Ballas, D. and D. Dorling 'Measuring the Impact of Major Life Events upon Happiness', *International Journal of Epidemiology*, 2007, 36, 1244–1252. http://ije.oxfordjournals.org/content/36/6/1244.full.pdf?ijkey=zOergXjDGRwK0G0&keytype=ref

47   On following the trajectory of the United States, see the graphs that were used to chart inequalities over the last century in my book *Injustice* (Dorling, D. 2010, Bristol: Policy Press). They are available open access at: www.sasi.group.shef.ac.uk/injustice/chapter5.htm

48   The death count was revised upwards in 2003 to at least 2,500, the quotation is sourced from: http://en.wikipedia.org/wiki/1928_Okeechobee_hurricane which continued (when accessed in October 2010): 'Around 75% of the fatalities were of migrant farm workers, most of whom were black. Black workers did most of the cleanup, and the few caskets available for burials were mostly used for the bodies of whites; other bodies were either burned or

buried in mass graves. Burials were segregated, and the only mass gravesite to receive a memorial contained only white bodies.'

49   The US Army Corps warning was found within the undated report 'Lake Okeechobee and The Herbert Hoover Dike: A Summary of the Engineering Evaluation of Seepage and Stability Problems at the Herbert Hoover Dike': 'When the lake is high, water finds its way through the dike from lakeside to landside – sometimes eroding soil from within or beneath the dike. This erosion of soil is technically known as piping. The piping of the soil creates a continuous open path through which water can erode even more soil. If this soil erosion is allowed to continue, it will eventually create large cavities in the dike. And those large cavities – with water from the lake running through them unimpeded – create a serious risk that the dike will breach, with large releases of water from Lake Okeechobee flooding the surrounding lands.' Published by the US Army Corps of Engineers. See: www.saj.usace.army.mil/Divisions/Everglades/Branches/ProjectExe/Sections/UECKLO/LakeOWatch/DOCS/LakeOandHHDike.pdf It sits on the website nearby the hurricane-warning report: http://www.saj.usace.army.mil/Divisions/Everglades/DOCS/HHD_FS_Hurricane_2010.pdf In between the two is a nice children's story about the rain cycle featuring 'Wayne Drop' the water droplet, which explains why unrepaired dikes erode and eventually collapse. Page eight of the 'Wayne Drop' report suggests that children need not worry as the dikes are very carefully managed. In fact in CAPITALS Wayne says: 'VERY Carefully Managed TODAY'. We don't want children to have nightmares, and so hope they don't click on the report meant for adults. All three reports can be found here: www.saj.usace.army.mil/Divisions/Everglades/Branches/ProjectExe/Sections/UECKLO/LakeOWatch/

50   This quotation is from the first report referenced immediately above (for adults); the army says the dike is leaking.

The lake is enormous, the dike was built from 1932–7 (creating jobs during the Depression); later strengthening was completed by 1961. It would be worth re-strengthening, work which would again employ millions of people looking for jobs in the US and the UK (should any of our Victorian-era dams require work we have not been told about). Unfortunately government capital spending is to be severely curtailed following the spending review of October 2010; thus, those who are out of work will not be employed to strengthen any dams in Britain any time soon, or doing other, similar work that could make us all safer, happier and more equal.

Chapter 6: A Nation Ever More Divided between Town and Country

1   'The Perfect Rural Idyll: As many dream of a peaceful cottage in the country, Matt Baker meets some of the people who have found their own slice of rural tranquillity', *Country File* magazine, issue 21: www.bbccountryfilemagazine.com/feature/country-people/perfect-rural-idyll

2   The first episode of the animated children's television series, *Camberwick Green*, was broadcast in 1966. The company which made it went on to create *Trumpton* and then *Chigley*: www.t-web.co.uk/trumpgo.htm *Postman Pat* is a modern-day equivalent, as is *Balamory*.

3   The M40 motorway has been built between the canal and the village. For details see: www.waterscape.com/canals-and-rivers/oxford-canal/map

4   On retiring so far away from the city, here is the problem. One day, you slip and your hip joint goes; or did your hip joint go and then you slipped? You'll never know. What you do know is that you quickly discover that the local district hospital doesn't do hips and it is a sixty-mile round trip to one that does. Your friends can't travel that far – more and more of them are getting too infirm to drive. Many of their hips have gone already. What was the point

of having the garden and all those walks nearby? Isn't the countryside a little wasted on the retired?

5　In 2008 the residents of Radipole were still fighting enclosure of the last bit of community land to prevent it from being built over, which would cause more flooding. See: www.radipole-dorset.co.uk/SaveOurSouthill.html and on the original Act of Enclosure see: www.parliament.uk/about/living-heritage/transformingsociety/towncountry/landscape/overview/enclosingland/

6　In Thomas More's *Utopia* (1515–51), in one of the longest sentences ever translated into the English language, the evils of enclosure and the amassing of property are explained in his discussions with Raphael Hythloday www.gutenberg.org/ebooks/2130: 'As if forests and parks had swallowed up too little of the land, those worthy countrymen turn the best inhabited places into solitudes; for when an insatiable wretch, who is a plague to his country, resolves to enclose many thousand acres of ground, the owners, as well as tenants, are turned out of their possessions by trick or by main force, or, being wearied out by ill usage, they are forced to sell them; by which means those miserable people, both men and women, married and unmarried, old and young, with their poor but numerous families (since country business requires many hands), are all forced to change their seats, not knowing whither to go; and they must sell, almost for nothing, their household stuff, which could not bring them much money, even though they might stay for a buyer.'

7　Thomas Hardy's *The Mayor of Casterbridge* (1886) and *Tess of the d'Urbervilles* (1891) are two of the most widely read portrayals of rural life during the long depression of 1873–96.

8　On the 'church and the pub' and so on, all this is gleaned from the village website: www.fringford.info/history.html

9　The claim concerning 1960 was made in Mabey, R., 'Diary of a Country Woman', *Guardian*, 13 December 2008. www.guardian.co.uk/books/2008/dec/13/lark-rise-candleford-

flora-thompson. On Fringford see: http://en.wikipedia.org/
wiki/Fringford

10   These prices and quotations on junctions of the M40 are
     found on the Teamprop website. For example, see this
     property advertised as: '3 Bedroom House For Sale in
     FRINGFORD, BICESTER, OXFORDSHIRE'(note it is 'in'
     and not 'near' Fringford) found on www.teamprop.co.uk/
     properties/TMB1883/Details.aspx, October 2010 (and
     going for £389,950).

11   Bicester itself is far from a cheap place to live. Nowhere
     around that part of the country is easily affordable any
     more. Only the firemen who also moonlight can really
     afford to retire along that stretch of the M40. They may
     now have to move away from children, grandchildren and
     where they grew up and worked all their lives. They are
     public-sector pensioners.

12   Thompson, F., *Lark Rise to Candleford: A Trilogy*,
     (London: Penguin, 2008). Originally published by Oxford
     University Press as *Lark Rise* (1939), *Over to Candleford*
     (1941) and *Candleford Green* (1943).

13   Osborne, V., 'Literary Landscapes: Juniper Hill', *Telegraph*,
     8 June 2002, www.telegraph.co.uk/gardening/3301349/
     Literary-landscapes-Juniper-Hill.html

14   *Ibid.* It is worth saying that the switch here from poverty to
     affluence has been very fast.

15   *Ibid.* Continues, 'was a favourite saying that occurs fre-
     quently in the book'.

16   For more details see: www.youngfoundation.org/general-/
     -all/news/sinking-and-swimming-understanding-britains-
     unmet-needs

17   A version of the truth which suggested that if rural locals
     did not vote Tory, then black and brown people from the
     cities would come to steal their jewellery, scare their sheep,
     and impregnate their daughters.

18   And even back then there were still dirty tricks to be
     played to try to secure apparently democratic victory by
     holding back progress legally as long as was possible. The

Conservative party had a manual back then which told them that 'no more than two such joint occupiers may be registered in respect of one set of lodgings', which is how they tried to get people cast off the electoral role if they thought they might not be their supporters. See: http://en.wikipedia.org/wiki/Parliamentary Franchise in the United Kingdom 1885%E2%80%931918

19 Give yourself extra marks if you knew it was the three that people always forget. They were: Robert Arthur Talbot Gascoyne-Cecil, 3rd Marquess of Salisbury; Archibald Philip Primrose, 5th Earl of Rosebery; and Henry Campbell-Bannerman (the first man to actually be called Prime Minister and by far the best of the bunch). The last time a majority of the electorate voted for a single political party in Britain was when the first of these three, the Marquess of Salisbury, led the Conservatives to win 50.3 per cent of the vote in the Khaki (post-Boer War) general election in 1900, but he only managed that because the Liberal Unionists did not oppose him in many seats. One great fear is of that history repeating itself: http://en.wikipedia.org/wiki/List_of_Parliaments_of_the-United_Kingdom. Incidentally it is reported that Robert was a descendant of the Cecil Family, being the great-great-something grandchild of another Robert Cecil (1st Earl of Salisbury). The Canadian Prime Minister said of the later Robert that he had 'what I regard as a very stupid and worthless life'. (Public Archives of Canada, Gowan Papers, M-1900, Thompson to Gowan, 20 September 1893). On the Cecils in general see: Dorling, D., 'The Darwins and the Cecils Are Only Empty Vessels', Environment and Planning A, 2010, 42, 5, p. 1023–25 www.sasi.group.shef.ac.uk/publications/2010/Dorling 2010–EaP.pdf.

20 At some point the voting age will fall to 16, or even lower, to the age of criminal responsibility (which itself may rise to, say, 12 or 14), and be extended to current groups who are still disenfranchized, but that will initially be opposed as strongly as were votes for women:

www.parliament.uk/business/publications/parliamentary-archives/archives-highlights/archives-the-suffragettes/archives-the-first-women-in-parliament-1919–1945

21 Rowntree, B.S., and M. Kendall, *How the Labourer Lives: A Study of the Rural Labour Problem*, (London: T. Nelson and Sons, 1913).

22 The recording was done by Benjamin Seebohm Rowntree whose surveys of poverty in York in 1936 and 1951 allowed a direct comparison to be made and the effects of the 1945 Labour government to be quantified. Although subsequent reanalysis of his 1951 results suggested poverty was a little higher then, and even though Peter Townsend and his colleagues' work on the 1968–9 survey found abject poverty had not been eradicated as the earlier trend suggested it might, the period 1936–69 remains that of greatest reduction in poverty – ever.

23 Like Mr McGrew from *Chigley* we can call Harold by his first name – in this case not to maintain a rhyme but because Harold was the first Prime Minister for many years not to have attended a public school, where first names were eschewed. He was followed by Edward Heath, whose first name was occasionally shortened to 'Ted'. Contrast that with how nowadays Ed Miliband is never called Edward Miliband (although David Cameron failed to shorten his name to 'Dave' and whereas Mr Osborne did successfully rebrand himself as 'George' despite being christened 'Gideon').

24 The ice-cream was so cheap and affordable that no doubt millions of poor children have been made obese from it. Thatcher married a richer, older man, which thankfully saved us from more of her food chemistry, and further cheap artificial inventions aimed at an increasingly laissez-faire food industry that mistook entrepreneurship for quality or caring. Unfortunately Mr Thatcher's money allowed Maggie to play at politics. She then further watered down health-and-safety laws; her successors hated 'regulation'.

25 Dorling, D., 'Our Divided Nation', *New Statesman*, 14

June 2010. www.newstatesman.com/uk-politics/2010/06/election-seats-support-tory

26   Maggie achieved her victory despite screeching like a banshee in 1979 and so 'shortly after she became Prime Minister, she underwent training to lower her voice-tone as her advisers had decreed that she sounded too shrill'. Pierce, A., 'New Documents Come to Light about Margaret Thatcher', Telegraph, 22 February 2009. www.telegraph.co.uk/news/newstopics/politics/conservative/4780515/New-documents-come-to-light-about-Margaret-Thatcher.html. Thus, it was not her voice or manner, nor her personality (far from it) but the end result of twenty years of very slow and not too steady increase of geopolitical polarization (with that jump during 1974) that resulted in Maggie's first national victory .

27   Heirarchies both Oxford university colleges and in nearby still-near-feudally-obsequious Oxfordshire villages.

28   Professor Philip Rees (incidentally the same man as I quoted as saying that the UK's ethnic make-up is 'evolving significantly' in chapter 4. See text quoted from the BBC, this volume, on page 105.

29   Dorling, D. and P. H. Rees, 'A Nation Still Dividing: The British Census and Social Polarization 1971–2001', Environment and Planning A, 2003, 35(7), pp. 1287–1313. http://sasi.group.shef.ac.uk/publications/2003/Dorling_and_Rees_nation_still_dividing.pdf

30   For our story to work, an urgent solution was needed to get people back into the right places. This was a scenario not unlike the way rationing was introduced, within a year of the outbreak of the Second World War, but having been four years in the planning, and lasting much longer than the war. Petrol had been rationed since September 1936; butter, bacon and sugar not until January 1940. The planning had begun in secret, as far back as 1936. The seventieth anniversary of the introduction of rationing was marked on 8 January 2010. See: http://food.iwm.org.uk/?p=296

31   On the exodus see endnote 41 on page 274. People on

Job Seekers' Allowance are to have their housing benefit reduced by 10 per cent after a year unemployed, which may force them to move home. Others claiming over £400 a week to house a large family will have to move to a cheaper area even sooner. On a much more minor scale and having the opposite effect, movement was curtailed when the US introduced its 50mph national speed limit in 1973 to reduce gasoline consumption, a move that lasted much longer than the initial oil crisis and was not repealed completely until 1995. There have been calls recently to revert again to the limit (most prominently from Hilary Clinton in 2006): http://en.wikipedia.org/wiki/Speed limits in the United States#National 55 mph limit

32   Dorling, D. and P. H. Rees, 'A Nation Still Dividing', p. 1287.

33   The figures are taken from: Dorling, D. and P.H. Rees, 'A Nation Still Dividing', p. 1312, table 6. The number 2,452,021 is the difference between the 1971 and 2001 totals, which were 5,350,122 and 7,802,143 people respectively. These were the numbers who would need to move if every district were to have identical age, marital-status and work-status population profiles. The number rises as areas polarize (and only a little as population grows).

34   It is usually not possible to commute by bus in many directions from many rural areas. If you live in such an area and lose your job, cannot find another and cannot afford to run a car, then you might well also lose your home. The implication of Ian Duncan Smith's call, in 2010 for the jobless to get on buses is thus a further call to cleanse the countryside of people who fall on hard times. Beattie, J., 'Iain Duncan Smith Echoes Norman Tebbit by Telling the Jobless to "Get on a bus" to Find Work', *Daily Mirror*, 23October 2010. www.mirror.co.uk/news/top-stories/2010/10/23/iain-duncan-smith-echoes-norman-tebbit-by-telling-the-jobless-to-get-on-a-bus-to-find-work-115875-22652814/

35   Dorling, D., *A New Social Atlas of Britain*, (Chichester: Wiley, 1995), pp. 37, 173; and Dorling, D., Human

Geography of the UK, (London: Sage, 2005), p. 54. See www.shef.ac.uk/sasi/hguk for data behind Figure 4.5.

36   See maps of unemployment by amalgamated office area from 1978 onwards in Dorling, D., 'CATMOG 59: Area Cartograms: Their Use and Creation', *Concepts and Techniques in Modern Geography* (University of East Anglia: Environmental Publications, 1996), series number 59. http://sasi.group.shef.ac.uk/publications/1996/dorling area cartograms.pdf (full colour section).

37   Dorling, D. and P. H. Rees, 'A Nation Still Dividing'; and Dorling, D., and Woodward, 'Social Polarization 1971–1991: a Micro-Geographical Analysis of Britain'. Monograph in the Progress in Planning series, 1996, 45, 2, pp. 67–122. Which is an earlier study that I was involved in did not find this because we could not look at the polarization of wealth. http://sasi.group.shef.ac.uk/publi-cations/1996/dorling_and_woodward_social_polarisation. pdf

38   Dorling, D., J. Rigby, B. Wheeler, D. Ballas, B. Thomas, E. Fahmy, D. Gordon and R. Lupton, *Poverty and Wealth across Britain 1968 to 2005*, (Bristol: Policy Press, 2007). www.jrf.org.uk/publications/poverty-and-wealth-across-britain-1968–2005

39   Had you tried to achieve the social change of recent decades in a single year there would have been a revolution.

40   The four-page summary of our findings, which is where we wrote these words on the breadline poor, can be found here: www.jrf.org.uk/sites/files/jrf/2077.pdf

41   Dorling, D., 'Mind the Gap: New Labour's Legacy on Child Poverty', *Journal of the Child Poverty Action Group*, Autumn 2010. www.sasi.group.shef.ac.uk/publications/ 2010/Dorling_2010_Poverty.pdf

42   Not Mrs Webb this time but the Beatrix who wrote about Mr McGregor attempting to murder Peter Rabbit. In the film of Miss Potter's life Beatrix was played by Renée Zellweger (as well as Bridget Jones, and like the two Beatrixes, Renée has a couple of walk-on parts in this book, see chapter

1 of this volume). For a detailed deconstruction of this particular work of Miss Potter, see the highly entertaining: Jesús Moya Guijarro, A., 'Multimodal Analysis of *The Tale of Peter Rabbit* within the Interpersonal Metafunction', *Atlantis*, 2010, 32, 1, pp. 123–140. www.atlantisjournal. org/ARCHIVE/32.1/2010MoyaGuijarro.pdf

43 Or, to be honest and slightly un-chivalrous, I thought my colleague Bethan Thomas had made a mistake, as she was the one who drew the first draft of this map, in: Thomas, B. and D. Dorling, *Identity in Britain: A Cradle-to-Grave Atlas*, (Bristol: Policy Press, 2007), p. 63.

44 I'm afraid you'll have to read all of Thomas and Dorling, *Ibid.*, to verify this claim, but in particular see page 21, which shows where young mums give birth; page 127 for marriage among those aged under 40; page 206 on where 60 to 74-year-olds live; pages 212–3 on how many are divorced, separated or remarried; and page 279 for who is still in good health aged over 74. All provide a useful cramming guide.

45 But it had to be possible for someone. That, after all, is what a market price is: what someone will pay. Maybe this hypothetical couple will have purchased the five-bedroom home for £500,000?

46 Hillyard, P., C. Pantazis, S. Tombs, D. Gordon, and D. Dorling, *Criminal Obsessions: Why Harm Matters More Than Crime*, (London: Centre for Crime and Justice Studies, 2005). The second edition is available here: www. crimeandjustice.org.uk/criminalobsessions2.html

47 Ibid. The overall numbers of murders, with age and sex structure taken into account, are shown in this report in chapter 2, table 1, page 32. This diagram is reproduced from Figure 4 on page 34 on that report.

48 Thomas, B., D. Dorling, and G. Davey Smith, 'Inequalities in Premature Mortality in Britain: Observational Study from 1921 to 2007', *BMJ*, 23 July 2010. www.sasi.group. shef.ac.uk/publications/2010/ThomasDorlingDaveySmith 2010 BMJ.pdf

49   The figures shown on the 'Injustice' website are a couple of years out of date now. (see www.shef.ac.uk.sasi/injustice) Bankers' rising bonuses and the further immiseration of the poorest in Britain due to the budget cuts of June 2010 and those announced in October 2010 means that we are probably now more unequal than we last were in 1918. For the story up to 2008 see: www.sasi.group.shef.ac.uk/injustice/chapter5.htm

Chapter Seven: Time to Put Them out to Grass? – What to Do with the Elderly

1   Conway, E., 'UK's Aging Population Is a Bigger Economic Threat than the Financial Crisis', *Telegraph*, 12 February 2010, www.telegraph.co.uk/finance/financetopics/financialcrisis/7216546/UKs-aging-population-is-a-bigger-economic-threat-than-the-financial-crisis.html

2   Treanor, J., 'Barclays Boss Diamond to Bank £14.8m Bonus', *Guardian*, 8 January 2010, www.guardian.co.uk/business/2008/jan/08/barclaysbusiness.executivesalaries

3   Fernandez, C., 'Rambler with an Interest in Bible Studies is the City's Highest Earner on £60m a Year', *Daily Mail*, 27 September 2010, http://www.dailymail.co.uk/news/article-1315366/David-Harding-Citys-highest-earner-60m-year.html?ito=feeds-newsxm (the article also gives the most recent estimate of Bob Diamond's annual salary that is used here).

4   The £11 is one half of the married couples' weekly pension of £156.15, further divided by seven days; thus, it is only a fraction above what those seeking work are allowed to live on (at £9 a day). Why do we begrudge people living on £9 a day Job Seekers' Allowance (and award pensioners so little) when if someone like Bob were to invest his bonus in government gilts we would be paying him £4,060 a day for the privilege?

5   Reece, D., 'If Anyone Should Be Protesting, It's the Put-upon Private Sector', *Telegraph*, 15 September 2010 www.tele-

graph.co.uk/finance/personalfinance/pensions/8003185/
If-anyone-should-be-protesting-its-the-put-upon-private-
sector.html

6   'One in Four Women Rely on Their Husband's Pension
    in Retirement', *Telegraph*, 15 September 2010, quoting
    Vince Smith-Hughes, head of pensions development at
    Prudential: www.telegraph.co.uk/finance/personalfinance/
    pensions/8003500/One-in-four-women-rely-on-their-
    husbands-pension-in-retirement.html

7   Monaghan, A., 'Parents Won't Have Wealth to Pass
    on, Report Says' *Telegraph*, 18 September 2010 www.
    telegraph.co.uk/finance/personalfinance/8010896/Parents-
    wont-have-wealth-to-pass-on-report.html

8   Greenwood, J., 'Do Children Need Pensions?' *Telegraph*,
    20 September 2010, www.telegraph.co.uk/finance/person-
    alfinance/pensions/8013002/Do-children-need-pensions.
    html

9   www.telegraph.co.uk/finance/personalfinance/pen-
    sions/8013002/Do-children-need-pensions.html#disqus
    thread

10 One thing we can do is point out repeatedly how precarious
    we have made our lives and by asking if there were not a
    better way we could arrange our affairs.

11 The United Nations figures for all countries is reported in
    simplified form here: http://en.wikipedia.org/wiki/List_of
    countries_by_infant_mortality_rate

12 Due to the risks of childbirth, women died earlier than men
    on average, from when we arrived over that land-bridge,
    through to just before my grandmother's generation –
    around 1900. Recent statistics reveal that women are now
    three times less likely to die year-on-year compared to
    men; however, this applies across almost all affluent coun-
    tries and is becoming more apparent with the advent of
    each of the 1970s, 1980s and 1990s economic recessions.
    See: Rigby, J.E. and D. Dorling, 'Mortality in Relation to
    Sex in the Affluent World', *Journal of Epidemiology and
    Community Health*, 2007, 61(2). http://sasi.group.shef.

ac.uk/publications/2007/rigby Dorling_mortality_sex_sub-mitted.pdf

13 The atlas was published when I was 27 and I felt smug when I saw the graph, which made me think I was far away from aging. But I was – it was a fifth of an average life-time ago. See: Dorling, D., *A New Social Atlas of Britain*, (Chichester: Wiley, 1995), p. 150, fig. 5.16. www.sasi.group.shef.ac.uk/publications/new_social_atlas/index.html

14 *Ibid.*

15 Freedland, J., 'Remember 1983? I warn you that a Cameron victory will be just as bad', *Guardian*, 5 May 2010. www.guardian.co.uk/commentisfree/2010/may/05/1983-cameron-victory-kinnocks-words

16 Willis, R. 'Pharmaceutical Products in the Environment in the Context of Demographic Change in the UK', Report of ESRC-Sponsored Internship Student at the Royal Commission on Environmental Pollution, February-April 2010. Also: Willis, R., 'Key Health Statistics from General Practice 1998: Analyses of Morbidity and Treatment Data, Including Time Trends, England and Wales' (London: ONS, 2010). www.rcep.org.uk/reports/29-demographics/documents/Pharmaceuticals and demographic change RuthWillis2010.pdf

17 Three quarters! How many people in their twenties are cap-able of entirely taking care of themselves? How many of the super-rich? 'Guidance for the Care of Older People: Facts and Figures', Nursing and Midwifery Council, 2010. www.nmc-uk.org/General-public/Older-people-and-their-carers/Guidance-for-the-care-of-older-people-Facts-and-figures/ drawing in turn from 'Office of National Statistics, Population of Older People', (London: ONS, 2004). A majority of the elderly aged 90 and over in private hous-ing live alone although sometimes in sheltered-housing schemes. My grandfather, to whom this book is dedicated, is a case in point at age 93.

18 The 150,000 figure is found by referring in turn to Age Concern's 'Older People in the UK – Facts and Figures'.

19　We can't all be as rich as Bob Diamond without aliens arriving from another planet to act as our servants.

20　What we are actually talking about here is wiping your bum after you have gone to the toilet when you are no longer able to do so yourself. Even if you are now rich, what future, what society, would be better for you? Would it be a society that respected its carers or one more like our current model, where these carers have no good reason to respect you other than the fact that you are paying their wages?

21　Taking responsibility for myself is how the spivs like to sell it. The definition of a spiv is someone who does not undertake useful work but makes money out of others through various schemes. All the schemes, they tell you, are in your interest and if you are gullible, you may end up believing in the schemes. I'm just 'going to have to "invest" in some of those schemes the *Telegraph*, Aegon UK, and Barclays Capital keep pointing me towards, to ensure I'll be all right'. That is what they want you to think. It was Vince Cable, the UK's Business Secretary in 2010 who used the word spiv to describe this kind of behaviour. In his 2010 conference speech he asked, 'Why do directors sometimes forget their wider duties when a cheque is waved before them?' I can't help thinking that the answer is obvious and that anyone who is the Business Secretary should be less naive about greedy behaviour. For the quote see Porter, A., 'Vince Cable Attacks Bankers as "Spivs and Gamblers"', *Telegraph*, 22 September 2010. www.telegraph.co.uk/finance/newsbysector/banksand finance/8018194/Vince-Cable-attacks-bankers-as-spivs-and-gamblers.html

22　'Improving the Outcome for Older People Admitted to the General Hospital: Guidelines for the Development of Liaison Mental Health Services for Older People'. Report of a Working Group for the Faculty of Old Age Psychiatry, Royal College of Psychiatrists, 2005. A copy is here: www.leeds.ac.uk/lpop/documents/WhoCaresWins.pdf

23　Gillan, A., 'In Iraq, life expectancy is 67. Minutes from

Glasgow city centre, it's 54', *Guardian*, 21 January 2006. www.guardian.co.uk/society/2006/jan/21/health.politics

24   'Improving the Outcome for Older People Admitted to the General Hospital: Guidelines for the Development of Liaison Mental Health Services for Older People', p. 5.

25   See also Oliver James's book, *Contented Dementia: 24-hour Wraparound Care for Lifelong Well-being*, (London: Vermilion, 2008). The book is a description of his mother-in-law Penelope Garner's approach to dementia care, known as SPECAL (Specialized Early Care for Alzheimer's). See also: www.selfishcapitalist.com/

26   Jardine, C., 'Dementia: The Past Makes Sense of the Present', *Telegraph*, 28 July 2008, www.telegraph.co.uk/health/elderhealth/3355743/Dementia-the-past-makes-sense-of-the-present.html

27   Wilkinson, R. and K. Pickett, *The Spirit Level: Why Equality is Better for Everyone*, (London: Penguin, 2010). See: www.equalitytrust.org.uk/resource/the-spirit-level which reported on young and old combined. In chapter seven of *Injustice*, I report on children, and the combination of these two sources makes it possible to see that the older-adult profile will be similar.

28   'Improving the Outcome for Older People Admitted to the General Hospital: Guidelines for the Development of Liaison Mental Health Services for Older People'.

29   We will almost all be living a miserable existence in our dotage if in our middle age we do not collectively recast our priorities. How and when and where I die will to a large part depend on what is going on around me socially at that time, on how we all behave. By the time we are elderly and frail, how we may be treated will depend mainly on what kind of a society we have nurtured.

30   The official website is: www.royal.gov.uk/Home.aspx

31   www.royal.gov.uk/HMTheQueen/ContactTheQueen/Overview.aspx

32   The long quote is from www.royal.gov.uk/HMTheQueen/Queenandanniversary messages/Factsandfigures.aspx

33   If you are under the age of 9 please note that I am, of course, referring to the elves who live in Lapland and sign the letters on behalf of Santa as he is too busy making sure the reindeer are well fed and watered. Actually, if you are aged around 9 and reading this book – go and play outside – now! Learning more about Britain, second-hand from books, can wait, as can worrying about your old age.

34   I find it hard to believe that he would still be able to send a telegram. Maybe he'll send a text? See also, 'Improving the Outcome for Older People Admitted to the General Hospital: Guidelines for the Development of Liaison Mental Health Services for Older People'. And: www.nmc-uk.org/General-public/Older-people-and-their-carers/Guidance-for-the-care-of-older-people-Facts-and-figures/

35   Cheaper than the cost of maintaining a civil list and failing to properly tax the royal estates. I also wonder, what must it feel like to know that almost everyone you have written a card to is now dead? It can't be good for your psychological health to act as if you were some kind of higher being.

36   The 1955 and 1965 based estimates are discussed in Shaw, C., 'Fifty Years of United Kingdom National Population Projections: How Accurate Have They Been?', *Population Trends*, 2007, 128, pp. 8–23: www.statistics.gov.uk/downloads/theme_population/PopulationTrends128.pdf

37   *Ibid*. p. 10, www.gad.gov.uk/Demography%20Data/Historicalpopulationprojections.html

38   Matheson, J., 'National Statistician's Article on the Population: a Demographic Review', *Population Trends*, 2009, 138, pp. 7–21. www.statistics.gov.uk/downloads/theme_population/Pop-trends-winter09.pdf

39   Mizutani, T., 'Robot Suits to Aid Elderly Japanese Farmers with Toiling in the Fields', 24 August 2010, www.physorg.com/news201894668.html

40   The Wikipedia page of the town mentions 'Denderano', which is a hut far from any houses where the elderly

were brought to die in ages past. http://en.wikipedia.org/wiki/T%C5%8Dno,_Iwate

41 Of all the countries of the affluent world, Japan has the lowest proportions of both young people and old people in work. The standard retirement age in Japan was 55 for most of the post-war period. It is 60 now, below France's 62, although a few Japanese companies have raised the mandatory age to 65 in recent years.

42 Simizu, K., 'Raising Retirement Age Eases, Adds Strains. Keeping Seniors on to Meet Labor Crunch May Foreclose on Younger Hires', *Japan Times*. http://search.japantimes.co.jp/cgi-bin/nn20040107b2.html

43 People do live slightly shorter lives now in Greece (although not according to Eurostat), Portugal (more economically unequal than the UK), Denmark (where smoking is still common) and in Slovenia. All these figures are from Table H of the most recent UNDP human development report (2009) and purport to be for around the year 2007. See: www.undp.org/publications/annualreport2009/report.shtml

44 In the above UN report life expectancy in the UK is reported as 79.3 years in 2007. It has risen since, but the key measure is: has it risen by as much as in the large majority of affluent nations? If not, why not? The Eurostat source mentioned above for Greece contains more recent data than the UN source. See: 'The EU in the World: A Statistical Portrait', (Luxembourg: Publications Office of the European Union, 2010). http://epp.eurostat.ec.europa.eu/cache/ITY_OFFPUB/KS-32-10-333/EN/KS-32-10-333-EN.PDF. See p. 14 – where by 2008 life expectancy in Greece is 80 and the UK 79.8 years, lower than everywhere else in Western Europe except Portugal. The US in 2008, according to the table, has an expectancy of only 79.2 years, the smallest of fractional increases on a year earlier.

45 Irvin, G., *Super Rich: The Rise of Inequality in Britain and the United States*', (Cambridge: Polity, 2008), pp. 87, 118.

46 *Economist*, 31 October – 6 November 2009, pp. 15, 35.

47 Shanley, D., R. Sear, R. Mace and T. Kirkwood, 'Testing Evolutionary Theories of Menopause', Proceedings of the Royal Society, 2007, B: Biological Sciences, 274 (1628), pp. 2943–49. http://rspb.royalsocietypublishing.org/content/274/1628/2943.full.pdf+html. Humans are thought to be unique among animals (there remains some uncertainty about the habits of some species of whale!). Humans have evolved to benefit from growing old, or at least from females growing old. This study revealed that in the Gambia between 1950 and 1975 children between ages 1 and 2 had twice the chance of surviving if their maternal grandmother was still alive – and that no other living relatives had a similar effect on survival in other similar circumstances. The belief is that menopause was timed to around age 50 because that seemed to be the optimum time to stop reproducing and to start advising, helping and assisting. See also: http://scienceblogs.com/primatediaries/2009/10/reply_to_moran_the_adaptive_va.php; http://tw3a.siuc.edu/431pubty.htm; and on apes: www.gan.ca/animals/chimpanzees.en.html. For us humans, 'Aunty' (the BBC) gives the best advice on puberty: www.bbc.co.uk/science/humanbody/body/articles/lifecycle/teenagers/growth.shtml

48 Middle-aged men are far from useless. One, Ian Dury (1942–2000), wrote the song 'Reasons to Be Careful' (1979), and 'Three is the Magic Number' (1990) is from De La Soul and the many folk they sampled.

Chapter Eight: The Future Is Another Place

1 Details of the various citizens' organization across Britain, and of how the London branch dominates, are given in: www.citizensuk.org. See also: Lawson, N. and J. Harris, 'No Turning Back', *New Statesman*, 5 March 2009. www.newstatesman.com/uk-politics/2009/03/labour-party-essay-society

2 Forty million might not sound much if you work in the City, but it is an annual fortune spread out over tens of thousands of people who were being paid the minimum wage and are now receiving the living wage. For the recent history of its work in these areas and the recent successes see: www.citizensuk.org/campaigns/living-wage-campaign/history/

3 Londoners also behaved differently to much of the rest of the population in the general election of 2010, swinging towards Labour while the rest of the country polarized towards the historical political preferences of their areas. The older political preferences of Londoners had, when averaged, tended to be Conservative in the past. See endnote p. 282, on *New Statesman* article of 2010.

4 Isherwood, C., *Goodbye to Berlin*, (London: Hogarth Press, 1939). See also: http://en.wikipedia.org/wiki/Goodbye_to_Berlin

5 Dorling, D., 'Mind the Gap: New Labour's Legacy on Child Poverty', *Poverty*, October 2010. See also: www.sasi.group.shef.ac.uk/ publications/2010/Dorling_2010_Poverty.pdf

6 And also more equally than is the case in almost all poor nations. In general, as humans become richer, they have shared more equitably. Inequalities are highest in some of the poorer countries of the world today, in countries such as Namibia, Chile and India (outside of Kerala).

7 These are taken from http://en.wikipedia.org/wiki/List_of_countries_without_armed_forces, which lists twenty-one countries, excluding Japan and a few other countries that are demilitarized but take part in 'peace-keeping' (a phrase George Orwell would have had fun with had he lived long enough to hear it used).

8 Frank, R. H., *Falling Behind: How Rising Inequality Harms the Middle Class*, (Berkeley: University of California Press, 2007).

9 This graph was first drawn for a lecture given at the Royal Geographical Society, London in May 2010. Data sources can be found from my university homepage where the

notes to the lecture and a recording of what was said are available. See: www.shef.ac.uk/sasi

10   An alternative, and links to many other alternatives are given here: Dorling, D., 'Should Government Have a Plan B; or, The inclusion of People in Society?' *Twenty-First Century Society*, 2010, Vol. 5, Issue 1, pp. 33–49. For more recent papers and links to alternative views to those of George Osborne's see the university website just referenced in endnote directly above.

11   Dorling, D., 'New Labour and Inequality: Thatcherism Continued?' *Local Economy*, August – September 2010, Vol. 25, Nos. 5 – 6, pp. 397–413. See also: www.sasi. group.shef.ac.uk/publications/2010/Dorling_2010_ LocalEconomy.pdf

12   Shaw M., S. Orford, N. Brimblecombe, and D. Dorling, 'Widening Inequality in Mortality between 160 Regions of 15 Countries of the European Union', *Social Science and Medicine*, 2000, 30, pp. 1047–58. See also: http://sasi. group.shef.ac.uk/publications/2000/shaw_Widening_ine- quality_160_regions.pdf

13   Overall life expectancy in Germany is higher than in the UK and the geographical divides are less extreme. This is possible because people in what was East Germany have better health now than do those who grew up and still live in Northern England, in Scotland, Wales and Northern Ireland: in the 'free' West. This is one of the clearest exam- ples of how the British made the wrong choices.

14   Some 500,000 of the 1.7 million being women in their twenties. For the most concise description of these changes see, as it existed in November 2010: http://en.wikipedia. org/wiki/New_states_of_Germany where it is also revealed that: 'In some regions the number of women between the ages of 20 and 30 has dropped by more than 30 per cent. In 2004, in the age group 18–29 (statistically important for starting families) there were only 90 women for every 100 men in the new federal states (including Berlin). In parts of the state of Thuringia, there are 82 women for every

100 men. The town of Königstein has the biggest demographic imbalance in Europe between young men and women.'

15   Tomáš Sobotka writing on 5 February 2010 in the 'Comment is Free' section of the *Guardian* suggested that: 'Spain witnessed an unprecedented immigration wave, and a gradual increase in birth rates. Despite low fertility, the Spanish population jumped fastest in Europe in the last decade, from 40 million to 46 million.' His article was written in response to Fred Pearce's vivid portrayal of population collapse in the town of Hoyerswerda in eastern Germany, including descriptions of the wolves returning from the forests to reclaim the lands now deserted by people. Fred's article is no longer available for free, but Tomáš's rebuttal of it makes the valuable point that when there are not punitive migration controls, immigration replaces reduced fertility. See:www.guardian.co.uk/commentisfree/2010/feb/05/europe-not-heading-for-population-collapse?showallcomments=true#comment-fold

16   Favato, G., 'Social Solidarity Can Compensate for Income Inequalities: the Case of the Public Italian Healthcare Service', *British Medical Journal*, 11 November 2007. http://bmj.com/cgi/eletters/335/7625/873#179440

17   See pages 145–146 [chapter 5] on the inverse care law in health in Britain.

18   See endnote, p. 14 [this chapter].

19   From 1984 onwards unemployment of people aged 25 and under stood at over a million when first counted as 'registered unemployed' and stayed at that level if we account for the various definition changes through to now, when the million unemployed are counted as 'not in employment, education and training', but only half a million of those can be registered as unemployed. Youth unemployment in the 1930s was far lower; it was older men who were then made jobless. By early November 2010 a further 1.6 million jobless, mostly among the young, were being predicted by personnel directors due to budget cuts and

their effect on employment figures. Emigration at higher levels would reduce those numbers.

20   See endnotes pp. 95–97 for what we know as this book goes to press. Net migration numbers are likely to change quickly and then be revised substantially in 2013 following release of the census taken in March 2011.

21   See endnote spanning pages 287–88 [Chaper 7] and the figure on cohort changes in the paper referenced.

22   See endnote 46 on page 285 [Chapter 6] and the final figure on cohorts in the chapter it references.

23   These figures are from the ONS survey of assets of 2008, released in 2010 and the Bank of England's estimates of both secured and unsecured personal debts in 2010. Both figures are likely to fluctuate in the near future as has already occurred in the US, where both have fallen considerably. See D. Dorling, *Injustice: Why Social Inequality Persists*, (Bristol: Policy Press, 2010). www.sasi.group. shef.ac.uk/injustice/chapter7.htm (on figures from the US Federal Reserve).

24   New Zealand, with about a fifth of the population overseas-born and a fifth emigrating, is the country of greatest population turnover and also a place with fairly stable population numbers. In Norway, in very recent years, about a tenth of young people have come in from abroad, which makes its population grow more quickly than New Zealand's. See: www.worldmapper.org for demographic accounting on lifetime migration (see 'movement' section of that website, at least for the older figures for New Zealand).

25   See second endnote on page 257 [Chapter 4], on what can go wrong if you get your insults confused.

26   See endnote at the bottom of page 255, [Chapter 3]. See also: Dorling, D., 'Glass Conflict: David Cameron's Claim to Understand Poverty and His Wish to "eradicate dependency" Seem Wide of the Mark', *Roof* magazine, 2001 35, 1, p. 10 www.sasi.group.shef.ac.uk/publications/commentary/dorling_2010-01_roof.pdf

27   The evidence is collectively known as the 'Flynn Effect';

Google it to learn more; if you can't Google, or think your way laterally around the web, discerning what may be fact from fiction and understanding complex diagrams, try asking a younger person for help, but please don't tell them how, in your day, standards were so much higher. If standards were, then you would know so much more than you do about a wider range of issues. Aging is wonderful, but each recent generation is aging with far greater resources in its collective mind. Hardly anyone in my grandfather's day carried on at school after age 14. Many never properly learnt to read and write.

28 Many of our beaches are wonderful, but the scope to appreciate them is a little limited by our climate. However, this does have the advantage that for much of the year they are abandoned and tranquil! There is much to appreciate about Britain, but I think an ugly culture can make a place much less inviting than it need be. A happier, more trusting, more equitable Britain could be a far less drab country to live in, even under our often cloudy skies, and despite how much we have partitioned our land for profit. Holidaying in Britain would be a far more pleasant experience if the country were less divided, if our seaside towns were not used to 'garage' so many of the poor that we create by sustaining some of the highest levels of inequality in Europe, if our cities were more welcoming rather than primarily being centres for commerce, and if our countryside were less exclusive and excluding.

29 On how living in a country as unequal as Britain or Israel can change how you view others, see: Dorling, D. 'Mean Machine: Structural Inequality Makes Social Inequality Seem Natural', *New Internationalist*, 2010 433, pp. 20–1. Available from: www.sasi.group.shef.ac.uk/publications/2010/Dorling_2010_New_Internationalist_2010.pdf

30 The current Health White Paper is privatization by stealth: if the multibillion-pound NHS budget is handed over to general practitioners many of them would subcontract

for-profit healthcare companies to manage services in their place. General practitioners were trained to be doctors, not managers.

31 Singapore is the world's most unequal country regardless of whether inequality is measured as the ratio of the extreme decile or quintile groups' incomes (see also: Dorling, D., *Injustice*, which uses data from 2009), or whether quintile groups are compared using data from a little earlier as in the study referenced above in endnote concerning Richard Wilkinson and Kate Pickett on page 290 [Chapter 5].

32 We were once much more than a tax-and-banking haven, but in Victorian times also, we were an unequal country. If you find it hard to imagine Britain becoming like Singapore then look at our current immigration rules for what level of wealth is required to immigrate (without other conditions) here from outside Europe. See also endnote on page 265 and text on page 121 [chapter 4], on how Nicolas Soames, and those like him, are ever more loudly suggesting that people from abroad be granted the right to work here, but must leave if they have children. Consider how so many of the rich in Britain view the poor to be different to them. Consider the source of the colonial attitudes in Singapore. It is easy to develop an insular view of the rest of the world if you live on an island. A more unequal Britain could be a country that becomes more like Singapore than like the United States. Even fewer people in Singapore share the wealth of that country than the proportion that share the wealth in the US. The most common job in Britain would again be to work 'in service'. The only job opportunities increasing in any number for the young in Britain, as recorded in the Labour Force Survey by 2009, were waiting on tables. Dystopia is not hard to visualize right now.

33 The last two items come from a poem written at the height of empire concerning exploitation of others: Carroll, L., 'The Walrus and the Carpenter', from *Through the Looking-Glass and What Alice Found There*, (1872). www.jabberwocky.com/carroll/walrus.html

34 See the maps of child (majority) and adult (minority) literacy on www.worldmapper.org

35 See endnote 38 p. 284 [Chapter 6] for the reference to the study including both rich and poor.

36 Just over a century ago they were labelled the 'Vicious semi-criminal' areas on Charles Booth's maps. On the fear growing again among the rich of those nearby who are poor, see: Minton, A., *Ground Control: Fear and Happiness in the Twenty-First-Century City*, (London: Penguin, 2009) extract at: www.guardian.co.uk/society/2009/jun/17/hous ing-regeneration-oldham

37 See the third endnote on page 236, [Chapter 1] on the play based on the book *Love on the Dole*.

INDEX

301